Writers of the 21st Century

JACK VANCE

Best wishes, Tim Underwood

Edited by
TIM UNDERWOOD

and

CHUCK MILLER

General Series Editors:
MARTIN HARRY GREENBERG
and
JOSEPH D. OLANDER

jack
vance

TAPLINGER PUBLISHING COMPANY / NEW YORK

First Edition

Published in the United States in 1980 by
TAPLINGER PUBLISHING CO., INC.
New York, New York

Library of Congress Cataloging in Publication Data
Main entry under title:

Jack Vance.

    (Writers of the 21st century)
    "Jack Vance: a bibliography, compiled by Marshall B.
Tymn": p.
    Includes index.
    1. Vance, John Holbrook, 1916–   —Criticism and
interpretation. I. Underwood, Tim. II. Miller,
Chuck, 1952–   III. Series.
PS3572.A424Z73   813'.54   79-57353
ISBN 0-8008-4294-4
ISBN 0-8008-4295-2 (pbk.)

CONTENTS

Introduction

TIM UNDERWOOD

"Beauty is difficult, Yeats."
— Aubrey Beardsley's reply to William Butler Yeats, when Yeats asked why he drew horrors.

NINETEEN SEVENTY-SEVEN may well be remembered as the year science fiction came in out of the cold. That year Hollywood found out, with the movie *Star Wars*, what the New York publishing houses had already discovered: science fiction can break out of its restrictive category and appeal to a *very* wide audience. *Star Wars* was both significator and catalyst of this new phenomenon. At the same time, the borderline between science fiction and "mainstream" literature, already stretched and broached in recent years by William Burroughs, Thomas Pynchon, Terry Southern, Kurt Vonnegut, John Barth, Jorge Luis Borges, William Kotzwinkle, and others, began to dissolve entirely.

At last, the "SF" label has ceased to inhibit a writer's commercial prospects. Indicative of this transition, in the late 1970s Big Money was finally being made available to many science fiction writers. Along "Publishers Row" in New York, these same writers were still considered minor league, if the truth be known, but now they were fashionable, marketable, and profitable — and thus very desirable. Record advances for science fiction authors regularly made headlines. Frank Herbert's third Dune novel became the first book with an SF label to reach bestseller lists in both hardcover and paperback. Subsidiary sales of American science fiction were booming (and still are) in Europe, Japan, and elsewhere.

Along with other established writers, Jack Vance has benefited from this sudden widespread acceptance and interest in science fiction. More than a dozen of his novels which were long out-of-print have been repackaged and reprinted. Today, nearly thirty of his SF novels and story collections are available in the United States. A good many of these have been translated and published overseas. The future for SF seems bright indeed.

But it was not always so. Most SF writers now currently popular and well-respected share similar commercial histories of limited success. Poul Anderson, Philip K. Dick, André Norton, Frank Herbert, Frederik Pohl, Fritz Leiber, Jack Vance: for many years these and others wrote for pennies-per-word and often less. When Jack Vance began his literary career at the close of World War II, pulp magazines and digests were virtually the sole marketplace for speculative fiction. As Robert Silverberg remarks about Vance's *The Dying Earth* (1950), when a science fiction book appeared in those days, it was an *event*. (In 1979, *Locus* magazine listed over seventy SF books published in the month of June alone!)

Still, it must be admitted that, as a genre, science fiction has seen more than its share of schlocky literature. Vance himself wrote hundreds of thousands of words for the pulps and digests of the 40s and 50s, often prefabricated "idea" stories with cute plots, cardboard characters, and a great deal of SF gadgetry. This last-mentioned element was a prerequisite, because while those ephemeral magazines offered easy money to any would-be writer willing to cater to their standards, their content was largely restricted to *science* fiction (a legacy of Hugo Gernsback's dictum that the business of science fiction is science).

Authors such as Philip K. Dick (who as a young writer felt

naturally inclined towards fantasy and horror), Fritz Leiber (whose best works deal with horror and the supernatural), and Jack Vance (whose first book, *The Dying Earth*, showed him to be fantasy-oriented in story treatment and imagination) were all to some extent forced to write "scientific" fiction — with physical science and technological hardware prominently displayed within the story — or cease to publish.

Yet within these confines (which finally began to disappear in the mid-60s, thanks to a change in readers' tastes and social temperament, and in publishers' editorial staffs) Jack Vance produced some very worthy science-backgrounded speculative novels and, eventually, some science fiction masterpieces which may last as long as his best works of fantasy.

Vance not only learned to write *science* fiction, he learned to write it well, though rather differently than it had been written in the past. Gradually, his craft evolved. Having finished *Big Planet* (1952), *To Live Forever* (1956), and *The Languages of Pao* (1957) — along with some other less interesting novels — Vance successfully harnessed his fanciful imagination, his yen for innovation within traditional structure, and his taste for eclectic ornamentation. Great works resulted — *The Dragon Masters* appeared in 1963 and won a Hugo; *The Star King* appeared in 1964, the first book in the Demon Princes series. Both are masterpieces of their kind. Within the following three years he had published two more extraordinary examples of stylized imagination, this time "classical" fantasies — *The Eyes of the Overworld* (a sequel to *The Dying Earth*) and *The Last Castle*, which won a Nebula Award in 1966 and a Hugo Award in 1967.

This collection of essays on Jack Vance's speculative fiction is therefore timely and extremely apropos. As Poul Anderson points out in this volume's Afterword, despite having won a Nebula and two Hugos (and an Edgar for his mystery writing), Vance's work has received little critical attention. Probably no other author in the field has received as much acclaim and as little analysis.

In "Jack Vance and *The Dragon Masters*," Norman Spinrad contrasts this invisibility of Jack Vance as author with the very visible and distinctive literary style displayed in his mature works. *The Dragon Masters* won the Hugo in 1963; Spinrad explains how Vance's sardonic posture and richness of style transform what in other hands would be straightforward science fiction into "a kind of sophisticated Grimm fairy tale" which was worthy of this award.

In "Fantasms, Magics, and Unfamiliar Sciences: The Early Fiction of Jack Vance, 1945–50," Peter Close details the very beginning of Vance's career as a prolific journeyman-writer for the pulp magazines of post-World War II. Close sees these magazines as providing a useful format for apprenticeship. Vance's exotic early stories are examined and Close summarizes their plots, points out their flaws and highlights, and defines their successes as period pieces.

Arthur Jean Cox, in "Jack Vance—The World Thinker," depicts Vance as an enormously talented writer who is not temperamentally suited to the metaphysical preconceptions which, Cox says, lie at the heart of traditional science fiction. Cox notes the lack of message and ideology in Vance's fiction and the ineffable and timeless quality of his best novels. Significantly, Cox addresses himself to the way in which Vance accomplishes some very unusual effects in his later fiction.

In "The Double Shadow: The Influence of Clark Ashton Smith," Don Herron discloses the major influence which *Weird Tales writer Clark Ashton Smith exerted on Vance's writing— an influence still evident today. Jack Vance is in fact one of very few contemporary writers whose imagination bears the imprint of Weird Tales*, an unusual pulp magazine which had its heyday in the 30s. Today, just as much as when he began in 1945, Vance is concerned and fascinated with all the applications of that singular expression: *weird.*

In "Tschai: Four Planets of Adventure," Mark Willard summarizes the Tschai series: *City of the Chasch, Servants of the Wankh*, *The Dirdir*, and *The Pnume*. Tschai may be the most fully realized alien planet in all of science fiction, and Willard explores this accomplishment. Various themes throughout the series are isolated and examined, especially the situation that is basic to all four books: humanity being forced to adapt to an alien environment.

Robert Silverberg recalls the publication of Vance's first book in "*The Eyes of the Overworld* and *The Dying Earth*." He discusses the milieu of the early 50s and Vance's impact on that period. *The Dying Earth* is then contrasted stylistically with *The Eyes of the Overworld*, its more mature sequel of 1966. By comparing specific passages from both novels, Silverberg makes clear how Vance's stylistic temperament and voice have changed.

Terry Dowling, in "Jack Vance's 'General Culture' Novels: A Synoptic Survey," sees Vance as being primarily concerned with humanities and the "soft" sciences. The term *xenology* (also called *exobiology*) is introduced and defined as alien "anthropology"—the study of the stranger. In the realm of speculative literature, the xenographical novel portrays alien worlds in such sufficient detail for the portrayal itself to have been one main reason for the writing of the book—a concept as applicable to Vance as it is to Tolkien. With this line of thought, Dowling ties together all of Vance's major works.

The first critical work on Vance's fiction was Richard Tiedman's monograph, "Jack Vance: Science Fiction Stylist." A revised version appears here. Tiedman's essay overviews Vance's literature; Vance's growth as a novelist is illuminated, and his work is compared to that of Isaac Asimov, A. E. van Vogt, and some others of his contemporaries.

Which of Jack Vance's many books will endure the test of time? My own guesses are as follows: *The Dying Earth*, *The Eyes of the Overworld*, *The Dragon Masters*, *The Last Castle*, and probably the four Tschai books and the Demon Princes series.

(Naturally such premature selection is a chancy business. In Melville's time most readers neglected *Moby Dick* completely; it was *Typee* and *Omoo* which made and sustained Herman Melville's reputation among his contemporaries. And Melville himself, like Thomas Hardy, dedicated the latter part of his career to writing volumes of poetry, in the erroneous belief that his verses would outlive him.)

I met Jack Vance in the course of publishing an illustrated edition of *The Dying Earth*. All of this recent excitement surrounding his profession has left him untouched. While he has always studiously avoided self-promotion and publicity, I can report that as a man, he is not unlike the protagonist in many of his novels. On the sunny side, he does his share of good works, cultivates good company, engenders and enjoys good cheer, and appreciates natural scenery and beauty where he finds it. His rendering of the truly strange identities of people and places and his attraction to the mysterious qualities of Beauty in all of its forms arises from an almost mystical fascination with environment. This is essential to his inner nature. For Jack Vance, especially as seen in his later writing, this fascination has assumed the function of religious awareness.

With his wife Norma and son John he has travelled to nearly every corner of the globe. But as this collection of essays will indicate, his best books are not reflections of the world around us, they are rather distillations and transmutations. When they do reflect, it is of images from within, from the realms of imagination and beyond, from Poe's "weird clime that lieth sublime, Out of Space—out of Time."

Vance takes you there and back again. This book attempts to shed light on how such a thing is possible.

1. Jack Vance and "The Dragon Masters"*

NORMAN SPINRAD

How CAN ONE explain the relative obscurity of a writer whose work has twice won the Hugo Award for best science fiction of the year in its category? A man who has been writing and publishing science fiction for over a quarter of a century. A man whose prose style is so unique that a random paragraph taken out of almost any piece of science fiction or fantasy he has written is sufficient to identify itself as unmistakably the work of Jack Vance:

> In the first place, the Rhune is exquisitely sensitive to his landscapes of mountain, meadow, forest and sky—all changing with the changing modes of day. He reckons his land by its aesthetic appeal; he will connive a lifetime to gain a few choice acres. He enjoys pomp, protocol, heraldic minutiae; his niceties and graces are judged as carefully as the figures of a ballet. He prides himself on his collection of sherliken scales; or the emeralds which he has mined, cut, and polished with his own hands; or his Arah magic wheels, imported from halfway across the Gaean Reach. He will perfect himself in special mathematics, or an ancient language, or the lore of fanfares, or all three, or three other abstrusities.... (*Marune: Alastor 933*, IV)

Yet Jack Vance seems to be an invisible man. Academics have written at great length and Byzantine complexity about science fiction writers with a far less substantial body of work and far less stylistic interest than Jack Vance. About Vance little has been written and even less is known. The science fiction readers, who twice have given Vance their award, seem to look right through him too. Not only will you seldom hear his name mentioned in a discussion of the major writers of the field, but there was a time in the 1950s when many fans were convinced that he did not exist.

In the late 1940s and early 1950s, Henry Kuttner and his wife Catherine Moore wrote under a bewildering number of pseudonyms, singly and together. Henry Kuttner, C. L. Moore, Lewis Padgett, Laurence O'Donnell, and any number of other regular contributors to the science fiction magazines were really Kuttner and/or Moore in one or another of their permutations. And it was thought for a time that "Jack Vance" was but another pseudonym of the Kuttners. This rumor was not scotched until Henry Kuttner died and his wife went into retirement and Jack Vance continued to produce works. Even today some libraries still erroneously catalogue the books of Jack Vance as pseudonymously written by Kuttner, and there they sit on the shelves with the "Ks." How's *that* for the invisible man?

And far from chafing under this anonymity, Vance seems to cultivate it. He does not contribute to fanzines; he does not go to science fiction conventions; he does not lecture at colleges; he does not give interviews; and even his agent has not been provided with an official biography.

In one of Vance's stories of the magical twilight of man, collected in *The Dying Earth*, Liane the Wayfarer finds a magic ring through which he can step into a private universe and thus render himself invisible to passing eyes: "Once more Liane tried his bronze ring, and this time brought it entirely past his feet, stepped out of it, and brought the ring up into the darkness beside him. What a sanctuary! A hole whose opening could be hidden inside the hole itself!" (*The Dying Earth*, IV). It would appear that Vance himself has deliberately done the same thing. A thirty-year stream of work has steadily appeared in our own continuum, but the intelligence behind it remains inside its invisible hidey-hole.

Rest assured, however, that Jack Vance does indeed exist, no matter how hard he may try to obscure the fact. Officially, his full moniker is John Holbrook Vance, which form of his name he uses on his mystery fiction (*Bad Ronald*, 1973; *The Fox Valley Murders*, 1966; *The Pleasant Grove Murders*, 1967), which has won him an Edgar Award. Unofficially, I was his anonymous agent for a time when I worked at the Scott Meredith Literary Agency for a time in 1965, and once I met him at Poul Anderson's house in Orinda, California. Jack Vance is really Jack Vance.

Turning from the man to his work, the invisibility act looks even more the amazing feat of prestidigitation, "Phandaal's Mantle of Stealth." As near as can be accurately counted, Jack Vance has at this writing published twenty-six novels and seven collections of short stories, not counting the mysteries published under "John Holbrook Vance." Many of these thirty-three books have gone into multiple printings. One of them, his first, *The Dying Earth* (1950), has been considered a classic for twenty years. Its sequel, the stories of Cugel the Clever, published as *The Eyes of the Overworld* (1966), eclipses it thoroughly as a work of literature. Both *The Last Castle* (1967) and *The Dragon Masters* (1963) won Hugos in their magazine novella versions. We have here one of the longest-working and prolific authors in the science-fiction genre, a multiple award winner, and, moreover, a writer whose production has been more or less consistent for over a quarter of a century, and who has maintained a similarly consistent style, elegance, and craftsmanship. *The Dying Earth*, *The Eyes of the Overworld*, *The Blue World* (1966), and *Emphyrio* (1969), for example, which did not win awards, are by no means inferior to the works that did. Vance's fiction is of a piece, a high plain of crafts-manship with few peaks or valleys.

The science fiction genre has produced but a handful of true stylists—that is, writers whose sentence-by-sentence prose is fine enough, idiosyncratic enough, subtle enough, and consistent enough from page to page and book to book to become the major interest in reading their work. Ray Bradbury. R. A. Lafferty. Alfred Bester. Perhaps Harlan Ellison and Cordwainer Smith.

But the list is tiny. It does not include Theodore Sturgeon, Brian W. Aldiss, or Philip José Farmer, for instance, who are masters of several styles, who match their prose to their content, work by work. Nor does it include writers like Roger Zelazny or J. R. R. Tolkien or Samuel R. Delany, whose prose styles derive from the consistent iconography of their content. Few science fiction writers indeed have chosen to develop style-as-content, to concentrate on how more than what, to write, in this sense, in a baroque mode.

And no science fiction writer does it with the Roman luxuriousness and razor-edge control of Jack Vance. Vance cavorts in his own words like Scrooge McDuck in his money bin swimming pool. Like a painter, he endlessly describes clothing, architecture, landscape, and qualities of light for the purely aesthetic joy of it:

> Phade ran down the passage which presently joined Bird Walk, so called for the series of fabulous birds of lapis, gold, cinnabar, malachite and maracasite inlaid into the marble. Through an arcade of green and gray jade in spiral columns she passed out into Kergan's Way, a natural defile which formed the main thoroughfare of Banbeck Village. (*The Dragon Masters*, I)

Whether he is describing an expiring millennial Earth steeped in magic born of rotting history, or a galactic cluster of 30,000 stars, or the planet Aerlith under the baleful eye of the wandering lizard star, Vance creates baroque tapestry. Not content to limit himself to the mere world-creation of traditional science fiction, Vance adds those graceful superfluities that give his times and places baronial richness, late Renaissance grandeur, and the weight of cultural and aesthetic substantiality.

Out of this baroque prose style arise the baroque realities that Vance creates in his science fiction and fantasy. Vance's *oeuvre* may superficially be divided between "fantasies" like *The Dying Earth* and *The Eyes of the Overworld* in which the texture of reality is interwoven with magic, and works like *The Dragon Masters*, which justify every conceivable technical definition of "science fiction." I say *superficially* divided because the cleavage is technical and not something one experiences as a reader. Vance's "fantasy" has the same feel as Vance's "science fiction." Indeed, both have generally been published as "science fiction," and no one has seriously objected. For Vance's tone, his outlook on reality, and the flavor of his work arise from his style and mode, not from whether his material is "science fiction" or "fantasy."

Vance's worlds arise out of his own unique tone whether he's writing "straight" science fiction or "magical" fantasies. It's obvious in the Dying Earth and Cugel the Clever stories, where sorcery is treated something like a degenerate technology, where making miracles has become a science, where magic is a hand-me-down from a lost golden age of Faustian greatness. His fantasy is too detailed, convoluted, and realized not to be called science fiction, and his science fiction realities have the magical complexity of his fantasies.

The Dragon Masters, Vance's Hugo-winning short novel, for example, is science fiction by any reasonable criteria. Yet it retains the quality and tone common to all of Jack Vance's imaginative work. Just as Vance's tone arises out of his baroque prose style, so does that tone create story and character — especially when combined with Vance's characteristic sardonic viewpoint and his relentless sense of irony.

The Dragon Masters has a conventional space-opera plot, if one were to define it by simply capsulizing the story line. Lizardmen have captured all human planets except Aerlith by using genetically-altered humans as specialized brainwashed slave warriors. On Aerlith, humans have captured a party of invading "Basic" sauroids, and bred them into the same sort of specialized slave warriors. The Banbeck and Carcolo clans eventually use these "dragons" to destroy an invading party of Basics and their human warriors and seize their ship.

But such a conventional plot summary is hardly adequate, for it doesn't really describe what *The Dragon Masters* is all about. For Vance, plot and even character are skeletons upon which to hang his overriding concern for place and time, for a sense of history always imbued with a mordant irony reminiscent of the late Mark Twain.

Like many of Vance's societies, Aerlith has a political structure that is hereditary and feudal. The feuding forces of Joaz Banbeck and Ervis Carcolo battle each other for abstract advantage even as the Basics attack them both for the purpose of enslaving the last free men in the universe. To add another level of irony to the situation, the sacerdotes, a tribe of Aerlith humans who live in huge and eerie cave cities, consider themselves the only true humans and attempt to live out an insanely ex--treme philosophy of detachment in the face of the Basic assault. Vance's view of religious mystics is no more sanguine than his opinion of political leaders.

In *The Dragon Masters*, we can see how Vance's baroque style and sardonic stance transform what in other hands would be a straightforward science fiction story into a kind of sophisticated Grimm fairy tale entirely of a piece with works like the Cugel stories or the Dying Earth tales.

We can see this most clearly in the "dragons" of the title and the Basic-molded humanoids. Here are creatures out of some wizard's vat arrived at through the conventions of science fiction. *How* human and Basic flesh is transformed into Giants and Heavy Troopers, Blue Fiends and Termagants, is never scientifically explained — nor need it be, given the story's far-future context. If Vance *could* explain it, he'd get a Nobel Prize in biology. The difference between this kind of "science fiction" and the fantasy that produces Magnatz, Chun the Inevitable, deodands, and leucomorphs is something only an aged mandarin could distinguish.

What counts in both cases is the reality, the verisimilitude, the three-dimensionality of the fantastic creatures the writer has created, not how they were technically arrived at. And here Jack Vance's richness of style serves to best advantage, creating gothic creatures that reverberate with the mythic dimensions of the Brothers Grimm, but which have the solidity, believability, and even upon occasion the psychological depth of well-realized science fiction.

> A palpable aura was cast up, a weft in space meshed of varying depravities. And the demons swooped like birds alighting and joined the delirium. Foul face after face T'sais saw, and each burnt her brain until she thought she must scream and die—visages of leering eye, bulbed cheek, lunatic body, black faces of spiked nose, expressions outraging thought, writhing, hopping, crawling, the spew of the demon-lands. And one had a nose like a three-fold white worm, a mouth that was a putrefying blotch, a mottled jowl and black malformed forehead; the whole a thing of retch and horror. To this Etarr directed T'sais' gaze. She saw and her muscles knotted. "There," said Etarr in a muffled voice, "there is a face twin to the one below this hood." (*The Dying Earth*, III)

No cardboard bug-eyed monsters, these. And in *The Dragon Masters*, we can see that the dragons and humanoids are not merely tour-de-force window dressing, but beings whose existence determines the plot—indeed, grotesques whose existence *becomes* the plot. A reality which contains such presences is clearly something other than what most of us experience from day to day—in quality, not only in content—which is why the work has fascination. This is fundamentally what people read both science fiction and fantasy for and what they seldom get—an altered reality with the cogency and verisimilitude of our own. And a reality, moreover, more convoluted, more ornate, more paradoxical more slippery—more magical, if you will.

But even as Jack Vance builds his ornate cathedrals around you, his viewpoint on his own creations remains mordant, sardonic, slyly misanthropic, perhaps even ultimately pessimistic. In the work of Vance, some enduring age is forever coming to a close, and men seem meaner and smaller than their ancestors:

> "In ages gone," the sage had said, his eyes fixed on a low star, "a thousand spells were known to sorcery and the wizards effected their wills. Today, as Earth dies, a hundred spells remain to man's knowledge, and these have come to us through the ancient books...." (*The Dying Earth*, I)

> Ervis Carcolo was an energetic man, intent upon restoring Happy Valley to the ascendancy it had enjoyed some twelve generations before. During these harsh times, before the advent of the dragons, men fought their own battles, and the men of Happy Valley had been notably daring, deft, and ruthless. (*The Dragon Masters*, II)

And in *The Dragon Masters*, men have been reduced to something truly less than human by the Basics—not only have they been bred into specialized serving animals like dogs, but their brains can no longer encompass the opposite concept to servitude. But Vance does not even let go of it there—he does not even permit humanity the moral superiority of the victim's position in such a degrading situation. For when men get the chance, they do exactly the same thing, breeding monstrous brute dragons out of their sapient Basic prisoners. Both men and Basics are guilty of a racial crime that goes genocide one better. And who is to say that the dragons, who snarl and bicker in their servitude, have not retained more dignity than the transformed humanoids who sincerely worship their masters?

Finally, after Banbeck and Carcolo have unwillingly combined forces to destroy the Basics, instead of a conversion to human solidarity, we have Carcolo pursuing his endless and in this instance powerless and therefore insane attempts to one-up Banbeck, and Banbeck—throughout the book the most sympathetic figure—executing Carcolo for expediency's sake, for "his duty to himself, his people, his ultimate goal."

A line from *The Dying Earth* sums up Vance's *oeuvre*, his

tone, his stance, his perspective on humanity perfectly: "Now, in the last fleeing moments, humanity festers, rich as rotting fruit...."

How then has such a body of work remained in such relative obscurity? Here is a writer who has been around for three decades, and who is perhaps the premier stylist in the science fiction genre in terms of fusing prose, tone, viewpoint, content and mood into a seamless synergetic whole. A writer whose *Weltanschauung* is unsurpassed in the genre for its maturity and unique for its mordancy. Why has Jack Vance not been recognized as the peer of Bradbury, Heinlein, and Aldiss, let alone of Ellison, Zelazny, or Delany?

Having looked at what the work of Jack Vance is, we might find it instructive to look at what it is not. Vance has produced no truly outstanding characters that are remembered long after the stories that contain them are forgotten, nor has he produced tales that live on as epic sagas, as instant myths. He has produced no quintessential single work to point to as a peak achievement — which is to say that he is not famous for any hero, nor for any story, nor for any book. But then, Vance doesn't seem to set out to do any of these things. He has chosen to write a sort of fiction not calculated to bring him fame and fortune, nor to make him an epic storyteller, nor a creator of magnetic characters, nor to produce sporadic masterworks. It is a kind of fiction that is definitely a minority taste, not a mass-market addiction — nor is it ever likely to become anything else. But that does not make Vance's work any less valuable, for the taste that it satisfies is subtle and sophisticated. To enjoy Vance, you have to enjoy words as sculpture on paper, reality as a baroque landscape, and sardonicism for its own elegance. You are offered this as the main course, hors d'oeuvres raised to smorgasbord.

And why not? This stream of literature has always been with us and always will be. It includes *The Tales of a Thousand*

and One Nights, the fairy tales of the Brothers Grimm, the Jerry Cornelius and Elric stories of Michael Moorcock, the work of Cordwainer Smith, and perhaps the best of Roger Zelazny. Mervin Peake's *Gorhmangast Trilogy* is perhaps the ultimate example of this architectural approach to fiction: in this case the major character quite literally is an aging castle.

In our modern Bauhaus age where form is supposed to follow function, Jack Vance is a man who makes style generate content. In what has been primarily a literature of logical positivism, he insinuates the metaphor of magic and the magic of metaphor into every nook and cranny, into every dark glade and dell of his fictional landscape.

But Vance's universe is not like the sanitary Fantasy Lands of Walt Disney or the smarmy heroics of J. R. R. Tolkien or the romanticized grandeur of the Galactic Roman Empire; his worlds have an existential and moral reality, and are informed by a mordant dubiousness about man and his works.

This is not the sort of fiction with the widest mass appeal, particularly within the science fiction genre, but it is the sort of fiction which in the long run continues to be read by generations of cognoscenti, and thus endures.

2. Fantasms, Magics, and Unfamiliar Sciences: The Early Fiction of Jack Vance, 1945–50

PETER CLOSE

IN ATTEMPTING an evaluation of the early work of Jack Vance, the first task must be to explain why the job is being undertaken at all. There are few writers who are proud of their earliest efforts, and although the current science-fiction boom has brought forward several collections of early stories from major names in the field, these are heavily freighted with apologia by authors, friends, critics, and editors. Vance himself has offered no encouragement to such a project. On the contrary, his only comment has been a courteous and laconic preference to forget all about it. In a 1976 interview he stated that he regarded his early stories, up to the publication of "Big Planet" in 1952, as an apprenticeship, and that he found it very embarrassing to look back upon them. So why should anyone else bother?

One reason, of course, is to see where Vance has come from. He has been in print since 1945, and his popularity has grown in mysterious ways. He is a writer who seems always to have been around, never quite rising from the known to the conspicuous. He did not write *The Demolished Man* or *The Space Merchants* or *The Left Hand of Darkness* or *The Forever War*. Instead, he wrote *The Dying Earth, To Live Forever, The*

Palace of Love, Emphyrio — all praised, all respected, but never quite reaching the wide vocal audience that makes the first rank of success. Only in recent years has his work begun to appear in respectable editions, and it is ironic that some of his earliest novels, published two-at-a-time in those garish Ace Doubles, should now be reissued and resold on a par with his most recent and painstaking books.

He has suffered, too, from his early identification with the pulps (specifically *Startling Stories* and *Thrilling Wonder Stories*), with their associations of gaudy superficiality and adolescent preoccupation. Although he made several attempts at publication before World War II (with the stories which eventually appeared as *The Dying Earth*), he first broke into print in 1945, at a time when John W. Campbell's legendary *Astounding* was the field's only standard of excellence. It was not until five years later that *Galaxy* and *The Magazine of Fantasy and Science Fiction* offered fresh markets to those who did not wish to confine their work to Campbell's idiosyncratic boundaries of theme, treatment, and style. Although Vance has said that he sent all his early stories to *Astounding* and submitted elsewhere only on rejection, he was clearly never a "Campbell writer" in the sense that Isaac Asimov, Robert A. Heinlein, and others were, despite the success of those stories which did crack the editorial barriers.

The first five years of Vance's writing career were thus spent almost entirely in the pulps. Much derided at the time, the pulps nonetheless represented a comprehensive apprenticeship for many authors. Always eager for material and unrestricted by literary pretention, the market demanded only that a writer should keep the reader reading. From the very first, Vance was able to meet this criterion.

He started with no technique except astonishing natural talent, and he learned quickly. In 1952, James Blish (writing as "William Atheling Jr.") said, in a comment on "Big Planet":

"Vance himself is a fascinating study in the technical development of a freelance writer. He started with three apparently natural gifts — a free, witty, unmannered style; an almost frighteningly fertile imagination, and a special talent for the visualization of physical color and detail. Any one of these gifts in excess in a young writer can prove fatal, as they can be and often have been used to mask or substitute for the essential construction problems of story telling. Exactly this happened to Vance in his early work: he tossed off ideas, wisecracks, splashes of color and exotic proper names like a Catherine wheel, while his plotting remained rudimentary or nonexistent."

Vance had, in fact, entered the field at a time when he could learn as he went along. Free of editorial biases or constraints, he was able to develop a personal style which has evolved into one of the most distinctive and rewarding in the field. At the same time, however, his strengths, by overshadowing his weaknesses, offered him no incentive to correct his enduring problems of construction, plotting, and resolution. As a writer who has never yet found an editor consistently able to bring out the best in him, Vance has had to rely on his own commitment to his craft and his own capacity (often formidable) for self-criticism.

In consequence of this, Vance's early stories are unusually illuminating in respect to his technical development. Successive stories are almost didactic in their illustration of increasing skills in specific areas of writing technique; Vance may fumble as every beginner does, but it is nearly always possible to point to a later effort which shows that he has learned better. Some weaknesses, sadly, seem inherent. Vance will never be famous for his plotting (the meticulous precision of *To Live Forever* being almost the only exception) and, ironically enough, his problems in this area are least noticeable when he settles for an elementary plot structure rather than attempting sophistication.

In examining Vance's early work, then, I have chosen, perhaps churlishly, to stop just when he reached a plateau of competence. In other words, it seems to me more instructive to look at what Vance did wrong, how he stopped doing it, and also to examine the ways he has been able, despite his technical naivete, to produce work which, after thirty years, retains color, verve, wit, and excitement. In the five years elapsing between his first publication and the appearance of *The Dying Earth* in 1950, Vance built the foundations of a brilliant and woefully neglected career. It is no disservice to him to display the intelligence, talent, and sheer hard work which went into that critical first phase.

1945

Vance's first published story, "The World-Thinker," appeared in *Thrilling Wonder Stories* (Summer 1945), although an accompanying letter indicates that it was probably written during the early part of the war and delayed by Vance's eventful spell in the Merchant Marine. The story has a curiously uneven texture, in which episodes of unremarkable formula fiction alternate with extraordinarily vivid scenes of surrealistic imagination, suggesting a lackadaisical draft extensively embroidered. This was to be characteristic of much of Vance's early work.

The story opens as routine space opera. The dauntless Inspector Lanarck of the Tellurian Corps of Investigation blasts off in pursuit of Kenna Parker, who has inherited a set of equations describing a new form of energy. Having declined the compulsory purchase suggested by the Empire, she has broken jail and made a run for it with the equations. Within a couple of pages, Lanarck has tracked her space-boat to a desolate planet, where a single ancient building stands in the desert. Inside dwells a mysterious alien, Laoome, who conducts a telepathic conversation. Laoome is capable of constructing entire worlds through mental effort alone, in alternate universes. In these created worlds, complete to the last detail, Laoome creates or destroys as he chooses, and he has chosen to create a refuge for Kenna Parker. He allows Lanarck to follow, leaving the two to resolve their conflict without intervention.

Laoome's motivations remain obscure, as does his background; he has been exiled from his home world of Narfilhet for milennia, although we never learn why. And he is aging; at one point, as he displays his powers to Lanarck, his control falters, with bizarre results to his created reality. With Lanarck's arrival on the created world, the story veers once more into formula: there's a shipwreck; exotic natives who worship Kenna Parker as a High Priestess; some slapdash action in which the only available "needlebeam" changes hands several times, etc.

There is little opportunity to carp, however; Vance suddenly takes off on a magnificent tour-de-force of imagination. In a splendidly ominous scene, a vast circular cloud erupts from the horizon; Lanarck realizes in terror that Laoome has once more lost control of his creation. Billions of tiny crimson animalcules rain from the sky, suddenly changing into blue manikins three inches high, which swarm singing over the horrified natives. Black pyramids sprout from the ground and shoot miles into the sky, which alters color to an unimaginable tint. The ground begins to dissolve. In an apocalyptic climax, the sun curdles into a segmented slug-like behemoth which crawls down the sky towards the planet. As gravity, matter, and light begin to mutate, Lanarck makes his escape with Kenna Parker (a routine impersonation plot-twist, preserving the romantic interest, goes almost unnoticed), and even as their space-boat turns into a living creature they reach the gate in space and return to Laoome's planet.

Only a few loose ends remain to be tied, strictly according to convention. Vance's explicit moral point, somewhat labored, is presented as an aphorism—"better that pins prick a million than that a sword be thrust into one"—and the story concludes abruptly with Lanarck's offstage killing of Laoome, justified by the pain Laoome has caused his created beings. Simultaneously, Kenna Parker, rather than to deliver such power to anyone, destroys the equations which originally caused all the trouble, and the story ends with the contrast of the two moral positions—her rejection of power and Lanarck's use of it to prevent a greater evil. Unsatisfactory and awkward though the resolution may be, the relationship of power and suffering is a recurrent moral conundrum in much of Vance's later work and is at the heart of all his major novels.

The story stands as an impressive debut flawed by formula plot, characterization, and pacing, but it revealed Vance's extraordinary imagination, gift for dialogue, and narrative skill. Recurring themes and preoccupations are already here—the concept of private worlds, strong female characters, the sea, paranormal powers, the pursuit of a criminal. Studded with exotic detail and elegant dialogue, powerfully vivid and fast-moving, disappointing and flat in resolution, "The World-Thinker" foreshadows the best and worst of Vance's writing.

1946

A year later Vance published "Planet of the Black Dust" in *Startling Stories*. An atrocious farrago of space-piracy, raking over most of the traditional seafaring clichés in a perfunctory manner, it did nothing to confirm his initial promise.

The story could usefully be included in a course on fiction writing, containing as it does almost every technical blunder imaginable. Vance changes viewpoint characters several times (occasionally within paragraphs), to no purpose and with none of the cues normally used to signal such a shift. Crucial aspects of the plot are wedged into the action in clumsy passages of exposition. Motivations are abrupt and sketchy. Characterization consists of physical descriptions and sinister stage directions. On top of all of this, the pace is frenetically confusing.

The plot concerns a space-freighter, described and handled exactly as if it were a tramp-steamer, on its way somewhere with a cargo of rare essences. The captain and mate, stamped as blatant hoodlums by Vance's crude characterization, have conspired to deliver the ship into the hands of notorious space-pirate "Killer" Donahue (although the details are not made clear until much later in the story). The constant exchanging of meaningful glances, mysterious and unexplained activities, and various unsubtle maneuvers make it obvious to the eventual hero, Holderlin ("second mate and quartermaster"), that all is not well. As Vance wisely admits, "Even a child would by now have been warned by the happenings aboard the *Perseus*."

So Holderlin suspects chicanery when given the order: "Take her five degrees closer to the star, Mr. Holderlin. We're somewhat off course, and the gravity will swing us back around." When the fake accident duly occurs — "Steering jets fused, Captain.... That cheap lining they put in at Aureolis has given out" — he allows himself to be maneuvered into a lifeboat with the "half-mad Callistonian cook," while the conspirators take the other one, which they believe is the only one with fuel and supplies (except that Holderlin has changed the fuel and supplies back, you see). In the next paragraph, the cook goes mad. Holderlin suddenly remembers a previous incident involving cannibalism in a lifeboat, which only this cook survived. The cook produces a knife and stabs himself "spasmodically" in the throat and dies. New paragraph.

After various nautical maneuvers (unconvincing in space), Holderlin disables the approaching pirate ship. He is able to do this because it happens to be identical to one of his former ships, and so he knows that it can be crippled by firing at "a small drain, the Achilles' heel of the heavy armor." Holderlin lands the *Perseus* by an unbelievable method which involves mooring his lifeboat to its "forward tow ring," then jockeying it down by means of two cords running from the lifeboat to the ship's controls. The planet turns out to be very black and dusty (hence the title) and also supports some silly-looking aliens, promptly filed away for future reference.

The pirates make contact by radio, bluster a bit, then retreat into the scenery. Holderlin goes off to find some clay (apparently the only raw material required to re-line those fused steering jets) and inveigles an alien into carrying for him. Enter the villains. After much chattering of needlebeams, Holderlin has them in his power. Both sides snarl away at each other in a remarkably juvenile manner, but eventually Holderlin blows up the pirate ship after a great deal of impenetrable scheming and a ludicrous scene in which one of the villains goes mad and attacks his crony with a cry of "You white-faced dog, you've ruined me!"

I have dealt with this story at cruel length to establish the level of Vance's technique at that time, although I am inclined to believe that this story possibly originated from an early stage of his pre-publication career. Occasional descriptive passages show some sparks of the later panache, but the dialogue is banal, the plot riddled with logical and motivational holes, and the style graceless, frantic, and wooden. The story also includes, disquietingly, the first appearance of a characteristic theme — the semi-intelligent natives who are moved hither and yon as the plot demands, with no suggestion of any moral imperative. In this instance, Holderlin blasts them down casually for no comprehensible reason; the remark "Can't have any talebearers" is meaningless in context.

"Planet of the Black Dust" is a far worse story than "The World-Thinker" and probably represents the lowest point of Vance's early work; later stories, while hardly more accomplished in technical terms, were at least partly redeemed by imagination and color. Vance's next story, "Phalid's Fate," appeared in *Thrilling Wonder Stories* in December and was at least an impressive failure. Though crudely plotted and executed, it included some thoughtfully characterized aliens and an ecological ingenuity which has since become characteristic of Vance. The story suffers from a mismatch of theme and plot, the theme itself being defined by Vance, in an accompanying commentary, as the nature of love and of idealistic love in its limiting case. The "limiting case" is that one partner wears the body of a different species.

While this theme was to be used, six years later, to revolutionary effect by Philip José Farmer in *The Lovers*, Vance's plot followed traditional lines. Ryan Wratch is seriously injured in a clash with the alien Phalids, and his brain is transplanted into the body of a captured Phalid as part of a sketchily described stratagem which does not become clear until late in the story. Wratch is returned to a Phalid ship by subterfuge and succeeds in releasing some human captives, although a girl remains through accident (and the need to introduce some romantic interest). Wratch evades detection until the ship arrives at the Phalid home planet, and he makes his escape with the girl. It is now revealed that he carries a disassembled transmitter to broadcast the location of the planet to Earth and, after an ingenious subplot involving the Phalid biology, the "cavalry" arrives. On his return to Earth, Wratch (and the reader) are amazed to discover that the girl loves him, and that his body has, after all, been repaired and is waiting for him. In a final mawkish scene, Wratch, restored to his body, clinches the girl and both exit.

The story reads better than this summary indicates, mainly owing to Vance's careful exploration of alien perception (gradually eroding Wratch's memories of humanity) and the intriguing life-cycle of the Phalids. The alien psychology is less successful, being constructed to fit the convolutions of the plot and to allow Wratch to carry off the flimsy impersonation. The romantic interest is not developed enough to be convincing, largely because Vance had to spend too much time moving the crowded plot along. He acknowledges frankly that he had found the task of describing Wratch's experience of alien perceptions too difficult and tedious and had given it up as a bad job. Certainly the story sags into unconvincing melodrama until Wratch discovers an ecological relationship between the Phalids and a forest which he has entered — having eaten of the "Fruit of Life," his body has become pregnant! The implications remain untouched, however, as Vance takes the easier option and produces Wratch's repaired human body.

On the whole, however, the failure of the story is due to in-experience and excess of ambition, and there's certainly no lack of imagination. The alien dialogue is elegantly bizarre, the action, while crowded and unconvincing, moves briskly enough, and the story indicates considerable potential.

1947

Perhaps in reaction to the failure of a major theme in "Phalid's Fate," Vance took a new direction in "I'll Build Your Dream Castle" (*Astounding*, September), a humorous minor piece which was to represent the course of his work for the following two years. Within its limits, it was highly successful, and its appearance in this demanding market at such an early stage of Vance's career was no mean achievement.

Vance has always been aware of the value of a strong opening paragraph, and this is particularly evident here:

> When Farrero first met Douane Angker, of Marlais & Angker, Class III Structors, something in his brain twisted, averted itself; and, looking down at the curl on Angker's tough mouth, he knew the feeling went double. Angker, short and solid, had concentrated in him a heavy unctuous vitality, the same way a cigar stump holds the strongest juices.

Such characterizations — terse, vivid, and unique — have become one of Vance's major strengths; the passage also indicates the beginnings of Vance's crisp, elliptical use of punctuation and detached clauses.

The plot is straightforward, slight, and ingenious, kept within the limits of Vance's technique at this stage. Farrero, a bright young architect, develops a cheaper method of house construction and passes the saving on to his customer. Angker, a senior partner, would prefer to take a higher profit. Farrero is scandalized, but soon finds himself blacklisted and unable to set up business for himself anywhere on Earth, the moon, or Venus.

Almost at once, however, customers begin to sign up with Farrero for contracts of fabulous cost, although the locations of his houses remain secret. Eventually a rival, posing as a customer, is taken out into nearby space, where Farrero has built gorgeous private worlds on tiny planetoids which, bewilderingly, have Earth-normal gravity and thus can hold a standard atmosphere. The plot denouement is intriguing and ingenious; Farrero has discovered a number of asteroids composed of collapsed matter ("star-stuff...matter crystallized at the heart of a star") and has established an unbreakable monopoly. However, in a final twist, he freely reveals the location of more of the collapsed matter—ten light years away in the dark companion of Sirius, at a temperature of twenty or thirty million degrees Centigrade.

By setting modest goals, Vance was able to produce a competent, entertaining, and colorful story which still retains charm today. The dialogue is crisp and authentic, while already elegant and witty; the plot moves briskly, with pacing and exposition well under control, in contrast to the breathless, meandering style of his previous efforts. The physics of the story is sound, if somewhat obtrusive, which may be the result of editorial pressure.

"I'll Build Your Dream Castle" is most notable for the exotic private worlds, meticulously worked out and described, and for the beginning use of Vance's personal technique for interaction; dialogue is interwoven with attitude, movement, and gesture to illuminate motivations, emotions, and responses. Such a technique—demanding skills of observation, description, and the construction of dialogue—far excels the multiple-viewpoint treatment of emotion and attitude generally found in beginning writers, and which Vance had attempted to use up to this point. In excess it can degenerate into meaningless details (as Hemingway and his imitators were to discover), and there is some slight tendency to this in the present story. On the whole, however, Vance displays a facility which has since become a cornerstone of his style, and this story set a high standard for his shorter humorous work which he has rarely failed to sustain.

1948

Having scored some success with his first attempt at this kind of story, Vance continued to develop his techniques within the framework of the short comic piece. For the next two years he was to publish only in *Startling Stories*, introducing the character Magnus Ridolph, an elderly dilettante detective with a sharp eye for the main chance. Ridolph is cautious, fastidious, and crafty; the characterization was highly unusual for the times. The heroes of pulp science fiction were, almost without exception, dense, fearless, upright young WASPs. Such characters, when they appear in Vance's work, are generally figures of fun; his protagonists, while certainly able to look after themselves, are given depth and character by their susceptibility to human weakness, self-doubt, and compassion.

The Ridolph stories, according to Vance, represented an early attempt to become a hack, a "million-word-a-year man." At first they appeared in *Startling* as fast as the magazine could be printed; Vance remembers them as first-draft work and describes them as absolutely awful. However, for this sort of story, an elderly character is something of an advantage as personality, attitudes, and history are already established. Romantic interest can likewise be set aside; Ridolph, who has some resemblance to Jules de Grandin (hero of an interminable *Weird Tales* series by Seabury Quinn), is too old for such follies and devotes his energies solely to personal enrichment and the enjoyment of good food, fine wines, and elegant clothes.

The first of the series, "Hard-Luck Diggings" (*Startling*, July), was apparently written in one sitting and reads accordingly. It has a peculiar, uneasy style which suggests that Vance was uncertain of the prevailing mood. It opens with Rogge, an obtuse and impatient mining engineer on a distant planet, who is experiencing undefined difficulties apparently of long standing. There are various comic reactions to bad news, the chewing-out of hapless subordinates, and the like, before a spaceship arrives with an eagerly-awaited inspector. At this stage we learn that Rogge's problem consists of an epidemic of mysterious murders, with men being strangled at the rate of three or four a day. The appearance of the mild-mannered Ridolph—not at all the expected beefcake—should be comic; however, it falls flat, overshadowed by the grimness of the situation.

Ridolph immediately tours the camp, asks a few questions, and almost at once deduces the solution to the mystery. Of course, he refuses to reveal it, preferring, in traditional manner, to put his theory to the test by inviting a murder attempt upon himself. This duly occurs and is unconvincingly forestalled by some technical gimmickry. It turns out that the murders are being committed by mobile roots of sentient trees threatened by the mining activities. Ridolph negotiates a settlement and is rewarded, oddly, by one of the trees with an excavated ruby.

Most "single-sitting" stories have pacing problems, and "Hard-Luck Diggings" is no exception, breaking down soon after the opening paragraphs. Ridolph's nearly instantaneous solution of the mystery fails to convince, and the attack on him, the climax of the story, is over in a few hasty paragraphs (and, logically, need never have happened). The final scenes are so crowded as to suggest editorial trimming for reasons of space (also implied by the layout of the magazine). In terms of the plot the story owes much to Sherlock Holmes, and an introductory quotation, attributed to Ridolph, is merely a restatement of Holmes's famous principle of eliminating the impossible until what remains, no matter how improbable, must be the truth. The solution of the problem is contrived but consistent; in later Ridolph stories the emphasis was to shift from technical deduction to more active and ingenious strategies, usually revolving around Ridolph's efforts to turn the tables on various tricksters and con-artists.

The macabre tone of the present story is inconsistent with its comic intent, and its general lack of polish makes it a minor and forgettable piece; Vance did not include it in a 1966 collection, *The Many Worlds of Magnus Ridolph*. However, it's interesting to note an early appearance of a recurrent theme — the conflict of man and alien is resolved by intelligent compromise. In John Campbell's magazine Earthmen would have been obliged to come out on top.

"Sanatoris Short-Cut" (*Startling*, September) is an early example of the elaborate, self-contained verbal scrimshaw which has become a major element of Vance's style. One of his favorite excursions is into the invention of games: often intricate, always colorful. In later work, most notably in *Trullion: Alastor 2262*, the game is integral to the story. In this case the game *is* the story for half its length, the other half being an inconsequential and slapdash melodrama.

Ridolph is brought on-stage with characteristic bravado:

> In the course of the years he had devised a number of money-making techniques. The first of these was profoundly simple. Surveying the world about him, he would presently observe a lack or an imperfection. A moment's thought would suggest an improvement, and in repairing the universe, Magnus Ridolph usually repaired his credit balance.

Short of funds, Ridolph visits a casino and takes an interest in a game called Lorango. The description of the game and an account of the factors involved in it occupy Vance for some five closely printed pages. Suffice it to say that the object is to predict which of twenty-four differently colored balls will bob to the top of a spinning globe full of water. Vance names every color with rare and evocative skill, lists the many physical parameters influencing the result, describes the calculation of the winnings, the house rules, the betting patterns, and so on.

Having analyzed the game, Ridolph promptly makes a killing, incurring the enmity of the casino boss, an obvious hoodlum named Acco May. Following some routine, if brisk, action and mayhem, Ridolph takes on the task of proving May guilty of a recent space hijacking, despite a convincing alibi. Much effort is expended by Vance on making the point that May's alibi can be broken if it is shown that a spaceship can travel from the distant planet Sanatoris in less than thirteen days. Even more laboriously, Vance resorts to a tiresome device which was to spoil several subsequent stories, as Ridolph inveigles May into a silly wager. If Ridolph can prove that the Sanatoris trip can be made in less than thirteen days, May will sign a full confession to the hijack; if Ridolph fails, May gets all his winnings back. Idiotically, May accepts the wager (even writing the confession in advance and lodging it with independent witnesses!), and Ridolph blasts off to prove his point. Far out in space, he zooms past waiting hatchet-men, apparently well off course.

In the next scene Acco May, duly convicted, is about to be marched off to "personality reconstruction." He confronts the complacent Ridolph, who has completed the journey in twelve days, sealing May's doom. Ridolph explains that:

> "Classical space charts . . . are constructed after the manner of a Mercator projection. The co-ordinates meet rectilinearally, the grid components running perfectly parallel but to infinity. This is an admirable system for short journeys, just as use of the Mercator system results in little error in a voyage across Long Island Sound.
>
> "However, on voyages of some duration, it is necessary to remember that the earth and — on a larger scale — space is curved, and to make the necessary correction."

This, of course, is balderdash. The errors of the Mercator

projection are implicit in the mapping of a spherical surface upon a flat one and have nothing to do with the mapping of three-dimensional space or the curvature of space-time through the presence of mass. Even if the explanation meant anything, it still requires Ridolph to have noticed an astrogational saving never before suspected—a situation roughly comparable to having all major airlines route planes from Los Angeles to New York via Cape Horn.

"Sanatoris Short-Cut" exemplifies Vance's talents for invention, color, intricacy, and weak plotting, with a fascinating doodle that makes a feeble story. With the development of his skills at greater lengths, Vance has been able to embellish and embroider as he wishes within the structure of a more involved plot, and the overall effect has been far more satisfactory. But I'd love to see a Lorango game in action!

"The Unspeakable McInch" (*Startling*, November) again failed to match a grim theme to lightness of touch and characterization, and was further damaged by maladroit plotting and a fundamental misapplication of the conventions of the detective story. The McInch of the title is a murderer, according to the first line. He is later described as a thief and a corrupt civic official who steals through graft, but it eventually turns out that he simply takes money at will from the municipal safe of Sclerotto City, a squalid township teeming with multifarious life and under the administration of the vaguely defined "Uni-Culture Mission," which commissions Ridolph to investigate.

Nobody knows who the thief is or how he steals; guards are invariably found dead of disease, with the safe rifled. Ridolph discusses the case briefly with the usual surly official, then proceeds to interview various suspects, a bizarre and fascinating collection of aliens (including a human Negro, a rare species indeed in pulp fiction, save as the protagonist of embarrassing parables). After a brief investigation, Ridolph deduces the identity of McInch and brings all the suspects together for the traditional confrontation. McInch, revealed, attempts to kill all present; foiled by Ridolph, he is torn to pieces by his enraged fellows in a grisly climax. It only remains for Ridolph to explain his reasoning and to depart with an appropriate snappy ending.

The failure of the story is mainly due to the excessive contrivance of the plot, and lapses of logic are evident throughout. Although McInch is said to steal through "civic corruption," there is no evidence for this — the safe is simply burgled. McInch could be anyone, in fact. Ridolph assumes that "McInch is one of the city officials; they would be the first to be exposed to temptation." This makes no sense but reduces the range of suspects to a manageable number. Although Ridolph deduces McInch's identity from his meetings with the officials, all the information which he uses is kept from the reader until the final exposition. Although it is imaginative and ingenious (based on the ways in which the various aliens spend their money), the problem has already been solved.

When McInch's identity is known, further problems appear. He is a huge alien creature resembling a sting ray, employed as a garbage-collector; in fact, the citizens bring their rubbish to him, as he wallows in organic refuse and absorbs it into his body. (The logistics of such an arrangement seem impossible. How much rubbish does a city produce? What do they do with their inorganic refuse? etc.) Vance makes no attempt to explain how such a creature could carry out regular robberies unobserved, or even why nobody notices the appalling smell lingering around the safe afterwards. McInch supposedly kills his victims with a squirt of virulent bacteria (Ridolph evades an early murder attempt through simple germicidal precautions). There's no explanation of why the guards of the safe could not do likewise, or, indeed, why they could not simply shoot McInch, hit him on the head, stand out of reach in a narrow corridor, or write a detailed account of events while sitting out the incubation period of the disease.

The main interest of the story, then, is an incidental detail: the haphazard architecture of Sclerotto City, the eerie daylight of twin suns of different colors (a recurrent embellishment in subsequent work), the fascinating aliens. However flimsy Ridolph's deductions may be, his fastidious self-regard and urbanity are developed with skill and economy, and his elegant dialogue contrasts well with the bluntness of the straight man, Boek, and the various modes of alien conversation.

1949

By the time "The Sub-Standard Sardines" (*Startling*, January) appeared, the "Ridolph format" had become clear—an intriguing narrative hook, an exotic locale, a flamboyant puzzle, and a snappy ending, with Ridolph's fastidious habits milked for comic relief. Not much was different in this story, but Vance's developing skills in background detail often lifted it out of formula.

The title is nearly the plot. Ridolph is commissioned by a friend whose sardine business is threatened by mysteriously contaminated tins of the product. He assumes the squalid identity of a sardine eviscerator on the planet Chandaria and soon meets the shifty partner in the business, obviously up to no good in a suspicious laboratory. This proves to contain various mutated sardines, including one of high intelligence who is able to communicate with Ridolph. After some routine mayhem, Ridolph is pursued by the villains to a colony established by the intelligent fish, whose unexpected independence has put them at some risk of attack. Ridolph helps them to outwit the corrupt fish farmers, and the obligatory punch in the ending is provided by his revelation that the intelligent fish are now partners in the business, much to his patron's comic astonishment.

As always, much of the interest is in the details—the menu, furniture, and decorations at a dinner; the desolate red-lit marshes of Chandaria; the disparate aliens in the cannery; the charts of the Barnett Method for Establishing Communication with Alien Intelligences. But it is also interesting to see traces of themes and concepts which Vance was to develop in later work. His interest in communication and language appeared again in "Gift of Gab" (1955), a more mature treatment of the theme, and was developed at novel length in *The Languages of Pao* (1958). In the present story, Vance's fascination with the sea is also apparent, as is his taste for moral paradox:

> Banish Evil from the world? Nonsense! Encourage it, foster it, sponsor it. The world owes Evil a debt beyond imagination. Think! Without greed ambition falters. Without vanity art becomes idle musings. Without cruelty benevolence lapses to passivity. Superstition has shamed man into self-reliance and, without stupidity, where would be the savor of superior understanding?

The story also includes the first appearance of the Vance "footnote," later to become an art in its own right. Dialogue, pacing, and viewpoint are handled with unobtrusive competence throughout, although Vance fumbles exposition on a couple of occasions, once through a clumsy snatch of overheard recapitulation, and again, at the end, in an ill-judged switch from third-person narration to Ridolph's own account. Nonetheless, though trivial, the story remains entertaining even to modern tastes.

Now that Vance's appearances in *Startling* with the "Ridolph" stories were a regular event, attracting enthusiasm from readers, he was learning to deal with errors which had marred earlier stories. "The Howling Bounders" (*Startling*, March) is a more assured story than any previously published and can be seen as a turning point in the sequence. Subsequent stories appeared less frequently (as Vance tired of the limitations of the form), but were more skillfully constructed; perhaps more important, they displayed a matching of style, content, and mood far superior to earlier efforts. "The Howling Bounders" is the last of the early short stories in which this basic mistake was made.

The story begins in the middle—a standard device often used by Vance as a narrative hook. Ridolph has bought a plantation on a remote planet at a knockdown price; of course, there's a catch. A brief flashback sets the scene. Pleading urgent cash-flow problems, a meticulously shifty planter has sold Ridolph half his plantation of ticholama, source of the versatile elastic fiber resilian. No sooner has Ridolph committed himself and his funds, however, than he discovers the depredations of the Howling Bounders — semisentient marauding humanoids which subsist upon ticholama and appear both savage and invulnerable. Gradually Ridolph's crop is laid waste; the former owner affects consternation, offering to buy back the holding at a derisory price. Once again, a pointless wager is made; the price of the plantation against Ridolph's projected profits, if he can defeat the Bounders.

After cryptic preparations Ridolph launches a campaign against the creatures, and here the problems of the story, so far constructional, become moral. The gimmick turns out to be the composition of the Bounders themselves; they are largely resilian, and so Ridolph traps them using a resilian bonding agent which glues them into a furious, unbreakable line. Fortuitously, they are rendered torpid by daylight, and so Ridolph goes out, kills them, and uses their corpses as sources of raw resilian.

The issue which arises here has been the theme of a number of good science-fiction stories; among the first that come to mind are Vercors' *You Shall Know Them*, Walter M. Miller's "Conditionally Human," Avram Davidson's "Now Let Us Sleep," and Robert Silverberg's "Sundance." Simply put, it is: how shall we decide what is human? If the Bounders are animals, Ridolph is ingeniously disposing of dangerous vermin. If they are intelligent, he is committing the atrocity of the Nazi death-camps — a genocide so efficient that it mines the bodies of the dead for raw materials. Some may say that this sounds like an excessive amount of significance to draw from a pulp science-fiction story, and a comic one at that. This, of course, is exactly the point. Vance, through inexperience, had written a humorous, lightweight story which happened to throw up a huge moral dilemma, and it became impossible for him to reconcile these elements.

As a humorous story, "The Howling Bounders" works well for much of its length. The opening scenes are thoughtfully laid out and carefully paced; there's an entertaining minor counterpoint involving the limitations of the native cook, tied up neatly in the last line; Ridolph's charged and circumlocutory encounters with the devious planter are excellently done. One may forgive the dubious chemistry of the scene in which Ridolph, in danger of suffocation during a fire, electrolyzes his water supply. However, the central problem remains. The Bounders may have language, are capable of organization, know the use of fire. Ridolph's band seems to be the only one on the planet, and by the story's end he has slaughtered 2,400 of them for the resilian in their flesh.

Nor is this the only occasion on which Vance's work has shown this disturbing blind spot. Many of his stories feature semihuman creatures whose sentience and status is never clarified—the mutations of *The Dragon Masters*, the puppets in *Emphyrio*, the merlings of *Trullion: Alastor 2262*, the morphotes and erjins of Koryphon in *The Gray Prince*, the ahulphs of Durdane, etc. Only once, it seems, has the issue been faced, in "Gift of Gab," one of Vance's best stories, in which the exploitation of the unhuman but eventually intelligent dekabrachs is uncompromisingly condemned. The omission of the problem in Vance's more ambitious work is disappointing; the fact that it occurs at all in "The Howling Bounders" shows clearly that, at this stage, Vance had not yet learned to keep control of his material.

"The King of Thieves" (*Startling*, November) is by contrast a mature and competent story which blends its theme much more satisfactorily with its mood and content. The theme is one of Vance's most pervasive preoccupations, and it is set out succinctly in an introductory epigraph:

In all the many-colored worlds of the universe no single ethical code shows a universal force. The good citizen on Almanatz would be executed on Judith IV. Commonplace conduct of Medellin excites the wildest revulsion on Earth, and on Moritaba a deft thief commands the highest respect.

For Vance, morality is a function of culture, and much of his later work explores the moral conflicts inherent in access to a multitude of social systems. In this story the issue is explored, light-heartedly but with ingenuity, by placing Ridolph in two social systems—one is the culture of Moritaba, the primitive jungle planet where accomplishment in thieving is the prime determinant of social status, and the other is encapsulated in Ridolph's relationship with Mellish, a shady entrepreneur who has already swindled Ridolph and now happens to be in competition with him for valuable mining rights on Moritaba.

Ridolph, of course, comes out on top. He succeeds by playing each social situation better than its other members, rather than by imposing himself upon it. He soon progresses from guarding his own property to stealing everyone else's (by a contrived modus operandi which does not bear excessive scrutiny) and becomes himself the King of Thieves. He outwits his rival Mellish (by means of another illogical wager), and when the villain attempts to turn the tables by means of extortion, Ridolph promptly turns them back again by extorting more skillfully.

In each situation, in fact, Ridolph's conduct is scrupulously moral; he plays by the ground rules, and when they are broken he plays by the new ones as well. Mellish, however, personifies the rigid boor who is incapable of seeing the world in any terms other than his own. Ridolph wins his mining concession from the King of Thieves by becoming King himself; Mellish offers bribes—a five-and-dime store, a merry-go-round—that recall the cynical bargaining for Manhattan Island. This blindness to other ways of living or the insistence that others live in one's own style is, time and again, the essence of evil in Vance's work and one of the major themes of his later story-cycles. Here, however, it is treated with a lightness of touch and a fine attention to detail; unlike "The Howling Bounders," the story never gets out of its moral depth. There are slipshod aspects, of course; Ridolph's method of theft is far-fetched and over-contrived, and the story piles up too many changes of direction in the closing pages. But generally it's an entertaining overture to much of Vance's more ambitious later work.

1950

"The Potters of Firsk" (*Astounding*, May) was Vance's second story in this prime market and represented a break from the amusing but eventually repetitive "Ridolph" series in *Startling*. There had been some tendency for Vance's work until now to include somewhat obtrusive chunks of science as turning points of the plot, and "I'll Build Your Dream Castle," his previous *Astounding* story, had suffered from this problem. "The Potters of Firsk," while less freighted with technology, was subsequently selected as representative of the science of chemistry in Arthur C. Clarke's anthology *Time Probe*. The chemistry content is slight but crucial; the main strength of the story lies in Vance's choice of subject — ceramics.

Vance has said that he and his wife were professional potters at this time; his expertise in the craft and his powerful visual sense were obvious from the opening paragraphs:

> The yellow bowl on Thomm's desk stood about a foot high, flaring out from a width of eight inches at the base to a foot across the rim. The profile showed a simple curve, clean and sharp, with a full sense of completion; the body was thin without fragility; the whole piece gave an impression of ringing well-arched strength.
>
> The craftsmanship of the body was matched by the beauty of the glaze — a glorious transparent yellow, luminescent like a hot summer afterglow. It was the essence of marigolds, a watery wavering saffron, a yellow as of transparent gold, a yellow glass that seemed to fabricate curtains of light within itself and fling them off, a yellow brilliant but mild, tart as lemon, sweet as quince jelly, soothing as sunlight.

The story is told by Thomm as a reminiscence of his youth in the "Department of Planetary Affairs," on Firsk. Entranced by the ware of the potters, he soon discovers that they exert a sinister control over the natives from their colony in the hills, using bodies (killed as necessary) to yield essential bonelime. Substitutes are rejected, as "the spirit of the person is in the bones and this passes into the glaze and gives it an inner fire otherwise unobtainable."

Thomm, conciliatory, attempts to negotiate, but his coarse superior, Covill, decides to end the kidnappings of the potters by dropping an atom bomb on their volcanic kilns. Thomm, attempting to mediate (and also pursuing a kidnapped girl introduced earlier for romantic interest), is about to become bonelime, but at the last moment manages to win over the potters by synthesizing the previously unobtainable yellow glaze using uranium salts derived from the atom bomb. In a fairly neat resolution, the oafish Covill attempts to retrieve the uranium and fails to return. Some weeks later, the potters inform Thomm that Covill, enraged, had finally caused violence; evading questions about Covill's fate, they present Thomm with the yellow bowl: "The fiery soul of the madman has given luster to an already glorious glaze."

"The Potters of Firsk" is a neat, competent story, enhanced by the strength of its visual passages and the intelligence of its cultural argument; once again the hero succeeds through his sympathetic understanding of the social priorities of the alien culture. The major problem is one of construction. The opening scene, despite its intrinsic merits, drains much of the tension from the narrative. Vance sets up two plot problems — what will happen to Thomm, and will the potters succeed in making their longed-for yellow glaze? The opening scene has already shown us Thomm alive and prosperous, with an impressive yellow bowl on his desk.

The technique of "framing" a story in this way, although very popular in the nineteenth century, is now rare, largely because of the greater premium now placed upon plot tension in popular fiction. Vance has not generally been very successful with it; the use of a "frame" is virtually the only flaw in *Emphyrio*, and the technique is also used to poor effect in the closing pages of *Marune: Alastor 933* and *The Gray Prince*.

"The Spa of the Stars" (*Startling*, July) is something of a potboiler—a rather perfunctory lightweight piece which attempted to ring some changes on the "Magnus Ridolph format." Ridolph, offstage for much of the time, is not the viewpoint character. The two lead characters, partners in the hotel venture of the title, talk in the unlikely sub-Runyon argot attributed to the lower classes by writers such as Robert Arthur. Vance (who claims never to have worked in a white collar in his life) knows better than this.

The Spa of the Stars is a grandiose beach resort, on a distant planet, which is unfortunately beset by ferocious animals soon after receiving its first guests; many of them, in fact, meet grisly deaths as a result. While a brisk indifference to carnage is an essential element in, for example, the milieu of the "Dying Earth" stories, it does not blend well with the light farce of the present piece. Ridolph is hired to solve the problem but in fact contributes very little. The partners, on their own initiative, prepare a foul-smelling paste which they believe will act as an animal repellent; Ridolph is used to test this out. In a far-fetched sequence, he is drugged, smeared with the malodorous paste, and left upon the beach. When the paste fails to repel an attacking beast, Ridolph saves himself by means of a supersonic whistle constructed a few moments previously. The natives, it seems, are able to produce such vibrations in their own vocal apparatus, hence their immunity to attack. In a closing scene Ridolph exacts revenge for the shoddy treatment given to him.

Ridolph's urbane dialogue and precise mannerisms redeem most of the scenes in which he appears, but otherwise the story veers too easily into slapstick or predictable comic routines.

There is an occasional touch of elegance, such as the reaction to Ridolph's crafty maneuvers:

> Joe and Lucky had turned their heads simultaneously, staring. Their faces wore the expressions seen on small animals, who, tripping a baited tiger, snap their own flashlight photographs.

"New Bodies for Old" (*Thrilling Wonder*, August) was by contrast a story of major importance and represented a critical turning-point in Vance's career. It was his longest, most ambitious, most accomplished story to date, and it displayed, in one form or another, most of the themes and techniques Vance was to develop in successive work in the next two or three years.

The story is set in a future society of economic prosperity; five bored young men, seeking adventure, sponsor one of their number to test the expensive and mysterious services of the Chateau d'If, whose publicity is as attractive as it is cryptic. A volunteer goes, disappears, is seen weeks later enjoying a playboy lifestyle; he refuses to talk to them but indifferently returns their money. The eventual hero, Roland Mario, is next to go; unable to learn what goes on at the Chateau, he nonetheless cannot resist the urge to find out. Drugged, he wakes to find himself trapped in the body of an aging and unpleasant businessman whose personality is now enjoying a fresh lease on life in Mario's body. The rest of the story is concerned with Mario's attempts to recapture his own identity.

To modern ears this may sound like a very tired plot; however, a close reading indicates sound and sophisticated development. For its time and milieu the plot serves well enough, and Vance has obviously put some thought into buttressing its weaker joints. For example, the difficulty of getting a character into such a situation in the first place is dealt with by a careful opening scene in which the five men discuss the aimlessness of their lives, the chance nature of worldly success, the possible motives of the managers of the Chateau d'If, the rumors surrounding the operation, and the safeguards against misfortune or treachery. The pace of the scene and the interaction of the characters build to a point where it is inevitable that one man will decide to try his chances. In the same way, his "success," despite its puzzling aspects, is sufficiently seductive to encourage Mario; his interview at the Chateau, while revealing nothing in the way of hard fact, is provocative, aggressive, and confident. The decision to plunge ahead thus becomes more credible. In earlier work Vance would simply have pushed his hero through the front door, and to hell with motivation; later stories have sometimes followed the same path, although Vance has been much more conscious of his effects and has used caprice as a deliberate, disarming dynamic of the plot.

Similar ingenuity appears in the resolution of the plot problem. How is Mario to regain his body? He cannot succeed against the powerful Chateau d'If—whose body-swapping has recruited influential old men from every sphere of life—by direct action; nor can he place his body at risk by involving the police. Subterfuge is his only recourse. However, instead of sneaking his hero into the stronghold through a fortuitous secret passage, Vance sneaks his hero into control of the firm of architects which *builds* the stronghold. This building itself, the Empyrean Tower, is one of the most imaginative inventions of the story. There are also lively subplots involving a charged sexual relationship and the invention of an interstellar drive.

In a story of this length Vance was able to allow himself the luxury of baroque extravagance, and "New Bodies for Old" offers some extraordinary flights of fancy, such as the lobby of the Atlantic-Empire Hotel:

> Here—if the guest cared little for expense—he could buy wrought copper, gold, tantalum; gowns in glowing fabric of scarlet, purple, indigo; *objets* from ancient Tibet and the products of Novacraft; cabochons of green Jovian opals, sold by the milligram; blue balticons from Mars, fire diamonds brought from twenty miles under the surface of the Earth; Marathesty cherries preserved in Organdy Liqueur, perfumes pressed from Arctic Moss, white marmorea blooms like the ghosts of beautiful women.

There's a similar exultant extravagance in the description of the splendid Empyrean Tower, crammed with artifacts from every field of human culture and enterprise. There are less flamboyant devices, too — the venomous insults of a deranged, sick enemy; the ingenious techniques of personality exchange; the intense and ambivalent relationship between Mario and the girls at the Chateau: "Her will is for destruction, death. A bright thing only on the surface. Inwardly she is as dark and violent as a drop of hot oil."

Vance also conveys a rare and chilling insight into the horror of Mario's predicament — his repugnance at the gross body which he now inhabits; his revulsion at using his host's razor or toothbrush, attending to his physical needs, living in his home; the grim realization that the glandular make-up of the body will itself distort and change his personality more and more as time goes by.

The flaws of "New Bodies for Old" are mostly honorable — perhaps an excess of extravagance and detail, a couple of plot-threads too many, a crowding of action into inadequate length. But it's a well-crafted, intelligent story, laced with tight elegant dialogue, insightful, thoughtful, and distinctive. It is probably the earliest published story in which Vance demonstrated the depth of his potential as a major stylistic talent in the field.

In contrast, "Ultimate Quest" (*Super Science Stories*, September) is mainly of interest as a curio. It is the only story widely known to have been published by Vance under a pseudonym, appearing by "John Holbrook," a variant of his full name (John Holbrook Vance), which he has used exclusively for his mystery novels. Vance has used other pseudonyms (which he now resolutely claims to have forgotten). He has said that his intention was to reserve his own name for his better stories, but finding that differentiation hard to maintain, he abandoned the practice. He could hardly have considered the present story comparable to contemporary work accepted by other markets, built as it is on the ludicrous premise of an attempt to circumnavigate the entire universe by travelling very, very fast in a very, very straight line.

The idea is mentioned again (in the Sons of Langtry conference in "The Five Gold Bands," published in November). Vance may have found it entertaining to develop the notion in another piece. In his later work, small vignettes and anecdotes are scattered throughout the main narrative with confidence and finesse; at this stage he had not yet learned fully how to measure the worth of an idea in terms of story length. This idea might work as a throwaway line or a paragraph; as a short story it runs into trouble very quickly.

Nonetheless, Vance tries his best. The opening sequence of "Ultimate Quest" is a press conference at which the project is discussed and all the obvious questions are asked. When the answers are weak or nonexistent — as so many of them are — the lead character's confidence, coolness, and disarming directness must suffice to leap the gap and keep going. Vance is aware of the problems involved in flying a straight course over intergalactic distances at speeds of "six or seven thousand light years per second"; he knows about the horrendous effects of Dopplered head-on radiation; he is aware that it would be difficult to distinguish the original galaxy from several billion similar galaxies along the line of flight. However, he has no choice except to respond, through his laconic hero, with the recurrent admission: "That's a good question. I'm sorry to say I have no precise answer."

There is also a lunatic spaceflight system which reads like the sort of idea writers invent after a convivial evening with other writers. It involves two spacecraft (Nip and Tuck), the former cylindrical, the latter tubular. They align themselves by means of "destriation fields." Nip accelerates for a while, shuts off power; Tuck accelerates, slides over Nip, shuts off power; Nip accelerates, shoots through Tuck, shuts off power; etc., etc. By this method the straightness of the course is ensured to a ridiculous number of decimal places.

Vance valiantly throws in some distractions. There's a sub-plot involving a bumptious young crew member who eventually learns better, and the tensions and anxieties of the voyage are handled rather well. At the end, however, all is bathos; the crew stand anxiously on the bridge; the cherished gyroscope of the matured tyro ticks around to the 360° mark which will indicate the complete circuit of the cosmos (although Vance makes one of the irritating arithmetical errors which occasionally afflict him, momentarily putting 370° into a circle). The gyro keeps turning, at one degree per paragraph, and, at last:

> 360. "There! The big one! Golly, it looks almost like the face of some-one you know!"... Ahead, like magic, the sky suddenly showed full of familiar patterns.
>
> "Dead ahead!" cried Chiram. "See—that's the constellation Cygnus; that's where we started for.... And there—dead ahead—that yellow star..."

The story stops there, unfortunately; it would have been interesting to see how they managed to decelerate from seven thousand light years per second in the few milliseconds that appeared to be available. While Vance deserves some credit for diligence, the story cannot be taken seriously. It is interesting, however, to note that the notion of the "destriation field" was later to emerge as the "Jarnell intersplit" in the "Demon Princes" sequence.

With "The Five Gold Bands" (*Startling*, November), Vance published his first competent attempt at the kind of story which has now become characteristic of him—the colorful action novel, moving through a variety of settings, with a strong female secondary lead, a conventional plot, and a sadly perfunctory ending. Vance was to publish many stories in this format, most of which were reprinted during the 1960s as Ace Doubles. His major novels have followed a similar structure, albeit considerably stronger in characterization, theme, and style, but even the least sophisticated are still entertaining.

The plot of "The Five Gold Bands" is traditional; a secret

has been divided into five parts which have been dispersed for security. The story is the quest for them. The gold bands of the title are bracelets belonging to the five "Sons of Langtry," descendants of the inventor of space-drive, and which contain cryptic clues to the hiding places of the parts of the space-drive formulae. The Sons, with their unbreakable franchise on interstellar travel, wield immense power over multifarious races of their respective planets. Paddy Blackthorn, a burlesque Irish adventurer, is caught trying to steal the secret, but accidentally kills all the Sons while attempting to escape. Paddy, accompanied by "Earth Central" agent Fay Bursill, sets off to piece together the formulae, pursued by the inheritors of the Sons and their minions.

By now Vance had developed a number of techniques for camouflaging the flimsiness of his plotting. The characterizations, while crude to modern tastes, are well-developed. Paddy, although given a strong line in whimsical blarney, is a colorful and sympathetic character; cheerful, vigorous, and fast-talking, he remains somewhat ineffectual and often has to be pulled out of tight corners by Fay. She, in turn, is the prototype of Vance's female leads — cool, demure, humorous, resourceful, dark-haired, bright-eyed, well able to look after herself on equal terms with men. The light and constant sexual byplay between the two is one of the story's mainsprings.

Vance keeps his characters on the move and the pace rarely slackens. Exotic settings crowd through the pages, suspending disbelief to excellent effect. The story moves quickly from the Sons' business meeting on a tiny asteroid where Paddy is forced to act as interpreter — a role of purely diplomatic significance (and where the tension of the event obscures more critical evaluation of the plot dynamics) — to the various planets ruled by the Sons: the Thieves' Cluster, where he meets Fay; the eerie planet of Alpheratz, where the secret is hidden beneath a multilayered "ocean" of dense amber gas; the Badau planet where Paddy's pose as a travelling entertainer falls atrociously flat (and where Fay redeems the situation with an impressive strip-tease routine); Loristan, and the comic paranoia at the safe-deposit box; the tourist planet of Shaul, where intrigue, deception, and technology are all needed; and the grim Koton planet where the heroic pair are captured at last, and the dreaded nerve-suits are wheeled into the interrogation chamber...

Vance eventually loses control of his story, and the closing sequences strain credulity; the plot takes convoluted turns and motivations become flimsy. In a disturbing climax Paddy tricks his enemy into an error in the space-drive assembly, resulting in a huge explosion on his home planet ("...stupendous crater... millions dead," according to a fragmentary news broadcast). However, as it's already been argued that they weren't very nice people anyway, Paddy wastes only a sentence or two in regret, and the final paragraphs find him pursuing Fay amorously around the cabin (having, of course, committed himself firmly to marriage on several occasions).

"The Five Gold Bands" is a good early example of "second-order" Vance, displaying most of his enduring strengths and weaknesses: color, stylish dialogue and confrontations, elaborate bargaining scenes, exotic settings, bizarre folkways, imaginative characterizations, humor, pace, ingenuity, formula plotting, strained motivation, inadequate and disappointing resolution, the perceptive display of moral ambiguities and their slipshod disposal.

It takes a determined critical intent to resist the verve and extravagance of such a story and to look more closely at the weaknesses of structure. There is a marked incongruity, for example, between Paddy's sophisticated penetration of the space-drive factory in the story's enthralling opening sequence and his disastrous bungling once he gets inside. There is no real reason for the Sons to gather in one place at all; they supposedly hate each other, their business seems trivial and equally amenable to long-distance communication, and the purpose of the gathering is solely to get them killed by Paddy so he can steal the five gold bands at his convenience. Despite the vigilance of the entire galaxy, Paddy and Fay evade capture at half-a-dozen space-ports; at one stage Paddy escapes detection by the "psychograph" because, as he happens to mention afterwards, he has a surgical plate in his skull. At the close, Paddy is able to outwit an enemy who holds both of them entirely within his power, only through their captor's consistent refusal to take obvious and safe courses of action which would accomplish everything he wants.

Vance's subsequent space operas rarely escape such pitfalls, although the continued development of his style and narrative skills redeems the story in all but a few extreme cases. In his mature work, novels such as *Emphyrio*, the "Demon Princes" books, *The Anome, Maske: Thaery*, and *The Gray Prince* conceal a formidable depth of speculation, social comment, character development, and exquisitely crafted prose beneath an apparently superficial space opera. He has never been able to work comfortably at novel length in anything other than conventional structures, although some of his more obscure experimental work, published in the early 1950s, remains breathtaking even at this time.

It was at this stage, however, that Vance published his most famous and influential work and stepped at once to a leading rank in the field of postwar fantasy. *The Dying Earth* appeared in the autumn of 1950 in a shoddy paperback edition, abominably distributed, and it must represent one of the least auspicious debuts of any modern fantasy writer. A muddy cover depicts a woman clad in a vague gauzy robe and a troubled expression, while men in the foreground look on, and an owl-like creature hovers clumsily above. The back cover lists other titles in the series, of no great distinction. The paper is dingy pulp, the binding poor, the typeface without distinction. But the reader who persevered to the first page was met with one of the most exquisite opening paragraphs in the genre:

Deep in thought, Mazirian the Magician walked his garden. Trees fruited with many intoxications overhung his path, and flowers bowed obsequiously as he passed. An inch above the ground, dull as agates, the eyes of mandrakes followed the tread of his black-slippered feet. Such was Mazirian's garden — three terraces growing with strange and wonderful vegetations. Certain plants swam with changing iridescences; others held up blooms pulsing like sea-anemones, purple, green, lilac, pink, yellow. Here grew trees like feather parasols, trees with transparent trunks threaded with red and yellow veins, trees with foliage like metal foil, each leaf a different metal — copper, silver, blue tantalum, bronze, green iridium. Here blooms like bubbles tugged gently upwards from glazed green leaves, there a shrub bore a thousand pipe-shaped blossoms, each whistling softly to make music of the ancient Earth, of the ruby-red sunlight, water seeping through black soil, the languid winds. In this waning hour of Earth's life no man could count himself familiar with the glens, the glades, the dells and deeps, the secluded clearings, the ruined pavilions, the sun-dappled pleasances, the gullies and heights, the various brooks, freshets, ponds, the meadows, thickets, brakes and rocky outcrops.

This is pure Vance dazzlement, one of the most identifiable passages in all his work. Every element of his style may be seen here — the overpowering visual imagery; the flood of exotic inventions; the mannered, elegant, incantatory phrasing; the absence of redundant conjunctions; the rich vocabulary; the deep empathy for landscape and weather; the unerring sense of mood and atmosphere.

The book is replete with similar passages, and the quality and elegance of the writing are almost unfailing. Vance is, in fact, a born fantasy writer; his talents are so appropriate to the field that it was inevitable that this early attempt should be a landmark. Once again, however, it is the magnitude of his talent which allows him to publish work so lacking in basic technique, and there are few books in the field at once so stylistically excellent and so technically crude.

The Dying Earth probably took at least ten years to write, on and off. The stories that constitute the book were, according to Vance himself, written at sea (presumably in the early 1940s) and failed to sell. Sam Merwin, then editor of *Startling* and *Thrilling Wonder*, recalls some "fascinating, but, alas, unpublishable, pseudo-Cabell [James Branch Cabell] fantasies" submitted at this time. They were subsequently rewritten into book form and eventually published by Hillman Books, who concurrently were publishing the excellent and foredoomed magazine *Worlds Beyond*, with Damon Knight as the editor. *Worlds Beyond* published part of *The Dying Earth* under the title "The Loom of Darkness" in its first issue (December) and was to publish a splendidly constructed short story by Vance ("Brain of the Galaxy") in its third and last issue two months later. Knight had also got another story from Vance, "The Secret," which seemed accursed, being lost twice and eventually reprinted in England in 1966 without Vance's knowledge. With the demise of the magazine, Vance lost probably his best chance to form a creative relationship with Knight, one of the finest and most intelligent editors in the field.

It seems likely that, in publishing *The Dying Earth*, Hillman and/or Knight were hoping to foster an obvious new talent. The book represents a recapitulation of Vance's entire writing career up to that time, from his earliest efforts, when he was simply incapable of telling a story, to the relative sophistication and competence of stories such as "New Bodies for Old" and "The Five Gold Bands." As such, it is sometimes excellent and sometimes very bad indeed.

It is inconceivable that there should be any reader of Vance who does not own a copy of *The Dying Earth*, and so a detailed treatment of the book can omit much expository detail. The texture and language of the work are, in any case, so seductive that a general overview offers more chance of evaluating it critically.

To begin with, the book has no structure. While Lin Carter has described the stories as opening into each other like intricate Chinese boxes, in fact there is no unifying theme and the overlap of characters is inconsistent and apparently virtually fortuitous. Even the time sequence of the stories is confused. "Mazirian the Magician" opens the book, but in fact takes place some indeterminate time after the event of "Turjan of Miir," which follows it (an order Vance thought useful at the time, with some justification in terms of exposition, but which has been reversed in subsequent editions). "Turjan of Miir" generates the central character of the first part of "T'sais," in which a parenthetical episode introduces the central character of "Liane the Wayfarer." "Ulan Dhor Ends a Dream" includes only the minor character Prince Kandive from earlier stories, while "Guyal of Sfere" is related only through some geographical references (and, of course, the common background of all the stories).

The background of the Dying Earth itself has few antecedents. In the far future of Earth the sun is growing dim, the moon has departed the sky, science has fallen, and magic, itself a declining and half-understood technique, is the only power in the world. There are similarities here to Clark Ashton Smith's "last continent" of Zothique, and, although Vance acknowledges Smith as an exemplar, the style and mood of his work have taken a different direction. Certainly Vance shares Smith's taste for elegant syntax, rare words, and sardonic humor; however, there is a cynical, misanthropic flavor to Smith's work which is rarely found in Vance without a compensating empathy and compassion.

The rationale put forward for the magic in the setting is initially physical; spells work by twisting space into appropriate distortions when certain sounds are uttered. The outlandish and difficult nature of the sounds is what makes magic hard work (a fantasy author must place some restriction upon his effect, otherwise no story is possible). Later in the book magic is discussed as an ultimate branch of mathematics, and the wizard Pandelume, mentor of Turjan of Miir, is a "Master Mathematician." In "Guyal of Sfere," we encounter a desolate and dangerous area which appears to be a radiation crater, and "Ulan Dhor Ends a Dream" is a science fiction story with no real fantastic elements.

"Guyal of Sfere," however, also includes a more Jungian explanation of the origins of demons and other monstrous creatures; they appear to be tangible manifestations of the accumulated dark side of the race's unconscious. The book abounds in magical devices and artifacts whose origins remain vague to good effect; in Vance's world, magic, like science, is decaying from a peak of accomplishment, and the book is steeped in a twilight sense of decline and decadence. Everything is left over from long ago; history has become so vast and impenetrable that nothing but trivia can be drawn from it; the hopeless cold future pins Vance's characters into the frantic present, day by day, like struggling butterflies.

Magic and wonder, however, are only the backdrop (at least in the present work) for the struggles of the human characters, and the problems of the book's construction arise in part from Vance's tendency to forget this. With no consistent protagonist or viewpoint character, the book sags into an uneasy compromise between a novel and a collection, and there was to be some argument as to what Vance's intention had been. While Vance has always maintained that it is a collection, I think it likely that he was, at that stage, simply not aware of the reading problems which he had generated. In contrast, his later *The Eyes of the Overworld* is a firmly unified book with the circular plot which has generally represented Vance's greatest sophistication in this area of technique.

There is a corresponding limitation in Vance's plotting for *The Dying Earth*, which eventually becomes tiresome as the same plot is repeated in every story. Everyone in the book is looking for something: Mazirian pursues a mysterious woman, Turjan seeks the secret of artificial humanity, T'sais looks for love and beauty, Liane the Wayfarer tries to find Chun the Unavoidable (ironically enough!), Ulan Dhor seeks the lost city of Ampridatvir, and Guyal of Sfere is curious about *everything*. In some cases Vance drops one quest and picks up another, as when the crowded adventures of T'sais are suspended in order to follow the career of her rescuer Etarr (who is trying to get his own face back), and when both of these characters then go off in search of a fortuitous god who can give them both what they want.

The construction of individual stories improves steadily throughout the book, although Vance tends not to notice when one story is over and another has begun, creating a broken-backed effect which is most intrusive in "Guyal of Sfere." "Mazirian the Magician" is so enthralling in its furnishings and atmosphere, and advantageously placed as the first story in the book, that its disintegration in the closing pages goes almost unnoticed at first reading. After the duel in the lake, the viewpoint shifts abruptly to the fleeing woman T'sain, forcing a change of outlook and orientation upon the reader at an awkward moment. Improbabilities come thick and fast after the death of Mazirian, as the fatally injured T'sain returns several leagues through the deadly forest, at night, walks into Mazirian's mansion without magical hindrance, finds his keys in a cabinet, locates his most secret room several floors underground, throws Turjan's glass prison to the floor without harming him, and happens to have a magical rune on her wrist which will restore him to normal size. Turjan's mawkish soliloquy, while explaining T'sain's origins, does not reveal how this elaborate and improbable scheme was arranged. Nor does the reader stop to reflect upon the perfect fit between Mazirian's magical preparations and the circumstances which he encounters.

"Turjan of Miir" also succeeds through style alone, with particular strengths in dialogue and confrontation. While the plot lurches from one encounter to another, looking very aimless in between, the set pieces themselves hold considerable excitement. Unfortunately, the central problem of the story (Turjan's quest for the secret of artificial life) is solved several pages before the end, and another abrupt change of viewpoint is needed to bring T'sais on stage and focus attention upon *her* problem. The naive conversation between T'sais and T'sain at the end of the story, while forced upon Vance by previous developments, carries little conviction.

The third section, "T'sais," is technically the weakest in the book and is completely shapeless, badly paced, infuriatingly and rewardingly discursive, grossly reliant upon happenstance, and resolved by a literal *deus ex machina*. The power and imagination of individual scenes make these faults all the more frustrating, like a necklace of exquisite jewels whose string has broken. The story is over-packed with detail, and scenes follow each other too quickly for full effect, like a hastily told fairy tale. The quest of T'sais begins the story but is dropped after she finds safety with Etarr (and after suffering three horrific encounters over eight pages in the time frame of a couple of hours). Etarr's quest then becomes the theme, while T'sais' problem is resolved slickly on the last page. The story throws off entrancing fireworks in all directions: the mesmeric evil of Liane the Wayfarer's atrocities, the murderous politeness of the confrontations, the deodand's pursuit, the ancient massacre on Modavna Moor, the Green Legion of Valdaran the Just, the fantastic revels of the Sabbath, the ancient god of justice. Unfortunately, all these things are more interesting than what happens in the main plot of the story, such as it is, and Vance had not yet learned how to embroider his stories without concealing their form altogether.

By contrast, "Liane the Wayfarer" is much more soundly constructed, and Vance moves the plot smoothly through to resolution with unusual assurance. There is an intriguing opening hook in Liane's discovery of the talisman of invisibility, and Vance establishes the motivation of the plot (vanity and lust) with extravagant panache, in a delightful confrontation between the arrogant Liane and the competent witch Lith. There is a straightforward plot development pinned to Liane's journey to the lair of Chun, and the colorful scenes attached to it (in particular, the tour de force of displayed magic at the inn) are not allowed to obscure the direction of the story. The appalling and unforgettable climax, and the final twist, are strokes of mastery.

The only real flaw of "Liane the Wayfarer," in fact, is the continuing obtuseness of Liane in the face of unmistakable warnings that Chun is a powerful adversary. Liane fails to ask Lith why she cannot recover her own tapestry, or what has already been done to retrieve it. He seeks no information about Chun from the wizards at the inn, although they obviously dread Chun despite their magical skills. Even when surrounded by seven eyeless corpses, he neglects to ask what sort of creature Chun is, or how he defends himself so competently.

Vance makes this as credible as he can, however, by endowing Liane with a magical amulet and a gigantic conceit; without such foolhardiness there is no story, and a certain simplification and inflation of motives is permissible in the genre, and is in fact a consistent feature of the "Dying Earth" stories. Indeed, lunatic motivation, always intensely personal, is one of the most rewarding and individual aspects of Vance's work.

"Ulan Dhor Ends a Dream" is a long, closely plotted science fiction story that is one of the best in the book, and in some ways it represents a change in direction. The theme moves to another level of sophistication, from the elementary conflict of two characters to the development of an exotic social situation. In later years this was to become the major direction of Vance's fiction.

Some lengthy initial exposition is well-handled by framing it in a prickly and closely observed dialogue between Ulan Dhor and Prince Kandive. Vance, for once, exercises some self-restraint in allowing Ulan Dhor to reach the scene of the story proper without having several distracting adventures on the way. The bizarre social order of Ampridatvir is competently detailed through direct and reported exposition, dialogue, action, Ulan Dhor's own reflections and deductions; Vance shows here that he is learning how to present a strange and wonderful setting without boring the reader or lecturing him. The story moves smoothly to a resolution, avoiding the meandering subplots which occur so frequently earlier in the book; and although the overblown super-science ending becomes far-fetched and over-paced, the vigor of the conclusion goes a long way towards redeeming this. The style at times carries a little more atmosphere than the narrative can support, but generally Vance achieves a competent matching of form and content.

"Guyal of Sfere" is the longest story in the book and the best, in my opinion, moving firmly into the area of exotic sociology which Vance has now made his own. Richly detailed, atmospheric, sharply characterized, and splendidly inventive, it ends the book on a sustained and near-flawless peak of excellence. (It is unfortunate that the story, as reprinted in Vance's 1969 collection *Eight Fantasms and Magics*, has been trimmed in a number of passages, and some of the names have been altered. Occasionally this is for the better, as in the substitution of the fictional Lost Book of Caraz for the extant Book of Kells. More often, passages are elided or shortened to worse effect — for example, the splendid entrance hall of the Museum of Man is stunningly described in the original and dismissed in an abridged paragraph in the later version. Vance has said that he made the changes himself, wishing to "eliminate overblown expressions and extravagance"; such an excess of misplaced self-criticism underlines his need for a sympathetic and skilled editor.)

The story follows the quest of Guyal for the source of all human knowledge in the fabled Museum of Man; his motivation is simple curiosity, and he is sustained throughout by his purity of intent. While he keeps to the trail, no harm can befall him, thanks to his father's blessing (one might almost argue that, at this stage, Vance was in need of a similar restriction upon his plotting and story construction!). On the whole, however, the simplicity of the story's direction enables Vance to avoid foundering in side issues, and the wealth of subsidiary scenes is controlled by a meticulous sense of atmosphere which never loses touch with the central theme.

The misfortunes which befall Guyal have all been echoed

and redeveloped in subsequent work: the villainous ferryman, the baroque bargaining scene with the raffish and pretentious augur, the unctuous, sinister villagers and their brutalized oasts, the dreamlike musical interlude in the bewitched empty city, with its strange and terrible occupants, and the long ordeal of Saponce, where Guyal is tricked into captivity and subjected to the eccentric formality of a cynical trial, with legal arguments of the most perverse logic. Similar fates, or course, were to be encountered by Cugel the Clever in *The Eyes of the Overworld*, but Guyal is too sympathetic to be consigned to the mortifying reverses which befell Cugel in the last scene of that book. From this point on, however, the plot comes under pressure, and successive events seem ever more hurried. The restoration of Kerlin the Curator to sanity, the over-elaborate stratagem used to defeat Blikdak, and the last-minute revelation of the mode of operation of the memory-banks — all seem excessively contrived, as if Vance had been in a hurry to get the story over with. The ending has now become standard for Vance: the two protagonists, their preoccupations resolved, now find their future directions open and experience a disconcerting sense of aimlessness. In this case, at least, the white stars overhead indicate an obvious future, but many of Vance's later novels end on a note almost of foreboding, as their leading characters realize that they may now have nothing left to aim for, and that they have been changed for better or worse and can never return to the lives they left. "What shall we do?" is a question which recurs time and again, and in later work there is often the disturbing implication that morality is no longer available and that characters have lost forever their innocence and their certainties.

The Dying Earth thus remains a chaotic, shapeless, uneven book — often brilliant, occasionally crass, bejewelled with splendid descriptive passages, exotic invention, polished dialogue, vivid metaphor, rare vocabulary. In its range of themes and settings, it displays almost all of Vance's talents and weaknesses. In the ten years which elapsed between its inception and its publication, Vance developed (entirely through his own efforts) from a gifted amateur totally lacking in technique to an accomplished freelance writer. The plotting and resolution of his stories have always presented major problems, and it is one of the most saddening aspects of his career that he should have been unable to find an editor who could work with him at this time to overcome these weaknesses.

Perhaps, however, these flaws are unimportant when set beside the accomplishments of his talents and meticulously crafted style. It's only to be expected that his first book should reflect the development of his craft — here he loses control of pace, there he stumbles from one viewpoint to another, now the plot becomes nonsensical, this or that character is drawn too boldly for his place. But always Vance gives us color, imagination, splendid language, rich words, an unerring and perceptive eye for wonder, beauty, and strangeness, an enduring and sympathetic fascination with the varieties of human adjustment. By the end of 1950, five years after his first publication, the brilliance of his talent was beyond doubt.

3. Jack Vance — The World-Thinker

ARTHUR JEAN COX

I

JACK VANCE is the best writer in science fiction.

Let me elaborate on that, now that I (presumably) have your attention. You will notice that I don't say that he is the best writer *of*, but the best writer *in*, science fiction — these prepositions making a subtle but powerful distinction.

Science fiction has been notoriously difficult to define, but perhaps we can agree that there is something there to be defined — that it is a discrete fictive form (just as is the mystery story), and that we are actually referring to an identifiable entity when, in speaking of either one, we use that unpronounceable word *genre*. It follows from this (although it may not be immediately obvious) that a writer can have a superior command of language and powers of characterization, even superior story-telling abilities, and yet not be the best writer in the *genre* of ... well, let us say mystery fiction. Despite his superior abilities, he may not have that special talent for creating a baffling murder-puzzle that is essential to the mystery story. His style is more than good, his characters live and breathe, he has wit, charm, atmosphere; but his writings, although their virtues are recognized, always seem somewhat peripheral—E. C. Bentley may be taken as an example; whereas some brother (or sister) writer, whose prose is perfunctory and whose characters are strictly "functional," comes to be regarded over the years as a Giant (or Giantess) of the field—Agatha Christie is an example.

The equivalent phenomenon in science fiction would be the superior writer who is not temperamentally or otherwise inclined towards those metaphysical preoccupations that lie at the heart of science fiction. ("Metaphysical" is the missing word in nearly all discussions of science fiction: most commentators, hung up on "scientific," seem never to have heard of it.) The reader no doubt sees the drift of my thought here, but may object that it is not all that applicable to Vance. After all, he is not exactly an unappreciated writer. He has a faithful, and probably a large, following. He has won awards. He is often praised, especially by his fellows, who know a writer when they see one. His name frequently appears above the titles of his books and, very often lately, in larger letters. If not a "Giant," he at least has considerable stature. All this is true; nevertheless, we may feel that he is underappreciated, that his virtues as a writer are greater than those of some others who have received a larger share of the public esteem and the public purse. My immediate purpose is not to deplore this situation but simply to recognize and to account for it.

Trying to account for it, we are confronted at the outset by what would seem to be the most salient fact: that Vance is, mostly, a writer of colorful adventure stories, such as *Big Planet*, the Durdane trilogy, the Planet of Adventure series—stories that sometimes threaten to dissolve into exotic travelogs, or into straight "action" stories, or into "space opera" (this last being the term we use for writing that has the trappings of science fiction but only a routine or nonexistent theoretical element). In most highly regarded science fiction, the theoretical element is very strong: it is decisive in determining the events of the plot. But it seldom does in Vance's fiction. While there are strong thematic motifs and more ideas in his work than generally are recognized, he usually tells a story motivated by something other than a thesis. The result *is* science fiction, however. Vance's background—the world against which the hero moves in his quest for knowledge, wealth, love, revenge—has been brought into existence by speculations of the sort essential to science fiction. That background is not specious; a wealth of invention has gone into it. Neither does it have that makeshift quality often found in similar writings by others in the field. In Vance's best work we have the feeling that after the hero has moved on to some other scene, the culture, society, or planet he has been visiting will go on existing. One of the best things in *The Anome* (first published as "The Faceless Man") is the description of Garwiiy, the city of glass, a glittering set piece in the story. Consider, also, how much detail is lavished upon Eiselbar in *Maske: Thaery*. Even though Eiselbar is merely a side-trip in the novel, it is an exercise in virtuosity and we are delighted by it. That does not alter the fact that this sort of thing is less esteemed than science fiction that is more immediately and centrally speculative, or "extrapolative"; that is, science fiction whose main purpose is to explore and expound some scientific (or metaphysical) idea.

Clearly related to Vance's choice of subject matter, in determining his reputation, is the way in which he chooses to write. Most of his fiction is cast in the more familiar forms of story-telling, embodying what are usually called "traditional story-values"—sympathetic characters, exciting action, atmosphere. *Emphyrio* (in my opinion the best SF novel of 1969) could have been published in *Astounding* in 1940 or 1941 with very little change. This could possibly be said of other recent novels—Arthur C. Clarke's *Rendezvous with Rama* might have been perfect for a 1929 *Amazing Stories Quarterly* (if the sex orgy at the end were deleted and some Wesso illustrations added). But it would not be true, I think, of many. Norman Spinrad's *Bug Jack Barron*, published the same year as *Emphyrio* (and so aptly contrasted with it in Joanna Russ's review in *The Magazine of Fantasy & Science Fiction*), could never have seen print in that earlier time; nor, one supposes, could have Frederik Pohl's *Gateway* or Ursula Le Guin's *The Dispossessed*, two novels based upon assumptions not at all self-evident to readers of that period. But there is not much in Vance that would either offend or puzzle a reader of the "Golden Age" — and that, of course, is precisely what would be held against him in some quarters; it would be thought a vice rather than a virtue (I would say that it is neither).

All this may seem obvious enough, but perhaps I may be permitted to harp on this one string a little longer. In recent years many readers, mostly young, seem to have turned to science fiction not merely for novel entertainment, exciting fiction, and the modest pleasures of speculation, but also to satisfy a need for profundity — for what is often called "relevance," and for general human experience and insight. I fear such appetites are going to be but imperfectly satisfied; they would be better advised to turn to Shakespeare, Dickens, Tolstoy, Joyce, Proust, Jane Austen, or others. Such readers are unlikely to turn to the unpretentious writings of Jack Vance. In most of his writings, especially those of the 1950s and 1960s, one senses a deliberate shunning of "significance," and a refusal to draw what would seem to be, in some instances, legitimate political or moral conclusions.

One guesses that Vance might wish above all things to avoid a sententious and humorless earnestness. In his rare prefaces, his habitual reserve and irony prevent any confidential response; does Vance mean it literally or is he simply teasing the reader? He has been the opposite in this regard to, say, Ray Bradbury, whose fiction seems to have a vague ideological coloring; Bradbury's stories strike certain attitudes and much of their appeal and charm derives from that. It is only in recent years (if we overlook "DP!" and perhaps "The Devil on Salvation Bluff") that Vance has allowed himself any ideological animus, and this too has had its effect in limiting and qualifying his reputation.

So Vance's underrated status involves no great mystery, really. But something else might also puzzle us. How does it happen that Vance gives us fantasy- and science fiction-adventure stories of this quality? There are many stories of this type by others which, to the casual reader, no doubt appear to do exactly the same thing that Vance's stories do. With rare exceptions, however, they are neither the same nor something just as good along somewhat different lines. Such stories are often shallow, meretricious, mindless fantasies, but Vance's work is infused with something much more significant. Why, we may then ask ourselves, have those qualities associated with Vance — intelligence, tact, inventiveness, strong syntax and narrative, a style at once vivid and cool — converged in stories probably meant for an audience that would have been satisfied with so much less?

II

"The World-Thinker" is of course the title of Vance's first published piece of fiction, appearing in the Summer 1945 issue of *Thrilling Wonder Stories*. I suppose he would not care to see it reprinted now; and, glancing through it, one sees that the writing is unmannered and imprecise — in short, un-Vancian. All the same, one cannot help but recognize it as the paradigmatic Vance story. The "world-thinker" is an egotistical inhuman entity, Laoome, whose godlike talent and special delight are to imagine worlds, worlds that then come into a kind of independent existence. It seems appropriate that this story, with its very apt title, should stand at the portal of Vance's career, for he is *the* world-thinker in a field that has specialized in the creation of worlds.

Of course, the term "world-thinker" does not so much mean a planet-maker, like his friend Poul Anderson (Vance's planets are no more substantial than they need to be, perhaps), but rather a deviser of cultures. The word *culture* is used here in its modern, or anthropological, sense, "which comprises," to quote the handy definition in Lionel Trilling's *Beyond Culture* (1965), "a people's technology, its manners and customs, its religious belief and organization, its systems of valuation, whether explicit or implicit." This succinctly describes what has been Vance's subject matter for quite a few years; indeed, he has been providing a pyrotechnic display of "manners and customs . . . religious belief and organization . . . systems of valuation, whether explicit or implicit" for the last quarter of a century. One thinks immediately of "The Moon Moth," of the amusing Kirstendale society in *Big Planet*, of the Eiselbar muzakologists and the social combinations of the Djan in *Maske: Thaery*, of the taboo against mentioning death so cleverly sketched out in *Clarges* (the original manuscript title for *To Live Forever*), of the color-symbology of the Durdane stories, of the murky social customs of *Marune*. Vance has staked out this rather large territory as his own and — though there are rival claimants — he is the writer most identified with it by knowledgeable readers.

This preoccupation with cultures is grounded, I need hardly say, in *terra firma*: in our, and his, experience of the cultures of this planet. The concept of "culture" has affected many of us in something more than an intellectual way; it is not merely an abstract notion, but has come to play a cherished part in our imaginative life — or an aspect of it has anyway, and that is the idea of The Other Culture. I mean by this that other country or people or political system, over the seas or in the past, to which so many of us have given a part or all of our loyalty. The discovery of The Other Culture usually is made during high school or college. We become aware of that wonderful society that seems to us so much more congenial than the one into which we have been, almost accidentally as it were, born: the world of ancient Greece, of France, of communist Russia or China, of Elizabethan or Victorian England, of modern or

Heiian Japan, or — a recent discovery — of the American Indian. Our allegiance to The Other Culture, sometimes proudly boasted of and sometimes hidden (the Anglophile Sigmund Freud kept his schoolboy journal in English), enables us to keep a part of ourselves aside, free from the pressures to conformity flowing from family and school, and safe from the terrible judgments of our peers. The ignorant and the xenophobic despise this attraction to The Other Culture as a form of treason, even when it has no political aspect and no practical bearings. But this affinity for The Other Culture, the way it enlarges the sympathies and develops the intellectual and imaginative functions not only of individuals but of mankind, has probably been invaluable. (The Renaissance, it has been said — by Kenneth Clark, for one — was made possible by the rediscovery of ancient Greece and Rome by a few gifted individuals.) And it has played a part, or such is my guess, in the development of the mind and writing of Jack Vance.

His Other Culture would seem to have been that of Europe in general and, I suspect, of France in particular — the attraction being suggested partly by the word *tradition* and possibly by Vance's sense that "France, Europe" had a culture that was more supportive of or bore a more intimate relationship to the larger possibilities of human life, that it more closely resembled a living community, that it was perhaps even more organic — say, like a tree — than elsewhere. For one is reminded of how often trees, sentient, intelligent, or communal trees, have flourished in Vance's fiction (some early examples are "Phalid's Fate," with its Father Forest, and "Son of the Tree").

I recall the delight of a friend, a tremendous Francophile, to discover that Vance and his wife were migrating to France. This was made possible, it seems, by the sale of Vance's 1948 short story "Hard-Luck Diggings" — a story about trees, incidentally — to, I believe, Twentieth-Century Fox and the author's subsequent period of employment at that studio. But Vance apparently suffered a disillusionment in France, that dis-

illusionment to which any expatriate, of any nation, is susceptible: the discovery that his adopted country was not, after all,
all that he had hoped, that it was not, as the disappointed Charles
Dickens had said of another country more than a century earlier, "the Republic of my Imagination." I did not need Vance's
remark in his Foreword to *Vandals of the Void* (1953) to suggest
this to me: "We are in a period of change-over, from a civilization based on European ideas that has lost its momentum and
grown tired, to a new civilization on whose basic patterns we
are still working." I already had read the opening lines of the
story itself, in which the site of a colony on Venus is described
as if it were "indeed the petrified stump of an ancient and colossal world-tree," and had taken them to be a figurative description of Europe.[1] (At about that same time Margaret Mead
used the same image in speaking of Europe, although she called
it, less harshly, "the flowering stump.")

My friend was shocked by Vance's short novel, "The Houses
of Iszm" (1954). He had not been much disturbed by the fine
short story "DP!" because in that "telling-off of the world" the
author had spared the French (the French soldiers were "brave
in their blue shorts"). But my friend failed to see what "The
Houses of Iszm" portended. The protagonist of that story visits
Iszm (doubtlessly pronounced "ism," the familiar slang for
ideology and reminiscent of that breeding-ground of isms, Europe) and carries away from it, in his head, a portion of its
most precious commodity, carries it back, half-unwillingly, to
an unscrupulous American businessman (worse! to a Los Angeles entrepreneur), K. Pench. The story is here described somewhat abstractly so that the allegorical skeleton will show through.
Our hero has carried a seed—literally, as it happens—from an
organic old world to a commercial and mechanistic new one so
that it, too, may become organic, at least in part. The story
comes to an ambiguous ending of a type not unusual in Vance,
but not before the pursuing Iszics, seeking to recover the seed,
are brutally slaughtered. It was this that so shocked my friend,

for he recognized the Iszics for what they were — representatives of The Other Culture — and he had extended his largest sympathies to them. He nevertheless declined to recognize what it meant: that Vance had declared a reshifting of allegiances.

Despite this declaration (considering it as such), not all was right with the world. The disaffection from Europe was followed by something that looked like disorientation, judging from the few stories by Vance that appeared in the magazines during the mid-1950s. Something of importance was missing; Europe, in vanishing, had left a void. Glancing back at these stories now, one senses an insufficiently assimilated violence of feeling and sometimes an inadequate resolution of problems. I am thinking not only of "The Houses of Iszm," but also of "Sjambak" (1953); "sjambak" being a form of berserker activity; of the rather striking "Shape-Up" (1953); of "The Devil on Salvation Bluff" (1954), which, when I first read it, I took to be chiefly an exercise in liberal or humanistic piety (but which I now see to have been a darker thing, a precursor of "The Men Return"); of "Where Hesperus Falls" (1956), a story of determined suicide; and of that almost nasty short story "Phantom Milkman" (1956).

Granted, when I speak of the violence of feeling in these stories, I can do so only by discounting the habitual abstraction and detachment of Vance's manner; yet I think that's legitimate, and my remarks cannot be dismissed as mere hindsight. I distinctly remember fearing for Vance's sanity when I read "A Practical Man's Guide" (1957), but I needn't have worried. The year that saw the publication of that story also gave us "The Men Return," in which the crisis of orientation — I am tempted to say the crisis of faith — reaches its deepest intensity and is resolved.

The world of "The Men Return" (a story novel enough to be announced as "A new KIND of story" on the cover of the July 1957 issue of *Infinity* in which it appeared) is one in which the fundamental physical laws have no consistency. The ground cannot be relied upon from moment to moment to give support. All is chaos, or nearly so. But, just as the situation verges upon total disaster — when the young have, in effect, slain the old, and when the last two surviving women are about to turn upon the last man; that is, when even the most basic human relations have become disturbed — the world passes out of the pocket of noncausality into which it has blundered. It steadies itself, order is reflexively reasserted, and nature comes home. And the sole surviving man turns with the two women towards the future, saying, "Let us make plans."

There duly followed the excellent stories Vance wrote during the 1960s, beginning with *The Man in the Cage* (1960), the best, I would say, of his mystery novels (although I also liked his 1966 *The Fox Valley Murders* very much, partly because of personal associations); the Demon Princes series, which constitutes his best work in science fiction, in my opinion; *The Eyes of the Overworld* (1966); and *Emphyrio* (1969). These, the few shorter works accompanying them, and most of the novels of the next decade show a new sense of confidence.[2] Their distances seem to be filled, as in a cover-painting by SF illustrator Hubert Rogers, with golden light. Consider *The Man in the Cage*, *Star King*, *Showboat World*, *Trullion: Alastor 2262*, *Maske: Thaery*, and you will see that this is so.

III

In the previous section the main contention is that Vance's experience with The Other Culture — his attraction to and disaffection from Europe — gave him his subject matter, and in a way that guaranteed its abiding personal interest. He has since, as I've noted, provided a pyrotechnical display of other cultures. Most of these have been human societies and have had an easily recognizable and strong human appeal. Most of them are not fanciful faerylands but are worlds in which human beings could actually live, work, hate, love, aspire, despair, and so on—worlds one could imagine living in. Many of us might gladly emigrate to Alphanor, Trullion, or carefully chosen parts of Big Planet.

What is especially attractive—to me, at least, and I suppose to others—is not so much any particular culture, any single world, as that general cosmopolitan scene of the novels published during the last fifteen years or so: the Oikumene of the Demon Princes series, the Alastor Cluster, the Gaean Reach; again, not so much any one of these alone (that would be too confining!) as all together. This wide and glittering prospect is immensely attractive. Looking out from the bridge of our Magellanic Wanderer (or from our easy chair), we seem to be drawn forward into endless depths, into that promising distance filled with light—in a word, into the Empyrean. There are no boundaries, no barriers, no horizons, but everywhere an inexhaustible novelty and variety, an unstructured and unimpeded freedom of movement. But after we have for the moment satisfied our thirst for novelty and for fresh modes of life, this heady vision —if we face the truth of our own feelings—is also a somewhat frightening one. Anxiety would seem to be lurking somewhere, for the Wide Prospect is not only exhilarating but dizzying. Since it is possible to go in any direction, and since there is no pressing reason to go in one rather than another, we may find it difficult to orient ourselves. Where anything is possible, nothing is more probable or more weighted than another; everything becomes random and absurd. We feel a lack of gravity. The atmosphere becomes too rarified to breathe.

But Vance has taken heed of this, too—or perhaps it is the logic of his craft. He has filled the universe with intriguing planets, and the main action of each story takes place on the surface of one. These planets are often remarkably homelike and real: Trullion, Halma, Thaery on Maske, Shant on Durdane. Each has its horizons and nearer prospects. Vance obtains some of his pleasantest effects merely from the simple homeliness of settings and people. There are scenes of quiet domesticity, of the problems of making a living, of loneliness and companion-ship. (I personally like the scenes in the taverns and inns, and the moments in which the reflective hero relaxes with a glass of wine on a terrace in Damar or Garwiiy or in one of the many places whose names I have forgotten.) In addition, there are poignant touches of nostalgia and homesickness that play a part in humanizing these far-ranging stories.

But there is a larger effect, too, which is that much of the interest of the stories comes directly from the conscious con-trast between some charted homelike world and the universe at large. However closely occupied he may be with some quasi-mundane setting, Vance rarely loses sight of that larger per-spective. It is as though we were on an island so small that no matter how far inland we go, we never stop hearing the sea.

By way of illustration, let me offer one or two instances of Vance's specific use of this contrast. Gastel Etzwane, of the Durdane series, is a skilled musician from a rural province. But in the second book, after he has travelled widely and has become keenly conscious of the existence of Earth and of other planets, his playing undergoes a curious change:

> His fingers moved of their own accord up and down the buttons [of his instrument], but the vantage was higher, the perspectives were longer; and he played with an almost imperceptible elongation of the tension of the beat. (*The Brave Free Men*, VIII)

Some things cannot be counterfeited — this Vancian "touch" is one of them. It shows Vance's complete immersion in the imag-ined world of his story. Another example is the ending of the third book of the series, in which Gastel Etzwane is abandoned by the admirable but exasperatingly ambiguous and unreachable Earthman, Ifness, and left stranded on his own planet, home-less at home. The effect is well brought off and rather curious, for Etzwane does not dislike his home, his friends, his art, nor has he, apparently, gained a taste for travel — and yet there is conveyed a tangible sense of being forever limited, cut off from real though undefined possibilities.

This fear of being marooned appears in other stories, too. Especially memorable is "Golden Girl," in which a beautiful girl from another and probably superior culture is cast away on this backward planet Earth, and finally takes the only way out left open to her. Even where characters are not marooned, as such, there may be a sense of limited possibilities, as with the citizens of Halma in *Emphyrio*, most of whom know and are resigned to the fact that they can never attain to financial independence and to the freedom represented by interworld travel.

Freedom — the dream we may prize above all others; freedom — that is to say, freedom of movement... to travel into the populated Empyrean, among the teeming worlds of the Oikumene and the Alastor Cluster, into that empty, infinite, glowing distance. What a glorious prospect! And yet we are right back where we were, conscious as before that there is something we have put aside or even out of sight: a longing for stability, peace, even passivity; or, as people sometimes say, "roots." "I don't want to be free," D. H. Lawrence wrote, "any more than a tree is free." We are reminded of the fate of the adventurous Ramus Ymph of *Maske: Thaery*, who breaks the bounds of his provincial world to wander freely among the worlds of the Gaean Reach and (to conveniently quote what I have written elsewhere) whose "horribly appropriate fate is to become a tree: rooted, stationary, drawing nourishment from his native soil."[3] Horrible... and yet it appeals to some dark, sympathetic thing in ourselves.

There seems to be no escape; we oscillate, back and forth, back and forth. Living quietly our placid daily life with wife and bairns, sitting comfortably beside our ain fireplace, and, staring into the flames, we find ourselves longing for the limitless freedom of boundless space. Achieve that freedom and it is not long before we are dreaming of the thatched cottage, the fence overgrown with ivy... or perhaps of the corner of 42nd Street and Broadway, or of Geary and Powell.

The point, of course, is not that one or the other is the better. It is the contrast itself between the exciting freedom of the infinite world on the one hand, and the detailed homelike charms of some peaceful and harmonious place on the other, that gives to many of Vance's writings their thematic tension. Much of their interest is derived from that polarity. Vance has no sooner imagined the Oikumene and the cosmic triumph of urbanity than he has called it into question by contrasting it with that idyllic pastoral earth-like planet discovered by the locater, Lugo Teehalt. Vance shifts the weight of his theme now this way, now that; but never heavily, or for long. In *Maske: Thaery* the man of restless adventure is the villain and in the end he is firmly planeted where he belongs. In *Emphyrio* he is the hero who, rejecting an identification with a humbler plant ("Why should I," he asks, "be born, live and die and make no more imprint on the cosmos than a blade of grass on Dumkin's Heights?"), breaks the bounds of *his* provisional world and achieves a kind of apotheosis: he becomes Emphyrio. Should Vance ever cast a decisive vote one way or the other, I suspect a part of the fascination we feel for the stories would be diminished.

IV

We now approach a more delicate matter, one which is somewhat more difficult to explain. To explain it at all, I will have to venture into what Vance has called (in *Star King*) "the morass of psychology trampled by generations of incompetents."

There is a quality of what might be called the temper of Vance's writings which not many have marked, and that is the absence in them of any trace of paranoia. At first thought, this may seem a curious comment, but it is worth making because it is so singular: there is no other science-fiction writer of whom I would say the same. At second thought, the above comment may seem to be glaringly untrue, for Vance on at least two occasions has handled material that would seem to be the very stuff of paranoia. *The Brains of Earth* would be one instance. At first reading it could be taken to be a paranoid fantasy; but the actual working-out of the story to its conclusion (which involves the virtual acceptance of the passenger life-form) convinces us of that error. (The still skeptical reader is invited to compare this novel to Eric Frank Russell's *Sinister Barrier*, which has a premise not unlike it.) Or, to take the other case, notice the treatment in the Durdane stories of the Asutra — a small, repulsive, parasitic life-form that seizes upon intelligent hosts and controls them — and contrast it with Robert Heinlein's treatment of the Puppet Masters in the novel named after them. There are similarities, but the fascinated loathing, fear, and hatred in the Heinlein novel are not present in the Vance books — or, more accurately, are present only nominally. The Asutra are by no means treated with awe. Quite the contrary: the Ka, a nonhuman people who were once victim-hosts of the Asutra, in time come not only to tolerate them but to co-opt them, to put them to various practical and even humiliating (to the Asutra) uses. A writer with more paranoid leanings might have realized more fully than has Vance the morbid fascination of this subject, and he might have worked out the Ka–Asutra–Human relationships with a more urgent logic; but in doing so he would have sacrificed those quieter and less common effects that Vance achieves.

The basis of paranoia, as everyone knows, is projection: attributing to persons and objects in the environment those feelings, thoughts, traits, and attitudes which actually belong to oneself. The opposite of this would be introjection: the taking, or mistaking, as parts of oneself what really belongs to the environment. This, too, exists. No one will dispute that we all project at times; it is equally true that we all introject. After all, we did not, as individuals, invent our language, customs, manners, modes of dress (all Vance's subject matter), but assimilated them more or less whole. Most or us would recognize a situation the narrator of *Strange People, Queer Notions* describes — a translucent moment when he and his girl sit drinking wine on a terrace in Italy: "I tried to encompass the instant wholly, to absorb it, to make it part of myself, so that I might have it with me always..." (an example of normal introjection). Only in their extreme forms, when each strives to dominate, do projection and introjection become obviously pathological. The projector, eyes averted, abandons himself to his fathomless suspicions and to his restless confirmation of them: he becomes paranoid. The insatiable introjector surrenders himself to complete subjectivity, to immobility (movement is pointless since he has succeeded in internalizing the whole environment): he becomes catatonic.[4]

Most of us are more conscious of the first predicament than of the second. We normally reject unfounded suspicions, and we usually refuse, contemptuously or amusedly, to go along with "crackpot" religious or political or other ideas. Vance, however, unlike most of us, has shown himself more keenly conscious of the second predicament. "What!" exclaims a mysterious personage in "'A Practical Man's Guide." "What could be more ludicrous, more tragic? A prisoner of self, so to speak!" But, as the author knows, that ludicrous and tragic fate may seem otherwise to the sufferer: "The world will be I, I will be the world!" gloats Lord Palafox in *The Languages of Pao* as he attains (or succumbs to) the condition known in that novel as "Emeritus." And in *Clarges (To Live Forever)*, Vance invents for his society a characteristic disease — catatonia-mania — and, as Gavin Waylock himself observes, a decidedly ingenious therapy for it; although, because of an unfortunate concatenation of circumstances, it failed to do much for the ill-fated "catto," Maximilian Hertzog, whose name one remembers after all these years. One suspects that Vance is sensitive to this condition because the natural bend of his mind turns in that direction opposite to ours — that is, towards introjection rather than projection.

Thus, what I take to be signs of the introjective temperament in Vance are simply those qualities of his writings which everyone recognizes — the abstraction of style and the detachment of viewpoint. This cool and reflective tonality of the prose gives to his writings a flavor such as one finds in no other popular writer I can think of, and the calm impersonality offers a welcome relief from so much else we read. It is, in fact, the very intonation of sanity. This abstractive turn of mind stylizes and strengthens the stories by creating a sense of consistent orientation and internal coherency rarely found in modern letters.

An awareness of Vance's affection for coherency will help explain one recent development in his work. Vance has written little in the way of polemical fiction, so it was something of a surprise to read "Assault on a City" (1974). In this story Vance attacks what he impressively calls "urbanity, the ultimate tragedy of mankind." "Urbanity" — a word he apparently derives not from "urbane" but directly from "urban" — is his epithet for a culture recognizably like our own: one characterized by, among other things, shallowness, narcissism, faddism, cynicism, and contempt for tradition, law, and custom. There is not much new in that, perhaps, as the city (the indefinite article in the title is misleading) has been under siege for the last two hundred years, ever since Rousseau.[5] But Vance's attack is also, more narrowly, upon what he calls "the exploration of inner space," which has reference, one assumes, to such things as our contemporary preoccupation with "the drug experience," with meditation, mysticism, various Eastern religions, and psychological cults. "The exploration of *inner* space...." Of course, one thinks, Vance would have to be on his guard against *that*; for in what other direction lies that danger hinted at in "A Practical Man's Guide"? That impossible but perhaps irreversible turning movement, inward and upward — ultimately, one imagines, "ullward," as in "Ullward's Retreat" (1958). My point is not that Vance is being, as is often too easily said, "projective" (which would involve me in a contradiction, anyway) or that what he

calls "the exploration of inner space" isn't a significant contemporary cultural phenomenon—I think it is.[6] The point is
that Vance is peculiarly sensitive to this aspect of "urbanity"
and brings it to the fore.

"The *exploration* of inner space..."? Yes, for what other
word would Vance use? Exploration is more than an important
activity in this writer's work: it is paramount. But it is the exploration of... well, one can hardly say "outer space" without
saying something other than what is meant. It is, nevertheless,
the exploration of what lies outside—the terrain, the landscape. A great many of Vance's books have maps at the beginning; he has allotted himself and us the rewarding task of exploring these countries, continents, worlds. Accompanying the
protagonist and narrator, the reader ranges back and forth over
the surface of some world, or portion of one, until he has covered all the significant ground. The fascination of Vance's invented worlds lies not only in their societies and their peoples,
but also in their topography. The coherence of this topography,
its worked-out particulars and overall configuration, orients
the reader and, giving him footing and a sense of direction,
provides a supportive substratum for the adventure story (although I should add this is as true of Vance's mystery novels as
it is of his science-fiction stories and so would seem to be essential at a level below that of subject matter). Often there is a
fusion of the two types; connected with the exploration, and
partly accounting for the sense we have of developing meaning,
is the unravelling of some element of mystery in the adventure
story. The exploring hero, while investigating the mystery,
reaches his destination (often his original starting point) and
the solution concurrently: the intellectual and the physical—the
topographical—converge.

This comprehensive, ranging speculation is one of the important strengths of Vance's work. It grows out of a characteristic impulse, a moving forward to explore and expropriate the
world. This impulse and its realization give his stories an inter-

nal consistency and satisfying shape, a coherence of thought and feeling which amounts, finally, to conviction.

V

Others will call attention to still other qualities, virtues, and strengths of the writings of Jack Vance. The three discussed here — his preoccupation with cultural motifs; the tension provided by the polarity between the lure of the Empyrean and the comforts of Home; the cool introjective temperament, unique in science fiction — for me constitute much of the sinew and tissue of his work. I have not allowed myself as much as I would have liked of the pleasures of praise. But then, as Nietzsche wrote, "To praise is as egregious as to blame." He might have added, "Or to criticize, analyze, interpret." So, in having risked one offense, I have spared myself some part of the other.

4. The Double Shadow:
The Influence of Clark Ashton Smith

DON HERRON

"I have, of course, read Clark Ashton Smith, when I was an adolescent. We lived in the country in those days; our mailbox was about a mile from our house, and on the day I might expect *Weird Tales* in the mail, I can remember walking down to that mailbox, peering in there, and being very unhappy if *Weird Tales* hadn't arrived." — Jack Vance[1]

CLARK ASHTON SMITH (1893–1961) has emerged, along with H. P. Lovecraft, Robert E. Howard, Robert Bloch, and Ray Bradbury, as one of the most important writers who regularly contributed to the famous pulp magazine *Weird Tales*. A California poet, artist, and fictioneer, Smith wrote stories that are regarded highly by *aficionados* of the weird fantasy tale, yet his work generally is disparaged by science-fiction readers. Considering that his fantasy and science-fiction tales form an obviously strong influence on Jack Vance, one of the most popular writers in the SF field, this lack of interest or open hostility toward Smith seems especially ironic.

Jack Vance (b. 1920) disclaims any major influences on his work. Still, his style, tone, motifs, and settings often echo elements found in Smith's stories. To be sure, authors other than Smith may be cited as influential: Peter Close, an English critic, mentions Olaf Stapledon, Edgar Rice Burroughs, Robert Chambers, James Branch Cabell, Robert Louis Stevenson, P. G. Wodehouse, Saki, and Jeffrey Farnol, among others. But Close offers these influences "as peripheral, although some affinities are recogniseable, such as Saki's talent for detached ironic humor and economic characterisation, Stevenson's color and themes, Farnol's handling of action, bargaining scenes and female characters, and Wodehouse's influence in *Space Opera*...."[2]

With most of these writers the influence *is* minor. Edgar Rice Burroughs, like Smith an author whose work was read by a youthful Vance, serves as a good example of this point. The John Carter of Mars novels by Burroughs are the obvious model for Vance's Planet of Adventure (Adam Reith) series: *City of the Chasch*, *Servants of the Wankh*, *The Dirdir*, and *The Pnume*. Each series places its protagonist on a hostile world with only his physical and mental abilities to help him survive, then chronicles his adventures. Burroughs' Mars and Vance's Tschai are planets given over to barbarism coeval with traces of superscience, with swordfighting prevalent as a means of settling disputes and flying boats commonly used as transportation. Burroughs' Tharks and Vance's Green Chasch are both gigantic green-hued nomadic warrior races. Adam Reith, the hero of Vance's books, often displays the same sort of naive romantic chivalry as John Carter does, although not to such an extreme degree. (Kirth Gersen of Vance's Demon Princes series occasionally suffers from it, too. Other of Vance's protagonists, though, are cads in this regard.) Aside from a few devices of setting, however, Burroughs' Mars books and Vance's Planet of Adventure series work very much on their own and share little, since Vance's concerns are not those of Burroughs. A small number of passing allusions to Burroughs may be found in other Vance stories. In *Star King* the race of Star Kings borrows a notion from a race of plant-beings in Burroughs' *The Gods of Mars*; for both races "the young develop as pods in the armpits" (*Star King*, VIII). Another possible acknowledgment to Burroughs appears in *The Eyes of the Overworld*, wherein ravenous monsters such as grues, leucomorphs, and erbs prowl by night. The "erb" acronym apparently honors Burroughs.

Clark Ashton Smith's influence, however, is more pervasive. In Vance's first published book, *The Dying Earth* (1950), the stories are set in the realms of Grand Motholam, a land existing in earth's far future when the sun is a sullen red disk soon to gutter and die, when the sciences are forgotten and magick is reborn. This same setting appears in a series of sixteen tales by CAS, published between 1932 and 1948, with the land called Zothique. Smith writes, "On Zothique, the last continent of Earth, the sun no longer shone with the whiteness of its prime, but was dim and tarnished as if with a vapor of blood.... Many were the necromancers and magicians of Zothique, and the infamy and marvel of their doings were legended everywhere in the latter days."[3] And Vance writes, "At this dim time, with the sun dark... Grand Motholam... swarmed with sorcerers of every description" (*The Dying Earth*, "Turjan of Miir"). As a contemporary reviewer of *The Dying Earth* noted, "One cannot help but compare the episodes in this book with the stories of Clark Ashton Smith."[4]

The six episodes in *The Dying Earth* may derive their structure from Smith also. The first five tales feature characters in common: Turjan of Miir appears in two; T'sais is a minor character in one of the Turjan episodes and the main character in a story chronicling her own adventures; Liane the Wayfarer is briefly seen in "T'sais" and is the protagonist in another story; Kandive the sorcerer is in "Turjan of Miir" and "Ulan Dhor Ends a Dream." The milieu is the dominant element which ties the tales together. This sort of structure is used by CAS in several of his fantasy series, which are series only by virtue of setting; Smith never had a series character such as Vance's Cugel the Clever. In his stories of Poseidonis, tales of the sinking continent now known as Atlantis, Smith features Malygris the magician in two stories. Malygris tries to conjure up his first love in one tale, with disappointing results. In the second tale he is *dead*, but a baleful scourge nonetheless. The sorcerer Eibon is mentioned in some Smith stories and appears as a main character in "The Door to Saturn." Other instances might be cited of Smith characters appearing briefly in one story only to star in another, but Smith's cycles of stories are all united by place rather than person as are—ultimately—the episodes in *The Dying Earth*.

Stylistically, the great influence Smith's writing has exerted on Vance may be seen instantly, unmistakably, in the kind of names both have used in their SF and fantasy work. Smith and Vance are considered masters at coining strange, evocative names, a quality in their work which cannot be denied. Consider the following names:

Ulan Dhor	Manghai Thal
Rogol Domedonfors	Zon Mezzamalech
Quantique	Zothique
Olliphane	Ouphaloc
Hildemar Dasce	Theophilus Alvor
Parsifal Pankarow	Satampra Zeiros
Tschai	Tasuun
Dadiche	Evagh
Pandelume	Fustules
Skerde Vorek	Kronous Alkon
Pharode	Phandiom
Robin Rampold	Allan Octave
Pallis Atwrode	Aristide Rocher
Rundle Detteras	Tirouv Ompallios
Jad Piluna	Ux Loddhan
Sibot	Saddoth
Vogel Filschner	Jasper Trilt
Hygen Grote	Avoosl Wuthoqquan
Paul Waunder	James Roverton

Viole Falushe	Ralibar Vooz
Lokhars	Lospar
Smargash	Cykranosh
Sarkovy	Lunithi
Lerand Wible	Rupert Balcoth
Mazirian	Gadeiron
Lugo Teehalt	Giles Angarth
Attel Malagate	Felix Ebbonly
Ben Zaum	Han Joas
Eridu	Evidon
Kislovan	Charmalos
Ao Hidis	Occlith
Tywald Fitzbittick	Francis Melchoir
Godogma	Ummaos
Kokor Hekkus	Maal Dweb

These names are taken from many different stories by Smith and Vance, stories written at various times in their careers. One might well believe that these names all spring from a single imagination to judge by their appearance and sound. (The names in the left column are taken from Vance's stories, those in the right column from Smith's.)

In *The Dying Earth*, and occasionally so in later work, Vance's prose shows definite affinities to Smith's.[5] In the "Ulan Dhor" episode we find this paragraph:

> I have known the Ampridatvir of old; I have seen the towers glowing with marvellous light, thrusting beams through the night to challenge the sun itself. Then Ampridatvir was beautiful – ah! my heart pains when I think of the olden city. Semir vines cascaded from a thousand hanging gardens, water ran blue as vaul-stone in the three canals.... But even in my life I saw the leeching of spirit. A surfeit of honey cloys the tongue; a surfeit of wine addles the brain; so a surfeit of ease guts a man of strength. Light, warmth, food, water, were free to all men, and gained by a minimum of effort. So the people of Ampridatvir, released from toil, gave increasing attention to faddishness, perversity, and the occult. (*The Dying Earth*, "Ulan Dhor Ends a Dream")

The feeling this description evokes is similar to the atmosphere in the following excerpt from Smith's "The Testament of Athammaus," as is the structure of the exposition:

> Lo! I am made young again when I recall Commoriom, when in this gray city of sunken years I behold in retrospect her walls that looked mountainously down upon the jungle, and the alabastrine multitude of her heaven-fretting spires. Opulent among cities, and superb and magisterial, and paramount over all was Commoriom.... And it was not, as men fable nowadays, because of that maundering prophecy once uttered by the white sybil from the isle of snow which is named Polarion, that her splendor and spaciousness were delivered over to the spotted vines of the jungle and the spotted snakes. Nay, it was because of a direr thing than this.... And though others forget, or haply deem her no more than a vain and dubitable tale, I shall never cease to lament Commoriom.[6]

Vance's luxuriant description of the garden in the first paragraph of "Mazirian the Magician" (see Chapter 2, p. 56) echoes similar richly detailed catalogs of flora by Smith in such tales as "The Maze of Maal Dweb" and "The Garden of Adompha." A phrase such as "others were decanting strange liquids and curious colloids" might unknowingly be attributed to Vance if one did not know that Smith wrote it. And in Smith's "The Coming of the White Worm," the passage where the sorcerer Evagh "Vainly, with numbing thoughts... strove to recall the exorcisms of Pnom"[7] suggests the action of the magicians in *The Dying Earth* as they strive to hold in mind spells created by the Arch-Necromancer Phandaal, spells so potent that only a few may be memorized at one time.

Smith and Vance share several motifs. One is a general disregard of scientific fact and possibility if it interferes with imaginative flights. Another is a recurring use of plant life, alluded to above, as in Vance's *Son of the Tree*, *The Houses of Iszm*, the vampire plants in "Mazirian the Magician," and other instances throughout the body of Vance's work. Smith also is somewhat famous for the plants in his stories; *Wonder Stories* for October 1930 devoted its cover to a scene from his "Marooned in Andromeda"—huge carnivorous flowers devouring hapless castaways from space.[8] Especially interesting is a comparison of Smith's "The Seed from the Sepulcher" with Vance's *Maske: Thaery*. In Smith's story two explorers in Venezuela happen on a seedpod in an old tomb. It bursts in one man's face, scattering spores over him. Deserted by their porters, the men try to reach civilization in a dugout canoe as the effects of the seeding become manifest:

> His features had grown as stark and ghastly as those of a dead man, and his whole aspect was one of mortal rigidity.... More dreadful than this... growths had issued from the eyes, and their stems, climbing vertically across the forehead, had entirely displaced the eyeballs.... They appeared to quiver with repulsive animations, nodding rhythmically in the warm, windless air.... From the mouth, another stem protruded, curling upward like a long and whitish tongue. It had not yet begun to bifurcate.[9]

In the Vance novel *Maske: Thaery* the villain comes to a similar end after angering a nature cult which places the welfare of its sacred trees before all else:

> On the following morning Ramus Ymph stood stiff on the hatch. His hair was totally gone; his bald pate showed a coarse and wrinkled texture... his eyes were already glazed over with a dim green crust. He had lost the flexible use of his muscles; he no longer uttered sounds. Small green sheafs protruded from the nodes; these, stimulated by the sunlight, began to burgeon. (*Maske: Thaery*, XVIII)

In the Vance episode the action also takes place on a boat, a ship on which the characters are fleeing the island of the tree cult. Like Smith's short story, this isolates the characters with the source of horror. The companion of Smith's doomed adventurer and the companions of Ramus Ymph have no recourse but to watch the slow metamorphosis of human into plant, a transformation that unnerves them by slow, budding degrees. Smith's handling of this theme is totally serious, since the atmosphere of doom is unrelenting; the plant-man's companion is lulled by the horror like a bird before a snake, and eventually he too becomes a victim of the seed from the sepulcher. Vance's treatment is considerably lighter: when the boat reaches shore, the treelike Ramus Ymph makes a final automotive effort and stalks stiffly from the ship to root himself permanently in the sod. The humorous conclusion of *Maske: Thaery* further contributes to lifting the tone of doom evoked aboard the ship.

Yet another motif Vance and Smith have in common is an unceasing ridicule of religion. This motif appears in brilliant, sardonic asides throughout the body of their writing. Sometimes they use ridicule to point out some of the hypocrisy prevalent in many organized religions or to make a statement on behalf of humane concerns which religious bigotry often overruns. Smith, relating the adventures of the fanatic Inquisitor Morghi, notes:

> Morghi, however, was not entirely happy. Though the Ydheems were religious, they did not carry their devotional fervor to the point of bigotry or intolerance; so it was quite impossible to start an inquisition among them.[10]

Vance, writing of some art, gives a capsule history of its origins:

> The nonhuman natives of Peninsula 4A, Lupus 23 II, devote the greater part of their lives to the working of these slabs, which apparently have a religious significance. Twice each year, at the solstices, two hundred and twenty-four microscopically exact slabs are placed aboard a ceremonial barge, which is allowed to drift out upon the ocean. The Lupus Salvage Company maintains a ship just over the horizon from Peninsula 4A. As soon as the raft has drifted from sight of land, it is recovered, the slabs removed, exported and sold as *objets d'art*. (*The Palace of Love*, IV)

Often their asides on religion are purely ridiculous, which makes a statement in itself, as when the minstrel-maiden Phade "gets religion" in the face of an enemy attack in *The Dragon Masters*:

> [Phade] sank slowly to her knees and began to perform the ritual gestures of the Theurgic cult: hands palm down to either side, slowly up till the back of the hand touched the ears, and the simultaneous protrusion of the tongue. Over and over again, eyes staring with hypnotic intensity into emptiness. (*The Dragon Masters*, X)

Or this instance of profound silliness from Smith:

They saw the Djhibbis, that apterous and Stylitean bird-people who roost on their individual dolomites for years at a time and meditate upon the cosmos, uttering to each other at long intervals the mystic syllables *yop*, *yeep*, and *yoop*, which are said to express an unfathomed range of esoteric thought.[11]

A good-sized book could be made of such excerpts from Smith and Vance; it would make amusing reading.

Another ability Smith and Vance are adept at is depicting aliens and odd societies. The ridiculous, bizarre antics of the Phung in Vance's Planet of Adventure series are a fine example of alienity, and the masked, musical society in Vance's excellent novelette "The Moon Moth" is genuinely unusual. In Smith's writing, a striking example of an odd society and a touch of pure alienity may be found in "The Dweller in the Gulf," wherein a culture of blind beings living in a deep cavern on Mars fondle an eidolon of their god, deriving strange sensual pleasures from running their fingers over its contours. Afterwards they fall asleep from the soporific effect of the experience and the original of the eidolon selects among them for its lunch.[12]

As noted, Smith's concept of a far-future earth in the Zothique stories is the major source for the landscape Vance employed in *The Dying Earth*. When Vance returned to this milieu in *The Eyes of the Overworld* (1966), he not only used a world-setting derived from Smith but a hero as well. Cugel the Clever, one of Vance's most notorious characters, comes in large part from Ralibar Vooz in Smith's "The Seven Geases." In that tale Vooz is engaged in a hunt when he accidentally disturbs the sorcerer Ezdagor at work:

> "May the ordure of demons bemire you from heel to crown!" cried the venomous ancient. "O lumbering, bawling idiot! you have ruined a most promising and important evocation.... Ill was that chance which brought you here: for They that you have frightened away will not return until the high stars repeat a certain rare and quickly passing conjunction; and much wisdom is lost to me in the interim."
>
> "How now, varlet!" said Ralibar Vooz, astonished and angered by this greeting, of which he understood little save that his presence was unwelcome to the old man.[13]

This sort of blundering interference in affairs beyond the ken of his knowledge or interest is one of Cugel's hallmarks, displayed in the episode where Cugel happens upon the amulet of the House of Slaye just before the true heir of the house would have reached it. This person had sifted the sands of the beach on which the amulet was lost for many years, and his fathers for four generations had spent their lives sifting the beach for this amulet they never found. Cugel accidentally kicks it into sight and appropriates it, despite the pleas of the rightful heir.

Another example occurs when hungry Cugel eats a creature the sorcerer Pharesm has been attempting to capture:

> Pharesm clutched at his head, hooking his fingers into the yellow down of his hair. He rolled his eyes upward and uttered a tragic cry. "Ah! Five hundred years I have toiled to entice this creature, despairing, doubting, brooding by night, yet never abandoning hope that my calculations were accurate and my great talisman cogent. Then, when finally it appears, you fall upon it for no other reason than to sate your repulsive gluttony!"
>
> Cugel, somewhat daunted by Pharesm's wrath, asserted his absence of malicious intent. Pharesm would not be mollified. He pointed out that Cugel had committed trespass and hence had forfeited the option of pleading innocence. "Your very existence is a mischief, compounded by bringing the unpleasant fact to my notice...." (*The Eyes of the Overworld*, "The Sorcerer Pharesm")

In tone and idea, this exchange closely follows the Smith model. And as in the Smith story, the sorcerer demands that the protagonist perform a task to amend his interference. This is the second geas put on Cugel in *The Eyes of the Overworld*; the first occurs early in the picaresque novel when Cugel is caught robbing the mansion of Iucounu the Laughing Magician. Iucounu sets Cugel to task and, to insure his unstinting cooperation, attaches a barbed being named Firx to Cugel's liver to spur the thief on in the swift completion of his appointed geas.

Both these episodes echo what happens to Ralibar Vooz when the angry Ezdagor says, "In retribution for the charm you have shattered, the business you have undone by this oafish trespass, I shall put upon you a most dire and calamitous and bitter geas."[14] The Firx creature is paralleled by the bird Raphtontis, Ezdagor's familiar, who guides Ralibar on his quest. When the bird begins its flight, "...Ralibar Vooz followed, driven by a compulsion that he could neither understand nor resist."[15] Lin Carter, who has done some Smith imitations, when reviewing *The Eyes of the Overworld* wrote that Cugel was "caught by the Laughing Magician while trying to steal some of his sorcerous treasures, slapped under a geas as in Clark Ashton Smith's tale, and dispatched on a long quest. ..."[16] It should be obvious that the germinal ideas for Cugel and many of the situations Vance uses in *The Eyes of the Overworld* may be found, more succinctly developed, in "The Seven Geases."

Vance, for all his use of concepts directly attributable to Smith, is nonetheless an original writer. The ideas he borrows from Smith are used in his own way. Cugel, though he may spring from the likes of Ralibar Vooz or the thief Satampra Zeiros or other CAS characters, ultimately comes into his own as a creation unlike any other in all of fantasy or SF literature. Vance's use of a dying earth is sufficiently distinct from Smith's Zothique tales that one need not worry about slavish imitation. Indeed, the reader can see from the various quotes in this chapter that Vance, owing much to Smith in terms of style and concepts, *absorbs* the Smith style into his own. I consider this absorption of style a more profound influence than any deliberate attempts to imitate Smith, such as Lin Carter's.[17] Any competent writer can mimic another, can borrow another's ideas, but absorption and transmutation of another writer's style into one's own is basic to true and lasting influence.

This underlying, pervasive influence may be seen more in the *tone* of Vance and Smith than in their style. Both writers are very sardonic; in fact, they are two of the most sardonic authors ever to work in the field of SF and fantasy. They employ irony at will, never hesitating to upset standard notions of story-telling. In various Smith and Vance stories the heroes and heroines meet sudden ghastly fates: in such Smith tales as "The Weird of Avoosl Wuthoqquan," "The Vaults of Yoh-Vombis," and many others or in the "Liane the Wayfarer" episode in Vance's *The Dying Earth* or the fates of the various damsels who encounter Cugel in *The Eyes of the Overworld.*

Consider the tone in this exchange, when police official Ben Zaum in Vance's *The Killing Machine* suggests that Kirth Gersen turn himself over to the villain lest twenty weasels (slang for spies) be slain in his stead:

> Gersen raised his eyebrows. "You suggest that I turn myself over to Kokor Hekkus?"
> "Not precisely, not exactly—well, think of it like this: it would be one man's life for twenty, and weasels are hard to come by—"
> "Only the inept are deweaseled," said Gersen. "Your organization is the sounder for their loss." He reflected a moment. "But your suggestion has a certain merit. Why not identify yourself as the man who planned the operation, and ask if he will spare fifty men for the two of us?"
> Zaum winced. "You can't be serious." (*The Killing Machine*, II)

A similar sardonic tone is evident in the following exchange from Smith's "The Door to Saturn," in which the Inquisitor Morghi follows the sorcerer Eibon through a magic door to Saturn in order to purge him:

> "Detestable sorcerer! Abominable heretic! I arrest you!" said Morghi with pontifical severity.
> Eibon was surprised, not to say startled; but it reassured him that Morghi was alone. He drew the sword of highly tempered bronze which he carried, and smiled.
> "I should advise you to moderate your language, Morghi," he admonished. "Also, your idea of arresting me is slightly out of place now, since we are alone together...and the temple-cells of Yhoundeh are many million miles away."
> Morghi did not appear to relish this information.[18]

To say the least! This sort of drollery and outrageous humor goes side-by-side with Smith and Vance. A reptilian chemist comments to Ralibar Vooz, "It was thoughtful of Haon-Dor to send you here. However, as you have seen, we are already supplied with an exemplar of your species; and, in the past, we have thoroughly dissected others and have learned all that there is to learn regarding this very uncouth and aberrant life-form."[19] The leader of a nomad tribe deals with Vance's hero Adam Reith after Reith incurs the tribe's wrath by flirting with one of their girls: "Traz Onmale summoned the butcher-woman. 'Bring a sharp knife. The slave must be made placid.' 'Wait!' gasped Reith. 'Is this any way to treat a stranger? Have you no tradition of hospitality?'" (*City of the Chasch*, II).

Of course, a great deal of Vance's prolific output bears no overt resemblance to Smith's writing. In some instances it bears little resemblance to other pieces Vance himself has written, as a comparison of the styles used in *Son of the Tree*, *The Eyes of the Overworld*, and *The Last Castle* will show. And of course not all the writing done by Smith and Vance has been good. Every writer produces some seriously flawed stories; these failures serve to keep praise for an author's truly great work within reasonable bounds.

Yet even in the good stories by Vance and Smith which are similar, even when the two are casting almost identical sardonic shadows across their fantastic scenarios, a basic rift separates their work. This rift was noted in the early review of *The Dying Earth* which pointed out Vance's indebtedness to Smith. "In certain respects, however," the review says, "Vance exceeds the writing of Smith. The former's characters are more human — a purely relative term in this application — and are moved more by actual emotions and motivations than Smith's protagonists."[20] Others have made essentially the same point since then and have reached the same judgment — that Vance, whose characters are more "human," is a better writer than Smith. When this judgment is made, invariably it overlooks the *reason* why Smith's characters are "less human" than Vance's: where Vance primarily is humanistic in his outlook, Clark Ashton Smith is cosmic.

A reviewer for a British fanzine, quite favorable to Smith,

commented on this point in a review of Smith's *Genius Loci*:

> To-day, many writers have succumbed to the realistic or humanistic trend of science fiction; and there is a disturbing schism between their work and the science fiction in this book. Even in the past, there was a bitter struggle between the two schools of thought. But Mr. Smith has remained faithful to the views he expounded in 1932: "One of literature's most glorious prerogatives is the exercise of imagination on things that lie beyond human experience — the adventuring of fantasy into the awful, sublime and infinite cosmos outside the human aquarium. The real thrill comes from the description of ultrahuman events, forces and scenes, which properly dwarf the terrene actors to comparative insignificance.... Science fiction, at its best, is akin to sublime and exalted poetry in its evocation of tremendous non-anthropomorphic imageries."[21]

H. P. Lovecraft, with Smith and Donald Wandrei one of the top-ranked cosmic writers in this century, defined cosmicism as the "capacity to feel profoundly regarding the cosmos and the disturbing and fascinating quality of the extraterrestrial and perpetually unknown"; and he noted that those "truly sensitive" to cosmic thought "will never be more than a minority, because most persons — even those of the keenest possible intellect and aesthetic ability — simply have not the psychological equipment...to feel that way."[22] Vance made a try at getting across the cosmic vision in *Star King*, in a passage purportedly quoted from one Jan Holberk Vaenz LXII (a pun on Vance's full name John Holbrook Vance). The fact that this passage is quoted under a takeoff on his own name is interesting in itself, because Vance comes close to capturing the same sort of cosmic perception that Smith had, as if he were consciously trying to come to grips with the notion of cosmicism:

> The most important fact of human life is the infinity of space: the bounds which can never be reached, the worlds without number still unseen — in short, the Beyond. It is my belief that the awareness of these awesome possibilities has somehow clotted at the core of human consciousness, and has diminished or dampened human enterprise. (*Star King*, VI)

This idea of space is presented as Smith or Lovecraft would present it. Where Vance shows his major concerns is in having this sense of infinity, of the wonder of the cosmos, a mere "damper" on human achievement! It is obvious that Vance, for all that he writes of interplanetary voyages, is concerned above all else about the *humans* making the voyages. For Smith the quality of the voyage would be sufficient reason for writing about it.

Another rift, not as profound, lies in the artistic intent of the two authors. Both can be totally sardonic, poking fun at any subject that comes along, but Vance is ultimately less serious than Smith. The example cited of the differences between Smith's "The Seed from the Sepulcher" and Vance's *Maske: Thaery* demonstrates Vance's lighter treatment of a horrific theme. When CAS sets out artistically to evoke a mood or create a doom, he enters the story without any personal or artistic reservations as to whether or not he should be coy or straightforward. If the story seems to demand a romantic ending, improbable or not, then romantic it is, as in "The Enchantress of Sylaire" and several other stories. If a realistic ending seems necessary, as in "The Dweller in the Gulf," then *all* the protagonists fall prey to the monster! "For Clark Ashton Smith," Harry Morris has observed, "the work of art is basically a work of the imagination while being at the same time true and real. This is perhaps the best way of defining what is meant by the sincerity of a work of art: the fidelity with which it adheres to the imagination of the artist."[23]

Vance does not seem to have this sort of commitment to the story he tells. He is known for his weak endings in many books, which I suspect are an outgrowth of his reservation about taking his invented worlds *seriously* as secondary creations. Vance seldom plunges totally into the story at hand; his viewpoint is detached, often completely unserious. *The Eyes of the Overworld* is essentially a very long joke with one punchline — that Cugel will end up where he started because of his blundering. (Of course, Vance's accomplishment in breaking down traditional considerations of the heroic fantasy novel by using this long joke device, his offbeat protagonist Cugel, and the continual abandonment of the damsels-in-distress makes up for any doubts one might have about reading such a book.) The attitude Vance has toward his fiction might be summed up by a sentence used to describe Kirth Gersen in the Demon Princes series: "Less angry—indeed, *half-amused with his own earnestness* he took stock of the situation [my italics]" (*The Killing Machine*, VIII). For Vance, especially the Vance of recent years, this point holds true: as a creator of secondary worlds he is never completely earnest, instead he keeps to himself behind a detached ironic perspective.

These rifts show how Vance and Smith are unlike yet are the only two basic departures between authors who are quite alike in most respects. In their best stories both writers have a rich style, full of words as strange as "cockalorum" or "mysteriarch"—and well worth reading for the sheer enjoyment of their fine prose. Once readers recognize the great influence Smith has had on Vance, perhaps Smith will gain his share of the popular appreciation which is deservedly coming to Vance.

5. Tschai: Four Planets of Adventure

MARK WILLARD

Two HUNDRED and twelve light-years from Earth hangs the smoky yellow star Carina 4269 and its single, ancient planet — Tschai. The Earth reconnaissance spacecraft *Explorator IV* penetrates the system and stands off Tschai. As a scout boat is prepared for launch, the *Explorator*'s officers examine the prospects; their conversation is wry, brisk, urbane, they contemplate the world below as a scientist contemplates an interesting petri dish. In the instant of the scout boat's departure, a torpedo from the planet intercepts the *Explorator*; in a dazzling flare the ship is obliterated save for skeleton fragments through which the old, old sun of Tschai shines knowingly. Officers, crew, and ties to Earth are no more than random atoms upon the solar winds.

Thus opens Jack Vance's Planet of Adventure series; and it takes no great imagination to view these first pages as symbolic. Officers Marin, Deale, and Walgrave may be taken to be representations of traits and attitudes inherent in much of Vance's previous work, and their uncompromising expungement as token that the story to come will differ in nature from what has gone before. Officers and ship did not die in vain; the promise is kept. The four Tschai novels (1968-70) are imbued with a greater vitality, a more down-to-earth urgency, a lesser detachment, and a more skillfull threading of fantasy through the framework of gritty reality than the body of Vance's earlier — and already excellent — work.

The Tschai series, comprising *City of the Chasch*, *Servants of the Wankh*, *The Dirdir*, and *The Pnume*, runs over six hundred pages. Scores of characters, dozens of locales, a seething wealth of events, attitudes, insights are paraded upon the stage; and four worldviews are provided in the brushes with the four alien races who give the books their titles. The landscapes of Tschai reek and radiate antiquity, and the human peoples live in the awareness that they are only the most recent of a near-infinity of generations whose lives were not perceptibly different. Throughout mankind's history on Tschai, humans have been pawns of the "great races." The native Pnume and Phung, three races of Chasch colonists, Dirdir and — the most recent arrivals — the Wankh all help set up a milieu incredibly rich and complex, a kaleidoscope of varieties of man and alien, vignettes of curious, specialized lifestyles each all-important to its practitioners. The surface of Tschai is a vast openness of steppes and far-flung continents, yet for contrast the reader gradually becomes aware of stifling traditions and the surveillance of the alien overlords.

Though the reader comes to know him well, the protagonist, star-scout Adam Reith, remains a somewhat unknown, ever-surprising quantity. Reith exists from the moment he steps into the scout boat in the prologue of *City of the Chasch*, and by casual mentions we learn that he has served on other missions, that aside from his avocation his life has not been out of the ordinary. However, of Reith's training, childhood, family, nationality, we discover nothing. On what does Reith base his decisions, his reactions? What cultural background does he bring to his evaluation of situations? All must be assumed, from Reith's actions and attitudes. Scouts in general are described

by Officer Deale before his death as "men who like a change";
Reith fits the description. His attention and the narrative's focus are firmly fixed upon the present.

So there is no extraneous clutter—no looks back, no detailed comparisons of Tschai's features with their Earthly
counterparts. Earth itself, even more than Reith, is a blank.
One's curiosity is piqued, but this paucity of background may
elicit admiration from a technical point of view: it must have
been more difficult than not to avoid mentioning incidents
about Reith's training, previous missions, friends and acquaintances on Earth, and so on, which could distract from the
story at hand. And, too, the situation allows a greater empathy
with Reith, since there is no strange futurian concept of his
Earthly background to assimilate.

As an Earthman, Reith is a unique specimen adrift upon a
vast world. He tends to transmute his emotions into purposeful
action and is relatively free of the malaise of homesickness.
While no stranger to doubt and despair, he rebounds from
them; his personality is not marred by experiences which might
have soured or maimed one less resilient.

Reith's companions contrast starkly with each other. The
Emblem nomad youth Traz is a straightforward, solid, rather
simplistic being whose personality is ingrained with a severity
and maturity unusual for his age through his carrying of the
chieftain-emblem Onmale. Anacho the renegade Dirdirman is
a civilized, cultured creature—didactic, petulant, verging on
the effete in mannerisms yet as harshly survival-oriented as any
other child of Tschai. Traz and Anacho regard each other
somewhat as one regards another person's pets—with faintly
amused incomprehension. To Traz, Anacho is freakish, garrulous, over-sophisticated, and tainted by the Dirdir; to
Anacho, Traz is blunt, dull, simple, and primitive. Their natural antipathy is used to good effect; frequently a comment from
one will stimulate the other to provide colorful background information. Each, in common with Reith, is a fugitive with no

life of his own beyond what he has shared with the other two. Traz's tie with Onmale remains strong; he hears the emblem calling to him from the spot where it lies buried and, finally, when he has gained the strength to govern it, reclaims the artifact. Anacho, on the other hand, has made a clean break with the Dirdir and gradually rejects his Dirdirman ideology as well. Traz is the more knowledgeable in the woods and steppes; Anacho is quicker to rebuff coercion and exploitation.

Beyond these three, each novel brings forward memorable characters, to be discussed at more length later: *City of the Chasch* introduces Ylin Ylan, the proud femme fatale; *Servants of the Wankh*, the saturnine Helsse and Zarfo Detweiler the Lokhar; *The Dirdir* the Dirdirman mongrel Alia Woudiver and the pensive Deine Zarre; and *The Pnume* the Pnumekin waif Zap 210 and the jovial philosopher Cauch the Zsafathran.

Several themes run through the four books; the strongest is contrast. Drab, somber Tschai, with its steppes and wastes, is circled by the pink moon Az and the blue moon Braz—twin symbols of gaiety and festivity! The Blue Chasch race is characteristically cruel, arbitrary, and sadistic, yet their dwelling places are gardens of feathery fronds and trees which refresh the air. On Tschai's surface the alien races rock and swirl in power struggles and combats; beneath the ground the Pnume historians pace their still shafts and caverns and make notes for their great records.

Another type of contrast is what might be termed anachronistic juxtapositions: the past and the future, and mud and the stars, tradition and antitradition, and so on are ever rubbing shoulders. Humans, barely civilized, make use of the cast-off and antiquated equipment of the Chasch, Wankh, and Dirdir, powered by ubiquitous Dirdir energy cells. Leap-horse riders charge into battle with motor-wagons and sandblasts; the Xar tribe journeys to festival upon a sky raft; an old woman sitting beside a tray of stale buns in a nowhere village looks up to see the aircraft of sons of other stars engaging each other above her head.

A certain realism might also be called a theme — delete some of the action and the series could almost become a fascinating travelog! A main thrust of all Vance's writing is sociological; there are no snapshot glimpses of tribes, cultures, or peoples, but somehow enough detail is introduced to show them in the round. Means of livelihood, outlook, natural features, the shaping forces of their existence — all are brushed on quickly but delicately. Rather than being noteworthy for curious character traits or personal foibles, most frequently the supporting characters are distinguished through their display of cultural attributes. As is often the case in Vance's work, cultures *are* characters; the rivalry between Thang and Zsafathran in *The Pnume* is far more entertaining than the actual encounters described in the narrative would be alone.

Antiquity and an awareness of the past are everywhere. In contrast to Earth, the inhabitants of Tschai are knowledgeable of the history of their world for tens of thousands of years — Anacho describes Dadiche as "... relatively old; twenty thousand years or so...." History on Tschai is comparable to geological ages on Earth. The records of the Pnume, and their monuments, reach back seven million years! The Pnume's present situation and the presence of the Dirdir have held sway in their tracts for sixty thousand. The Wankh forts have stood for "only" ten thousand years.

Though they share themes, the books in the series follow no formula. In *City of the Chasch* Reith attempts to recover his own spacecraft; in *Servants of the Wankh* he makes a stab at pirating one from a spaceport; in *The Dirdir* Reith resigns himself to building one; and in *The Pnume* he endeavors to escape the attention he has stirred up in his former activities. Similarly, to characterize each volume in a vastly simplified manner: *City of the Chasch* is a rushing explosion of new concepts raising possibility after possibility; *Servants of the Wankh* proceeds along more cautious lines and harks back to other Vance works and styles, setting up situations; *The Dirdir* is the Tschai concept in full bloom, the least episodic but having the strongest characters and plot; and *The Pnume* is a wrapping-up and fond farewell.

Tschai is an *alien* world. Vance establishes this simply in each of the opening chapters of the first three volumes by having Reith encounter a Phung, a solitary sapient creature of Tschai. The creatures "are the stuff of Tschai itself," alien to the borderline of our comprehension. Their eerie presence and bizarre actions (twice leading to their own destruction) fill us with a weird oppression and a tangible sense of the alien spirit. Clad in black felt hat and cloak, possessed of enormous strength and agility, feared even by the fearsome Dirdir, the Phung is a fairy-tale creature from an Arthur Rackham print. Its perversity, one feels, *must* be some utterly alien logic of behavior: a Phung dribbles pebbles down upon a sleeping man; a second, disturbed in its lair, comes forth to make short shrift of the armed intruders; a third disrupts a camp of Green Chasch then suddenly throws away its defenses, and later, its severed head, still wearing the felt hat, gazes into a dying campfire. The indigenes of Tschai—Pnume, Phung, and nighthound—are so estranged from the rest of the races that Chasch, Dirdir, Wankh, and man seem almost like kin.

In the last volume, the Pnume themselves set the atmosphere of Tschai; lost in their tunnels, Adam Reith feels a burgeoning hysteria, a desire to play tricks upon the Pnumekin he is following, a sense of invulnerability. Surely these are attributes of the Phung?

"Tschai is a world of anguish." This phrase is often repeated and often demonstrated. "Evil? On Tschai the word has no meaning. Events exist—or they do not exist." Yet this is spoken sadly, acknowledging that the lean, insecure life of Tschai is born of necessity and not in the nature of man. There is little pity and less squeamishness; sadly enough, the latter trait appears more strongly in the most civilized environs, the Yao lands and Sivishe. Life on Tschai is intensified; perhaps in the absence of massive material comforts and a structured society, the pains as well as the pleasures of life take on a stronger meaning.

Partly behind this driving intensity of life is the fact that the language of Tschai is near-universal; communication is a vital necessity where conflict is so frequent and its consequences so dire. Yet in contrast to the picture sketched above, a large portion of the human population consists of Grays, a hybrid mélange of many races and bleached in character as well as in coloring. This "Gray-ness" is protective. More than once it is emphasized that surveillance portends ill events; interest in the affairs of others is tantamount to a declaration of hostilities. Patrol aircraft of the great races monitor the doings of the human communities, this watchfulness ever reminding the humans of their place.

For all its anguish, Tschai is a marvelous world, its landscapes basking in a muted, vigorous age. The ethereal, pastel expanses of the steppes are desolate yet living — coarse dry soils, crumbling roads and ruins, sparse and hardy plants, sparser and hardier fauna. There are wild and lush seascapes, pink sand deserts with oases of white-plumed trees; coasts where mudflats and sandstone promontories alternate with awesome regularity out to the horizon haze. The colors of the dwelling-places are rich: old rose, old scarlet, dark gold, burnt orange, salmon. The fauna, too, is fascinating and all-too-briefly described: leap-horses, pull-beasts, herd animals, and many a curious wild denizen identified only by an exotic name are left to the reader's imagination.

Reith is an iconoclast. He is a shaking-up force, a breath from the human homeworld, and the representative of a fifth "great power." His mere presence embodies ideological disaster to certain sects upon Tschai; everywhere, like some natural force uprooting the landscape, Reith rearranges the social and political climate of Tschai. In *City of the Chasch* alone the Emblem nomads, the priestesses of the Female Mystery, the Gnashters and inhabitants of the Pera, and the Chasch and

Chaschmen of Dadiche are rocked by cultural upheaval, their ways irrevocably changed. The Wankhmen and Pnumekin are severed from their master races; only the Dirdirmen prove resilient enough or stubborn enough to survive Reith's passage.

Chasch is, as it must be, introductory. The reader and Adam Reith are thrust headlong into the seething possibilities and spectrum of Tschai's alienness — within moments of the scout boat's crash-landing appear the Emblems, Chasch, Dirdir, and their respective submen, along with strange and ornate flying craft and weaponry, and the hostilities among the races become apparent. Following this flamboyant, tumultuous glimpse at what is in store, Reith and reader are pulled back to recuperate and, on the relatively calm Aman steppes, the background is gradually filled in.

Reith's early sojurn on Tschai is made in false optimism; his unfounded hopes that the Chasch have preserved his spacecraft in operable condition are dashed when he stands before the eviscerated, completely dismantled hulk. His victory in Dadiche becomes a hollow triumph but one that prior events have schooled him to withstand.

Almost at once, before being fully recovered from the crash-landing, Reith must prove his worthiness to survive, first against the more obstreperous of the Emblems and then in a combat of wits with the magician caste. He provides the catalyst that breaks the boy-chief Traz Onmale free from his tribe, for Traz has already realized that a showdown and defeat at the hands of the magicians are imminent. He and Traz, and later Anacho, must survive eerie and dire visitations from the nighthounds, and after travels with a caravan they must escape from a pitched battle with the Green Chasch. The attack of the Green horde, coming just as a storm breaks and waged in the midst of lashing sheets of rain and thunderous lightning, is as vivid and brisk as any Vance has recorded. Then Reith comes as a fugitive to the fugitive city of Pera, where men live in the Chasch shadow.

The Blue Chasch are a stagnating, perverse, and cruel race, controlling their submen through a deception; their presence is all the more impressive after Reith's previous encounters with the brutish marauders the Green Chasch, and with the senile, humorous, and sinister walking-silverfish Old Chasch. The Blues' obsession with complexity as a beneficial end in itself is one with their — to humans — harsh and malignant attitude towards other forms of life; a brush with the Blue Chasch certainly complicates anyone's existence.

In *Chasch* Reith also encounters Ylin Ylan, the Flower of Cath — a peculiar, exotic, remote, pensive, fated personality. Reith's entrancement with her is credible, but her attraction scarcely extends into the reader's heart. Involvement with an attractive female is usually considered a staple of the adventure novel but it leads to pitfalls; the author walks a tightrope to maintain both the plausibility and force of his romance. Vance takes what is probably the best course this early in the game; after the relationship comes to full bloom in *Chasch*, it falls into a gradual estrangement in *Servants of the Wankh* that culminates in a dramatic and tragic parting.

In the close of *Chasch*, Reith adopts the position of leader and administrator, a role he manages to avoid in subsequent adventures. He must end the rule of the Gnashters in Pera to safeguard his companions and thus becomes the *de facto* government. When the Blue Chasch strike at Reith in reprisal for his intrusion into Dadiche, they strike at Pera. A revolutionary upheaval becomes the convenient, if somewhat messy, method by which Reith gains access to his scout boat.

Servants of the Wankh begins an interval after the close of *City of the Chasch*, skipping over the transfer of power in Pera and the first 2,000 miles of Reith's party's sky-raft journey. *Chasch* dealt mainly with nomads and barbarians; *Wankh* takes the heroes into more civilized climes and replaces the supporting cast by degrees. The pettish and flamboyant Yao cavalier Dordolio joins the party at Coad; Ylin Ylan exits during the voyage, and Dordolio drops away at Cath where the Wankh-man agent Helsse and Zarfo Detweiler the Lokhar are introduced.

The sea voyage to Cath and the earlier portion of the book are somewhat episodic; Vance indulges himself in detailing customs, curiosities, and items of cuisine, as well as in some brief but penetrating dialogue between the passengers of the *Vargaz* on the nature of religion and the enhancement of life through the institutions of formality. With the introduction of the second cast, the Wankh, the intrigues centered in Cath, and Reith's decision to steal a Wankh spaceboat, the story becomes gripping and fluid. Zarfo Detweiler is an enjoyable rascal, and Helsse has depths and qualities left unexplored by the narrative. The book might have benefitted from expansion of the later episodes; events whisk to a close all too swiftly.

Reith's attempted hijacking of a Wankh spaceship is slice-of-life writing. Weeks of plans and recruitment, torturous overland travel to approach the Wankh citadel from its blind landward side, the long wait for a suitable opportunity to move — and the effort concludes in a few frantic minutes beset by complications and surprises: a Wankh is aboard; the controls are a new modification; and, despite the heroic efforts of the Lokhar crew, the ship malfunctions and crashes.

The Wankh make the briefest appearance in the story of any race save the Phung; aloof and enigmatic, they have cultivated their submen as a buffer rather than as a tool (as have the other great powers). It is the Wankhmen, nevertheless, who are Reith's true adversaries. Their discomfiture, through Reith's manipulation of Helsse, clarifies the mysteries surrounding the destruction of *Explorator IV* and affairs in Cath; but the reader is left wanting to know more about the manipulations of the Dugbo necromancer which made the scene possible and about Helsse's sojourn underground where — presumably — he was interrogated by the Pnume.

Reith and his companions, after the debacle in Wankh territory, return with Zarfo Detweiler to his home, Smargash, where *The Dirdir* begins. The book courses from festival time in Smargash to the turmoil, adventure, and greed of Maust to the complex, sophisticated intrigues in Sivishe. In *The Dirdir* are to be found the strongest characters, the most vivid psychological insights. Reith's fortunes soar to the most exhilarating heights and take the most stunning falls.

The Dirdir figure strongly throughout the book, and our view of them is more thorough because of Dirdirman Anacho's comments and interpretations. Dirdir-Wankh and Dirdir-Pnume relations are made clear, as well as the social ferment which handicaps the race's expansion. The episode within the Glass Box is practically an expedition to the Dirdir homeworld, Sibol.

Vance's picture of the Dirdir seems to have changed between their first appearance in *City of the Chasch* as "tall attenuated creatures, hairless, pale as parchment, with... languid and elegant attitudes," "sheep-like length of visage," and "elaborate costumes of ribbons, flounces, sashes." Without directly contradicting any of this, Vance shifts emphasis in *The Dirdir* to portray them as "impressive creatures, harsh, mercurial, decisive... like lizards on a hot day," or "silver leopards walking erect."

The theme of anachronistic juxtaposition is strong in Dirdir from the outset; into the Smargash Fair, or "Unnatural Dream Time" — a wild and picturesque assemblage of primitive human tribes — drops a Dirdir hunting party, strong, sinister, and disturbing, with electronic tracking devices, energy weapons, and sky-cars.

An episode in the Carabas, early in the book, is a high point. Vance's heroes often gain riches through unorthodox means, but never has he skirted so close to the fairy-tale archetype of the search for wealth, skillfully grading it into shades of reality. Uranium compounds in the soil occasion the growth of nodes of chrysopine, which fragment into colored sequins used as currency. Treasure growing in the ground! Jewels sprouting from the soil in mushroom-like nodes! Find a node and there is still tension — is it royal purple, blood scarlet, or a lesser shade of value? And will the finder live to exit the Zone? Throughout the Carabas men hunt sequins and Dirdir hunt men, for the region is their game preserve, the allure of wealth assuring a constant stock of prey. Adjacent to the Carabas lies Maust, whose very name breathes antiquity, its polished stones and dry brittle air attesting to the length of time it has garnered wealth from sequin-takers in the manner that Las Vegas garners money from gamblers. Prospective sequin-hunters are destined "either for wealth or the experience of a Dirdir intestine," and the atmosphere is that of macabre carnival. Even the board game in a gambling house sounds a premonitory note; at its close the toy figures of sequin-takers have either departed or perished, and only the Dirdir roam the board.

With a fortune in sequins gained from the ambush of Dirdir in the Zone, Reith goes to Sivishe to construct a spaceship; the man who can be persuaded to assist him is Alia Woudiver. The evil Woudiver is perhaps the strongest supporting character in the series. His greed and malice blur the distinctions between goodness and wickedness; for reasons unknown he provides and then expunges technician Deine Zarre, a patient character seemingly existing only to suffer. About him is a web of influences and pressures; Woudiver lives by his beliefs but they bend to financial pressure, and dealing with him is like dealing with quicksand. He is certainly right when he reviles Adam Reith for exhorting him to illegal acts in the building of Reith's spaceboat, but he acts despicably in betraying Reith and his companions into the Glass Box.

The Dirdir is the best-plotted volume; it contains the strongest foreshadowing of its successor in Reith and Company's brush with the Khors and with spying Pnumekin, and also a musing summary bringing into focus Reith's other adventures on Tschai. The presence of the Dirdir and the evil genius Woudiver instill it with a vigorous atmosphere; the book even ends on a hot moment of confrontation and conflict, as if Vance simply had to force himself to cut off.

The presence of Woudiver is less imposing in *The Pnume* but still bizarrely sinister — a monstrous fat creature, chained yet plotting, placidly doing tatting as he suffers his confinement. Reith is undone by his Earthly scruples; he is reluctant to kill Woudiver in cold blood and thus gives his enemy the time needed to betray him into the hands of the Pnume.

The Pnume are a race apart in a different fashion from the Wankh; they "infest the ruined places of Tschai, like worms in old wood." Their hidden fastnesses are hushed places of layers and levels of knowledge as well as of passages and tunnels. The Pnume seem to a human observer to be unfathomable clock-work toys, possessed of inhuman strength and inscrutable emotions. The Pnumekin are less physically mutated than some of the other submen, but their intellects have taken another track; they are remote from humanity and the world above. The openness of above-ground oppresses the inhabitants of these tunnels; the broad brims of their hats hide them from the reaches of the sky.

Reith's sojourn in the Pnume caverns is even more intense and cloistered than his stay in Sivishe, and when it ends the story has come full circle. Upon departure from the underground world, Reith is once more a wanderer, accumulating companions and embarking upon an episodic journey.

The Pnumekin girl Zap 210 is paired with Reith by fate; the cataclysm which has landed him in the Pnume lairs strikes her from her place in life as well. At the outset she is an unlikely romantic interest, hostile towards Reith because he has kidnapped her, and desexed by name and by her conditioning. She acquires as deep and as swift a characterization as the Flower of Cath by a simple, masterful dodge. In their escape from the Pnume wardens, Zap 210 and Reith must make a long barge journey through an almost unlighted underground canal; in the shrouding darkness Vance is denied his usual palette of color and sight and so paints instead in psychological shades. When the pair emerges from the caverns at the end of the voyage, the release is palpable to the reader; but where a cultural cipher began the trip, a new female lead has completed it.

Poor Zap 210 is yanked out of her "cool gray existence" and, in the course of her companionship with Reith, thrust into a series of explicitly sexual situations. In the hands of writers like Philip José Farmer or Harlan Ellison the results might have been grotesque, but Vance succeeds in eliciting the reader's sympathy for the poor waif. Unlike Ylin Ylan she needs mental as well as physical assistance, and in receiving it her personality expands.

Following the oppressive interlude within the Pnume world-castle at the book's beginning, the delightful, less tense episodes in Zsafathra and Urmank are like icing on a cake, small treats bestowed on us as the series draws to a close. The wily Cauch the Zsafathran is of a kind with Zarfo Detweiler. A shrewd, worldly, mildly avaricious character, he is the fount of local knowledge in the absence of Anacho and Traz and the foil for Reith's daring and extravagant plans. The incident at the eel-races in Urmank is a return to a more usual (for Vance heroes) method of gathering funds: swindling a swindler.

The return to Sivishe is a farewell wave to the Dirdir episode, and the abrupt transition back to the Pnume caverns to recover Zap 210 holds an eerie, dreamlike, underwater quality. In his last brush with Tschai, Reith faces the personification of the planet's ancient spirit and its massive history in the form of Foreverness. His emergence with Zap 210 is like an awakening from a dream; Tschai is of the past, the way homeward is open, and the absence of opposition to the journey is like an emptiness.

Though Tschai is one planet, the series has taken us through four worlds, four environments, four spectra of alienness. In the passing the alien has become familiar; though Chasch, Wankh, Dirdir, Pnume, and Phung all remain strange and fearsome, we know their ways, at least enough to wish to know more. The Tschai series, at this writing, is Vance's longest, and it may be unseemly to hope that he might add to it; but the feeling persists that the more we are shown Tschai and its people, the more yet awaits to be seen.

6. "The Eyes of the Overworld" and "The Dying Earth"*

ROBERT SILVERBERG

OF ALL THE ephemeral science-fiction magazines that fluttered in and out of existence in the early 1950s — there must have been fifty of them, few surviving as long as twelve months — one of the most transient was Damon Knight's *Worlds Beyond*. It made its appearance in the late autumn of 1950, a small, neat-looking 25-cent magazine printed on rough pulp paper, published some excellent short stories, including several that have become standard anthology items, and expired with its third issue. Actually, it was virtually stillborn, for its owners, Hillman Publications, killed it a couple of weeks after the first issue was released, as soon as the preliminary sales figures had been received and found wanting. The second and third issues were distributed only because they were too far along in the production process to halt.

The first issue of *Worlds Beyond* offered many fine things — C. M. Kornbluth's "The Mindworm," John D. MacDonald's "The Big Contest," reprints of classic fantasies by Graham

---

*This chapter was first published as an introduction to *The Eyes of the Overworld* by Jack Vance (Boston: Gregg Press, 1977). Introduction copyright © 1977 by Robert Silverberg. Rerinted by permission.

Greene, Philip Wylie, and Franz Kafka, and some short, tren-
chant book reviews by editor Knight, harbingers of his later
brilliant critical essays. But for me, adolescent science-fiction
reader with head buzzing with dreams of distant tomorrows,
the most exciting thing of all was the advertisement on the back
cover, blue type on yellow background, heralding a novel by
Jack Vance called *The Dying Earth:*

> Time had worn out the sun, and earth was spinning quickly toward
> eternal darkness. In the forests strange animals hid behind twisted trees,
> plotting death; in the cities men made constant revel and sought sorcery
> to cheat the dying world.
>
> In this dark and frenzied atmosphere Jack Vance has set his finest
> novel, *The Dying Earth*, a story of love and death and magic and the re-
> discovery of science. Through this time, fabulously far from now, wan-
> der men and women and artificial creatures from the vats, driven by fear,
> lust, and the ever-present need for escape.
>
> One episode from Jack Vance's astonishing novel is printed in this
> issue of WORLDS BEYOND under the title, *The Loom of Darkness*. If
> you enjoyed this excerpt, you won't want to miss *The Dying Earth*.

I found threefold joy in that announcement. For one thing,
it promised an ambitious new series of original science-fiction
novels in paperback format — after the Vance book would come
Isaac Asimov's novel *Pebble in the Sky* — and that was heady
news, for the infant American paperback industry had not yet
gone in for science fiction in any significant way, and an increase
in the skimpy supply of my favorite reading matter was something to greet with enthusiasm. (It may seem hard to believe today, but in 1950 each new SF novel was an *event*.) Then, too,
the far-future setting of *The Dying Earth* held a special attraction for me. One of the first works of science fiction I had discovered was H. G. Wells' *The Time Machine* (1895), and I had
been so captured by the vision in that book's closing pages of
the last days of earth, that forlorn snow-flecked beach under a
black sky lit by a ghastly blood-red sun, that I had searched
through all the science fiction I could find for comparably powerful glimpses of the eons yet to come. Olaf Stapledon had met
that need in me, and H. P. Lovecraft, and Arthur C. Clarke,

and still I remained insatiable for knowledge of the end of time, and this new novel seemed likely to feed that strange hunger. And, lastly, I rejoiced because the author was Jack Vance, for whose voluptuous prose and soaring imagination I had lately developed a strong affinity.

In 1950 Vance had been writing science fiction only a year or two longer than I had been reading it; we were both newcomers. His first published story, "The World-Thinker," had appeared in the Summer 1945 issue of *Thrilling Wonder Stories*, a gaudy-looking pulp magazine that ultimately became far less tawdry than its outer semblance would lead one to think. Magazine science fiction in 1945 was pretty primitive stuff, by and large, and so too was "The World-Thinker," a simple and melodramatic chase story; but yet there was a breadth of vision in it, a philosophic density, that set it apart from most of what was being published then, and the novice author's sense of color and image, his power to evoke mood and texture and sensory detail, was already as highly developed as that of anyone then writing science fiction, except perhaps C. L. Moore and Leigh Brackett. A brief autobiographical note appended to the story declared, "I am a somewhat taciturn merchant seaman, aged twenty-four. I admit only to birth in San Francisco, attendance at the University of California, interest in hot jazz, abstract physical science, Oriental languages, feminine psychology." The magazine's editor added that Vance had been in the Merchant Marine since 1940, was serving somewhere in the Pacific, and had been torpedoed twice since Pearl Harbor.

Over the next few years a dozen or so Vance stories appeared, most of them in *Thrilling Wonder Stories* and its equally lurid-looking companion, *Startling Stories*. There was nothing very memorable among them — nearly all were clever but repetitive and formularized tales of the intrigues of one Magnus Ridolph, a rogue of the spaceways — but it was clear that a remarkable imagination was at work producing these trifles, for even the most minor story had its flash of extraordinary visual intensity and its moments of unexpected ingenuity. Would Vance ever produce anything more substantial, though? Finally, in the spring and summer of 1950, came two long and impressive Vance works. *Thrilling Wonder* offered the novella "New Bodies for Old," and a few months later *Startling* published his first novel-length story, "The Five Gold Bands." The first was a conventional adventure story in form, but the prose was rich with dazzling descriptive passages, sometimes to the point of purpleness, and the science-fiction inventions—the Chateau d'If, the Empyrean Tower, the technology of personality transplants—were brilliantly realized. "The Five Gold Bands" was even more conventional, a simple tale of interstellar treasure hunt, but it was made notable by its unflagging pace, the lively assortment of alien beings with which Vance had stocked it, and the light, sensitive style. Obviously 1950 was the year of Vance's coming of age as a writer, and *The Dying Earth* was a book I eagerly sought. The eleven-page slice published in the first number of *Worlds Beyond*, a delicate tale of wizardry and vengeance, whetted my appetite with its images of decay and decline, tumbled pillars, slumped pediments, crumbled inscriptions, the weary red sun looking down on the ancient cities of humanity.

"At your newsstand now," that back-cover ad in *Worlds Beyond* proclaimed, but where was the book? On dark and snowy winter afternoons I searched the paperback racks of Brooklyn for it, but saw no sign of it or of any other Hillman Publications books. A second issue of *Worlds Beyond* appeared, still advertising *The Dying Earth*, and still the book was impossible to find. Eventually—it may have been the last week of 1950, or perhaps it was just after the turn of the year—a friend gave me a copy that he had bought somewhere. It was the first chaotic winter of the Korean War, and paper supplies were tight, distribution channels confused; Hillman Publications had killed its paperback line, like *Worlds Beyond*, almost at the moment of conception; only a few thousand copies of *The Dying Earth* had gone on sale, in scattered regions of the country. The book, a shabby little item printed on cheap paper, with a crude, blotchy cover, was from the day of publication one of the great rarities of American science fiction. I treasured my copy; I treasure it still.

And yet I found the book obscurely disappointing. It was not a novel, I quickly saw, but rather a story sequence, six loosely related tales set against a common background, with a few overlapping characters to provide continuity. (Mysteriously, the first two stories were reversed, so that the central character in the opening chapter was a woman who is not created until the second chapter. This defect, which I assume was the publisher's error, has been corrected in later editions.) The loose-jointed structure didn't trouble me unduly, although I would at that time have preferred a more orthodox pattern with the familiar magazine-serial format of beginning, middle, and resolution; but what disturbed me was the discovery that the book was not truly science fiction at all, but fantasy.

What I wanted, in my literal-minded way, was absolute revelation of the far future. Wells, in *The Time Machine*, had meticulously described the climatic and geological consequences of the heat-death of the sun; Stapledon, in *Last and First Men* (1930), had proposed an elaborate evolutionary progression for mankind over the next few million years. But Vance showed no such concern for scientific verisimilitude. A truly dying Earth would be a place of thin, sharp air, bleak shadows, bitter winds, and all humanity long since evolved beyond our comprehension or else vanished entirely. But, though there are some strange creatures in Vance's world, his protagonists are mainly humans much like ourselves, unaltered by the passing of the millennia. Here is Liane the Wayfarer:

> His brown hair waved softly, his features moved in charm and flexibility. He had golden-hazel eyes, large and beautiful, never still. He wore red leather shoes with curled tops, a suit of red and green, a green cloak, and a peaked hat with a red feather.

And here is the world Liane inhabits:

> There was a dark blue sky, an ancient sun.... Nothing in sight, nothing of Earth was raw or harsh—the ground, the trees, the rock ledge protruding from the meadow; all these had been worked upon, smoothed, aged, mellowed. The light from the sun, though dim, was rich, and invested every object of the land, the rocks, the trees, the quiet grasses and flowers, with a sense of lore and ancient recollection. A hundred paces distant rose the mossy ruins of a long-tumbled castelry. The stones were blackened now by lichens, by smoke, by age; grass grew rank through the rubble—the whole a weird picture in the long light of sunset.

Liane wears medieval garb; the narrative action of *The Dying Earth* is largely a series of encounters among sorcerers; ruined castles stand at the edge of meadows. This is not science fiction. It is a continuation of the work of Scheherazade by other hands, a *Thousand Nights and a Night* romance of never-never land. To Vance, the dying Earth is only a metaphor for decline, loss, decay, and, paradoxical though it may sound, also a return to a lost golden age, a simple and clean time of sparse population and unspoiled streams, of wizards and emperors, of absolute values and the clash of right and wrong. If I failed to appreciate *The Dying Earth* when I first encountered it, it was because I had asked it to be that which it was not. I admired the music of the prose and the elegance of the wit, the cunning of the characters and the subtlety of human interactions; but it was something other than science fiction, except maybe for the sequence titled "Ulan Dhor Ends a Dream," and science fiction of the narrowest sort was what I sought.

The first edition of *The Dying Earth* disappeared and became legendary almost at once; Hillman Publications turned to other things, and no more books came from it, not even the promised Asimov novel; and Vance, perhaps expecting nothing more from the publication of his first novel than he had received—that is, a small amount of cash, prestige in exceedingly limited quarters, and general obscurity—went on like a good professional to other projects. *Startling* and *Thrilling Wonder* remained congenial markets for him over the next few years, and his narrative skills grew ever more assured, his style more dazzling, his mastery of large forms more confident. Now he worked almost entirely in the novella and the novel, with such magazine stories as "Son of the Tree," "Planet of the Damned," "Abercrombie Station," "The Houses of Iszm," and the immense odyssey "Big Planet." In 1953 came a novel for young readers, *Vandals of the Void*, and the ephemeral paperback publication of his earliest long story, "The Five Gold Bands," as *The Space Pirate*. By 1956, when Ballantine Books issued what may be his supreme accomplishment in science fiction, the powerful novel *To Live Forever*, Vance's position in the front ranks of science fiction was manifest. He had achieved no great commercial success, for his work was too "special," increasingly more dependent on a resonantly archaic, mannered style and a cultivated formality of manner, to win much of a following among the casual readers of paperbacks, but it was cherished by connoisseurs, and his popularity with the science-fiction subculture known as "fandom" was considerable. His novella, "The Dragon Masters," which had much the flavor of *The Dying Earth*, brought him his first Hugo award when it was published in 1962. The same year *The Dying Earth* itself was reissued in paperback by Lancer Books as part of a "limited edition" series of classic reprints. This second edition would go through several printings in the 1960s.

That Vance would choose to set another novel in the actual world of *The Dying Earth* came as a surprise, however. Except for the early Magnus Ridolph stories he had never been a writer of sequels or linked series of stories,* nor were any of his novels related to any other by a common background as are, say, many of the books of Robert A. Heinlein or Poul Anderson. And *The Dying Earth* was fifteen years old, a work out of a distant era of Vance's career, when *The Magazine of Fantasy and Science Fiction* unexpectedly announced in its issue of Novem-

---

*In recent years he has become quite fond of the multi-volume novel.

ber 1965 that it would begin publication the following month
of the first of five novellas in the same setting as that celebrated
book.

Over the next eight months the stories appeared, in this
order:

"The Overworld," December 1965.
"The Mountains of Magnatz," February 1966.
"The Sorcerer Pharesm," April 1966.
"The Pilgrims," June 1966.
"The Manse of Iucounu," June 1966.

And later in 1966 the complete work was published in paperback form as *The Eyes of the Overworld* by Ace Books, the
small but enterprising house that had previously brought out
most of the fine adventure stories that Vance had written for
Startling and *Thrilling Wonder* in the early 1950s. *The Eyes of
the Overworld* included all five of the *Fantasy and Science Fiction* novellas plus a sixth, "Cil," that had not been used by the
magazine. There were minor differences between the magazine
versions and the book: the chapter known as "The Mountains
of Magnatz" had been heavily and clumsily rewritten for the
magazine to repair the damage done by the extraction of "Cil"
from the fabric; small explanatory passages required by the
magazine to refresh the memory of readers from month to
month were deleted from the book; and the last of the five
magazine stories had combined two of Vance's chapters under
one title, so that in fact the book had seven episodes all told.

The new book was not so much a sequel to *The Dying Earth*
as a companion. None of the characters of *The Dying Earth* are
to be found in *The Eyes of the Overworld*, though a few historical figures such as the sorcerer Phandaal are mentioned in
both. There are references in *The Eyes of the Overworld* to
some of the geographical features of *The Dying Earth* — the
cities Kaiin and Azenomei, the Land of the Falling Wall, the
River Scaum — but most of *The Eyes of the Overworld* takes
place far beyond the Realm of Grand Motholam, in an entirely
new series of strange places. The bizarre quasi-human creatures

of *The Dying Earth*, the deodands and erbs and gids and such, do recur, and their presence among the fully human folk of the era is at last given some explanation; but mostly the world of *The Eyes of the Overworld* is created from new material. It is impossible to tell how the events of one book are related in time to those of the other, though the same feeble red sun illuminates both.

Structurally, too, the books are different. Both are episodic, but *The Dying Earth*'s six sections are virtually self-contained, each with its own protagonist. Characters recur from episode to episode—Turjan of Miir, Liane the Wayfarer, the synthetic girls T'sais and T'sain, the sorcerer Pandelume—but only occasionally do they interact across the boundaries of the episodes, and most of the chapters could have been published in any order without harm to the book's effect. Not so with *The Eyes of the Overworld*. Here all is told from the point of view of a single protagonist, a typically Vancian scamp named Cugel the Clever, and indeed *Cugel the Clever* appears to have been the author's original title for the book. The structure is that of the picaresque novel—the cunning rascal Cugel moves across a vast reach of the dying Earth, getting in and out of trouble as he goes—but the individual episodes are bound together by a theme as old as Homer (for Cugel is trying to get home). His task is defined, and the entire pattern of the novel made plain, in the opening sequence: Cugel overreaches himself by attempting a burglary at the manse of the magician Iucounu, is apprehended, and is sent by way of penance under compulsion on a difficult quest in a remote land. We know at once that Cugel will find that which Iucounu has ordered him to obtain, will undergo great hardship and tests of cleverness as he struggles to return to his homeland with it, and in the end will try to outsmart the magician and exact a vengeance for all he has suffered. Whereas *The Dying Earth* as a whole is plotless and subtle in form, *The Eyes of the Overworld* carries a rigid skeleton beneath its picaresque surface.

Where the books are one is in the texture of the world that

encloses them. *The Eyes of the Overworld*, like *The Dying Earth*, is a covert fantasy of the medieval. The first few pages bristle with artifacts of the fourteenth century A.D. — a public fair with timbered booths, amulets and talismans, elixirs and charms, gargoyles, a gibbet, a pickled homunculus. Cugel, in his wanderings, eludes archers and swordsmen, halts at an inn where wine-drinking travelers gather to trade gossip by the fire, joins a band of pilgrims bound toward a holy shrine. This is not the glittering clickety-clack world of science-fiction gadgetry. We might expect to meet Robin Hood in it, or Merlin, or Godfrey and Saladin, Tancred and Clorinda, but never Buck Rogers or Captain Kirk. Mysterious monsters prowl the planet, yes, flesh-gobbling deodands and dread ghouls, but they are only the analogues of gryphons and basilisks; they are aspects of the past, not the future. Everything in the world of these two novels of the remote future is old and mellowed, as, indeed, would medieval Europe be if it had survived intact into our own time, which is essentially the fantasy that drives Vance's imagination in these books. A sickly red sun dangles in the sky, said to be soon to go out, but the author is only pretending to be writing about the end of time. His dying Earth is moribund because *from his viewpoint* it is ancient, buried in the past, although he would have us believe he writes of a time yet unborn.

It is a perilous world, where enemies lurk everywhere and strike almost at random, and the chief activities of its denizens are theft, incantation, and chicanery. Power is all. No one lives at peace here, for danger is constantly at hand. The stories, ingenious and seductive, are built almost entirely out of conflicts; the war of wits, the contests of sorcerers, the ferocious struggles of rival rogues; and while conflict has been a wellspring of fiction since at least *The Iliad* and *The Odyssey*, it also in this case reveals a singularly bleak world-view made more palatable only by the elegance of the prose in which it is set forth and the unfailing courtliness with which the murderous beings of the dying Earth address one another.

That courtliness is an essential part of Vance's style. Cugel, having battered a sinister cannibal into serving as his guide, urges the creature to hurry, saying, "Why do you delay? I hope to find a mountain hospice before the coming of dark. Your lagging and limping discommode me." And the deodand replies, "You should have considered this before you maimed me with a rock. After all, I do not accompany you of my own choice." It is not the traditional language of magazine science fiction. And in another scene, wherein Cugel cruelly destroys a sentient crustacean that had annoyed him, the courtly manner is even more pronounced. "Why did you treat me so?" the dying shell-man asks faintly. "For a prank you have taken my life, and I have no other." To which Cugel replies, "And thereby you will be prevented from further pranks. Notice, you have drenched me to the skin." A curse is pronounced upon him by his victim, and Cugel responds in a manner that any experienced reader would instantly identify as that of Jack Vance: "Malice is a quality to be deplored. I doubt the efficacy of your curse; nevertheless, you would be well-advised to clear the air of its odium and so regain my good opinion."

If the tone of such exchanges owes nothing to the pulp magazines in which Vance first found publication, the prose technique is equally alien to that of Messrs. Asimov, Heinlein, or Clarke. A privately published pamphlet of 1965, Richard Tiedman's *Jack Vance: Science Fiction Stylist**, the most perceptive essay yet written on this author, suggests John Ruskin, Clark Ashton Smith, and Lord Dunsany as the chief influences on Vance's prose style. Certainly there is much of the ornate, congested approach of Smith in the early Vance, and the deftness of Dunsany, and the passionate pre-Raphaelite purpleness of Ruskin, though Vance's characteristic restraint and coolness temper excess. The two Dying Earth novels provide an instructive lesson in the evolution of style, for the first is

---

*See Chapter 8 of this book.

unabashedly romantic in a way that the second, written by a far more experienced and time-sombered man, is not. Consider this passage from *The Dying Earth*:

> The light came from an unknown source, from the air itself, as if leaking from the discrete atoms; every breath was luminous, the room floated full of invigorating glow. A great rug pelted the floor, a monster tabard woven of gold, brown, bronze, two tones of green, fuscous red and smalt blue. Beautiful works of human fashioning ranked the walls. In glorious array hung panels of rich woods, carved, chased, enameled; scenes of olden times painted on woven fiber; formulas of color, designed to convey emotion rather than reality. To one side hung plants of wood laid on with slabs of soapstone, malachite and jade in rectangular patterns, richly varied and subtle, with miniature flecks of cinnabar, rhodochrosite and coral for warmth. Beside was a section given to disks of luminous green, flickering and fluorescent with varying blue films and moving dots of scarlet and black. Here were representations of three hundred marvelous flowers, blooms of a forgotten age, no longer extant on waning Earth; there were as many star-burst patterns, rigidly conventionalized in form, but each of subtle distinction. All these are a multitude of other creations, selected from the best human fervor.

Vance has never lost his love of the feel and taste of colors, of the color of textures, and no book of his is without such passages of sensuous excess; but they have become more widely spaced in the narrative flow, and his raptures more qualified, as in this comparable passage from *The Eyes of the Overworld*:

> Cugel approached warily, but was encouraged by the signs of tidiness and good husbandry. In a park beside the pond stood a pavilion possibly intended for music, miming or declamation; surrounding the park were small narrow houses with high gables, the ridges of which were raised in decorative scallops. Opposite the pond was a larger building, with an ornate front of woven wood and enameled plaques of red, blue and yellow. Three tall gables served as its roof, the central ridge supporting an intricate carved panel, while those to either side bore a series of small spherical blue lamps. At the front was a wide pergola sheltering benches, tables and an open space, all illuminated by red and green fire-fans. Here townsfolk took their ease, inhaling incense and drinking wine, while youths and maidens cavorted in an eccentric high-kicking dance, to the music of pipes and a concertina.

The Dying Earth is, possibly, the more sophisticated work technically; its rolling structure seems a more delicate mechanism than *The Eyes of the Overworld*'s neatly calculated symmetries. *Eyes* is a single unified construct, heading forward from its earliest pages toward an inevitable end and the inevitable final ironic twist; one admires the perfection of Vance's carpentry, but it seems a lesser achievement than the relaxed and flowing pattern of *The Dying Earth*, which more fully portrays and entire culture from a variety of points of view. Cugel the Clever is an appealing rogue, but one misses the innocence of some of *The Dying Earth's* characters and the sublime skills of others.

Nevertheless the book is a worthy companion for the classic earlier novel: enormously entertaining, unfailingly ingenious, richly comic, a delightful fantasy now published in durable form for the first time. *The Dying Earth* has only recently attained hardcover publication for the first time too, albeit in a limited edition that may already be unobtainable. Taken together, they are two key works in the career of this extraordinary fantasist. Nor are they necessarily their author's last visits to the mysterious world of the reddened sun. Vance, now in his late fifties, is still an active writer and a sly one, much given to surprise. In the October 1974 issue of *The Magazine of Fantasy and Science Fiction* he offered without preamble a new exploit of Cugel the Clever, "The Seventeen Virgins," unconnected in content with *The Eyes of the Overworld*. Since then, no more in that vein; but a new Dying Earth book may at this moment be in gestation. I suppose I could telephone Jack Vance, who is my neighbor here in California, and ask him of his plans for Cugel, but that would spoil the surprise, and, in any case, he would probably offer me only some cunning evasion. Like the sorcerers who inhabit the dying Earth, Vance is not one to tip his hand without good reason.

7. Jack Vance's "General Culture" Novels: A Synoptic Survey

TERRY DOWLING

IN THE EARLY part of the novel *Emphyrio* (1969), Jack Vance's young hero Ghyl Tarvoke responds to a query:

"As I see it, the cosmos is probably infinite, which means—well, infinite. So there are local situations—a tremendous number of them. Indeed, in a situation of infinity, there are an infinite set of local conditions...." (VII)*

Vance's abiding concern is with such local situations. His is the art of xenography—the art of devising and exploring exotic and alien societies in a very distant future period when humankind has spread far from our own planetary system.

Vance is not alone in this sort of xenological enterprise. The art of the worldsmith—of the xenographical travelog—is firmly established. Larry Niven has contrived a most wonderful universe in his "Known Space" stories; Frank Herbert has put together his ConSentiency; and Poul Anderson has his own "future history," incorporating countless xenographical adven-

---

*Roman numerals in parentheses indicate the chapter of the work immediately being discussed or of the specific work cited in the following sections.

tures and xenological mysteries set in the years of the Poleso-technic League and the Terran Empire. Others like Hal Clement, Isaac Asimov, Keith Laumer, Cordwainer Smither, Ursula Le Guin, James Schmitz, and Lloyd Biggle, Jr., to name a few, have all turned their hand to it.

But in spite of an impressive checklist of authors and works, there still exists for many a very real difficulty in accepting and assessing science fiction works concerned with the "soft" sciences and the humanities, perhaps because the creation and exploitation of alien cultures and technologies was one of the main areas of abuse in the formative days of the genre. The Barsooms, Pellucidars, and Mongos were needed as contexts for the scientific adventure-romances, but the more "hard science" and technology-oriented readers were finally disenchanted with those writers who raged pell-mell along the road pioneered by Wells and who neglected the more sober approach of Verne and his successors. These same writers seemed to overlook the fact that Wells—himself the recipient of a scientific education from T. H. Huxley that was in some ways superior to that possessed by Verne—chose to be primarily concerned with sociological and ideological matters.

When Vance writes, in *Trullion: Alastor 2262*, of how the space-pirates fleeing Welgen failed to "go into whisk" or stardrive, this hyperdrive is merely hardware. In *Dune*, Frank Herbert does not bother to explain how his Heighliners or ornithopters function. They are furniture for the complex sociological-ecological stage he has set. Likewise with much of the technology displayed in Vance's writing.

For the purposes of this chapter I shall make one important distinction: *xenology* (also called exobiology) is alien "anthropology"—the study of the stranger. *Xenography* is the portrayal of that life-form within the physical and demographical environment that is its natural and/or chosen habitat. *Xenological* stories are those dealing with "First Contacts," initial pioneering confrontations, extraterrestrial visitations, and so on, and are most frequently puzzle stories relying on some sort of cultural analysis. Stanley Weinbaum's classic "A Martian Odyssey" (1934), Stanislaw Lem's *Solaris* (1961) and Arthur C. Clarke's *Rendezvous with Rama* (1973) are good examples.

The *xenographical* story, on the other hand, attempts to put together the alien world and lifestyle in all its "mundane" detail, to create the alien and exotic as commonplace. It could be described as conceptual, extrapolative, or speculative ethnography, but whatever term is used, it is the portrayal of alien worlds in sufficient detail for that portrayal to have been a major reason for the story or novel.

If we could speak of such a thing as a typical xenographical novel, we would probably say this: it is set in the reasonably distant future of the human race, when humankind has spread beyond the Solar System to other star systems. The continued homogeneity of this human stock would depend entirely upon the sophistication of communication and transportation links, and on whether or not there exist extraterrestrial cultures to encourage racial cohesion (or contribute to its breakdown due to cultural exchange and/or exploitation). Either way, local loyalties prevail, though there is invariably some sort of "federation" of these allied worlds, often coordinated from Earth.

Central to every xenographical novel is the local culture and the inevitable parochialism (and hence crisis-potential) that goes with it. Vance defines the problem:

> Should Alastor Cluster be considered a segment of the Gaean Reach? The folk of the Cluster, some four or five trillion of them on more than three thousand worlds, seldom reflected upon the matter, and indeed considered themselves neither Gaean nor Alastrid. The typical inhabitant, when asked as to his origin, might perhaps cite his native world or, more usually, his local district, as if this place were so extraordinary, so special and widely famed that its reputation hung on every tongue of the galaxy. (*Marune: Alastor 993*, I)

In each "general culture" novel, we are given such a local cultural "entry-point." On Maske, it is Wysrod on Duskerl Bay: "A small town in the center of the Great Hole — but for Thariots the focus of sentient life" (*Maske: Thaery*, IV), with its eccentric hacks, the Marine Parade and the Cham. On Trullion it is Welgen and the surrounding fens; on Big Planet the port of Coble on Surmise Bay, and so the pattern goes—whether it be Olanje, Garwy, or Ambroy. Even if we approach these foci from without, entering from the "general" (to some extent *shared*) culture first—as is the case with Axistil on Maz, and Port Mar on Marune—these centers remain the nodes whose distinctive cultural flavors permeate the works in which they are set.

Having established these astonishingly divergent nodes, Vance then engineers the confrontation that is the basis of most of his xenographical adventures. To borrow from the Glossary to *Maske: Thaery*: "When a general culture such as that of the Gaean Reach suffuses a local culture, there will be a mingling...." Vance's fundamental technique is to stage an enactment of this mingling—to have a member of either the local culture or the general culture brought into collision with the other. Rarely are we shown urban commercial districts anything like those to be found in contemporary Western cities. When we are given an industrial area, it invariably has that quaint old-world charm about it, and the distinctive modern elements are somehow distanced. In almost all of the "general culture" novels, we are dealing with frontier situations—the colonies, fringes, and outposts of human empire. Nevertheless, these locals and cosmopolitans alike live very much in a selectively delineated cosmos. The Outkers of Koryphon attend all manner of parties, fetes, discussion groups; they sit in inns and attend morphote-viewings. They do not sit at home and watch television.

Now it should be mentioned right away that Vance's novels are first and foremost exotic adventures. They are not meant to be ethnographical treatises (though in the course of presenting the adventure this becomes one of Vance's richest gifts to the reader), but rather they belong to the tradition of the peripatetic novel—tales of journeys and quests (and hence travelogs) with touches of the satirical and the picturesque.

Before turning to the novels of the "general culture" series themselves, we might first consider an earlier story, "The Moon Moth" (1961), for it is the definitive xenographical work and contains all the elements of the longer novels. First, there is the local focus—the town of Fan on the Titanic littoral on Sirene, a world of the star Mireille, itself located in the vicinity of Cluster SI 1-715. Sirene is a world occupied by an amazingly intricate terrestrial-derived human culture concentrated around Fan and by what are apparently autochthones or severely regressed human stock—the Night-men.

Sirenese society is highly individualistic, based entirely on the idea of *strakh*, or personal prestige (face, reputation, etc.). Because of a most benign environment and an abundance of natural resources, what would normally be regarded as "economic" affairs— the procurement and transferral of goods between individuals—is solely determined by the augmentation or diminution of *strakh* involved in a transaction. No one would dream of exceeding the entitlements of his particular level of "prestige."

But the culture of the Titanic littoral is far more complex. The cult of individualism has led to an equally strong desire for anonymity, and hence the citizens wear masks that totally conceal their faces. To go abroad in public unmasked is an act of unspeakable shame for which the penalty is immediate execution. Even slaves are masked. Inevitably, the style and quality of the mask worn must accurately portray the degree of *strakh* possessed by an individual.

An additional complication is the elaborate system of musical instruments that are an essential adjunct to civilized social communication on Sirene. Conversations are sung to the strict accompaniment of whatever instrument exactly suits that conversation. Only slaves sing unaccompanied. A visitor to Fan must therefore master at least six basic instruments before he can escape the contempt and derision of the locals, and one must constantly wear a mask that is strictly proportional to his minimal claims for *strakh*.

Having established his local situation, Vance then engineers the "collision" between local and cosmopolitan/off-world values and thus initiates the basis for his xenological mystery. Edwer Thissell has come to Sirene as Consular Representative for the Earth-worlds. He is one of four off-worlders on Sirene—a recent graduate from the Institute (presumably the Historical Institute)—and is hopelessly ignorant of Sirenese customs. After being set up with a houseboat, slaves, musical instruments, and an unpresumptuous Moon Moth mask by one of his fellow expatriates, Thissell withdraws eight miles to the south to practice his instruments, making only weekly visits to Fan.

It is on one such visit that he is notified of the pending arrival of a notorious criminal, Haxo Angmark, who must be apprehended and restrained at all costs. Because of his amazing gaucheries, Thissell fails to intercept Angmark on the latter's arrival at the Fan spaceport and soon loses his trail. Angmark has spent five years on Sirene previously and so has no trouble eluding the inexperienced Consular Representative.

In spite of further quite spectacular *faux pas* made in the course of pursuing his quarry, Thissell is correct in suspecting that the Sirenese themselves must eventually detect the presence of yet another off-worlder in their midst. Angmark, however, anticipates such an eventuality and simply murders one of the other three "cosmopolitans" and takes his place. Masked, protected by his already considerable expertise in the ways of the Sirenese, Angmark appears to have permanently eluded capture, until Thissel questions slaves from each of the other three cosmopolitan households as to the various masks most often worn by their masters. Working on the assumption that, as an impostor, Angmark would choose from among his predecessor's masks according to his own taste, Thissell is able to determine which of the three is Angmark, only to be captured himself by the exposed assassin, who then dons Thissell's Moon Moth and parades the unmasked Consular Representative in public, claiming that he is Angmark.

In a most ironical inversion of events, a classic case of poetic justice, the Moon Moth's earlier social indiscretions finally catch up with him, and Angmark is summarily executed by members of the very crowd he meant to deceive. Thissell, on the other hand, is acclaimed for his unprecedented bravery in going forth in public unmasked. As this is a feat no Sirenese would dare attempt, Thissell's *strakh* is immense.

In "The Moon Moth," we encounter that blend of the arcane and the commonplace, that balance of the alien and the exotic with the familiar and the mundane, that is so vital a part of Vance's writing. There are discursive passages carefully defining particular loci, peripheral footnotes, and placement of "Home Planet" names like Edwer Thissell and Cornely Welibus alongside the more homely names for slaves like Rex and Toby. Even the classification of the various masks (e.g., Forest Goblin, Cave Owl, Sea-Dragon Conquerer, etc.) releases their more traditional associations.

Emphyrio

According to Joanna Russ, *Emphyrio* is "not an adventure story but a *Bildungsroman* (a novel of the formation of a character, or the process of passing from childhood to adulthood, making oneself into a person) that describes a perfect curve from beginning to end."[1] It takes as its focus the ancient, half-ruined city of Ambroy, located on the Insse estuary in old Fortinone on the planet Halma, a world beyond the Mirabilis cluster — "a far planet, in the ditch at the edge of the universe," hanging below its "green moon Damar" (XX).

Halma is a world inhabited by men and the apparently indigenous Wirwans, "a race of semi-intelligent beings" who "existed in the Meagher Mountains at the time of the human advent." The moon, Damar, is the home of a race of small black subterranean sentients who are famous for exporting "live" puppets — creatures generated in the Damarans' artificial glands.

The city of Ambroy is now part of an impoverished welfare state, with an economy based on artisans and guild industries.

In this area, mechanization and mass production of any kind are strictly forbidden. It is a system of welfare rolls and guild regulations designed to maintain a status quo of "regulationary" behavior that benefits the elite minority of Lords responsible for controlling the basic public utilities restored to the city after a devastating war two thousand years before.

Born into this society is Ghyl Tarvoke, the son of a master woodcarver, Amiante Tarvoke. In Ghyl's growth to manhood, he becomes disenchanted with the harshness and futility of life under the Welfare system and is convinced that "there's something terribly wrong... in Ambroy" (X). He is sure that the key to this mystery is the legend of Emphyrio, an ancient hero who defeated the monsters sent down to his world, Aume, from the neighboring world, Sigil. Ghyl has partly managed to piece this legend together from the theme of a puppet show performance seen when he was seven years old, and from a fragment of ancient writing shown to him by his "irregulationary" father, Amiante.

After standing as candidate for the mayoral elections of Ambroy using the name Emphyrio — an abortive imposture meant to provoke the complacent citizens of the city, but which the Welfare agents interpret as a "malicious prank" (IX) and which leads to Amiante's "rehabilitation" and eventual death for having illicitly mass-produced election posters — Ghyl actively rejects the life of a "recipient" and, with a group of questionable companions, steals a spaceship. He intends to locate the Historian, "who knows the entire history of the human race" (XIII), so he can establish the true significance of the Emphyrio legend once and for all. Ghyl's companions, however, wish to "fly off in search of wealth and adventure," and this separation of interests leaves Ghyl marooned with a group of kidnapped Lords and Ladies on Maastricht, a world of Capella.

There follows the exacting cross-country trek to Daillie, where, true to the novel's ever-expanding focus, Ghyl learns from a local mercantilist that all trade dealings for Ambroy goods are handled by the Thurible Trading Cooperative, an organization dealing directly with the Lords responsible for controlling trade. He learns, too, that someone other than the "recipients" or the Lords is enjoying enormous profits. Working with the Maastricht mercantilist, Ghyl returns to Halma and attempts to break the Thurible monopoly, only to encounter suspicion and a most unnatural resistance to his proposals.

When he is apprehended and condemned to death for his part in the theft of the spaceship and the alleged murder of one of the elite, Ghyl manages to elude his fate and becomes the complete man of action. He ingeniously embezzles a vast fortune in handmade Ambroy goods which he carries to the markets of old Earth itself.

On Earth, Ghyl visits the Historical Institute and learns the true story of Emphyrio, of how long ago the Damarans were engaged in war with a race of star-wanderers and contrived synthetic warriors — the Wirwans — to drive these itinerant starfolk from Halma, only to discover that their mysterious enemy had already departed and that mankind had arrived during the lull in hostilities. The Wirwans thus began aggressions against the wrong adversaries, and it was Emphyrio who discovered the means of communicating with these Damaran invaders, telling them of their true origins and their great error, thus inducing them to cease hostilities.

With this knowledge, Ghyl returns to Halma and uncovers a further grim truth: that Emphyrio was ultimately unsuccessful in stopping the Damaran threat to his homeworld, and that it is the sybaritic Damarans who have in fact manufactured and instituted the Lords for the sole purpose of enforcing a state of "enslavement" on the people of Ambroy so that they might channel off the trade profits for their own use. The plot exposed, the Lords are overthrown, the Damarans proscribed, and Ghyl brings about a complete social revolution in Ambroy, thus fulfilling the Emphyrio legend himself.

Emphyrio conforms perfectly to the selective-and-expanding focus–exotic travelog–mystery format Vance has devised. Amiante, himself a clandestine observer for the Historical Institute, is there from the beginning to "complicate" Ghyl's parochial outlook. He subtly guides his son into acquiring the overview that leads him to question the Welfare system, the religion of Finuka, and the sovereignty of the Lords. By exposing Ghyl to Holkerwoyd's puppet show, the Emphyrio fragment, and the Great Charter of Ambroy, he accelerates the "collision" that makes his son perhaps the greatest "Chaoticist" of them all, implementing the crucial revolution in social forms and attitudes basic to all of the "general culture" novels.

By taking his protagonist to Maastricht, Vance is able to incorporate his planetary trek without compromising the sad beauty of ancient Ambroy, without damaging the "fragile" setting and its elusive backwater-planet charm — focused as it is on a young boy's reflections across estuarine mudflats, his journeyings through ruined precincts, his melancholy at the fading light in Undle Square (when thinking of Ambroy, I am always reminded of Birmingham's cover-painting "Spaceport: Backwater Planet" for the February 1962 number of *Analog*).

In direct contrast to these "intangibles," we are given the city of Daillie on the world of Maastricht, a chosen antithesis to all of Vance's preferred planetary foci:

> Daillie was a city vast in area and population, with a character peculiarly its own yet peculiarly fugitive and hard to put a name to. The components were readily identifiable: the great expanses of sun-dazzled streets constantly swept by wind; the clean buildings essentially homogeneous in architecture, cleverly built of synthetic substances; a population of mercurial folk who nevertheless gave the impression of self-restraint, conventionality, absorption in their own affairs. The spaceport was close to the center of the city; ships from across the human universe came to Daillie but seemed to arouse little interest. There were no enclaves of off-world folk, few restaurants devoted to off-world cuisines; the newspapers and journals concerned themselves largely with local affairs: sports, business events and transactions. Crime either was non-existent or purposely ignored. (XVII)

In other words, Daillie is a "neutral," modern, unimaginative city whose people have almost deliberately concealed their own unique and idiosyncratic character (though it is hinted at as being there all the same). It is the exception to Vance's rule, and intentionally so.

The Durdane Trilogy

This closed series primarily concerns the land of Shant on Durdane, a world "far to the back of the Schiafarilla Cluster" (according to the prologue to "The Brave Free Men" in the July 1972 issue of *The Magazine of Fantasy & Science Fiction*) and settled nine thousand years before by a group of Earth exiles who sank their ships in the Purple Ocean to ensure their isolation from the other Earth-worlds. In spite of these precautions, and like Halma in *Emphyrio*, this planet is also under the surveillance of the Historical Institute of Earth, but for reasons of far greater import than casual observation of the affairs of divergent offspring cultures. For now, a threat to the entire human universe is involved.

True to the widening focus, the three novels deal respectively with the metal-poor land of Shant, sixty-two cantons "each jealous of its unique identity" (*The Anome*, IX) and held together under the authority of the Anome or Faceless Man; the international crisis between Shant and Palasedra over the ownership of the rapacious Rogushkoi; and the resolution in far Caraz of an ancient off-planet conflict between two alien races, in which the Rogushkoi and Durdane humanity are merely pawns — a conflict which subsequently involves intervention by the other Earth-worlds.

In the first novel, *The Anome* (1971), the action centers on a small corner of Shant, Bashon in Canton Bastern, with the hero, Gastel Etzwane, endeavoring to locate the Faceless Man, first to appeal against the purely domestic matter of his mother's unlawful indenture to the cantonal religious institution of the Chilites, and then, after the marauding red savages known as the Rogushkoi are clearly seen as a national threat, to discover why the Anome has not acted against them. It is a quest whose outcome forever changes the face of Shant, for unlike that other anonymous ruler — the Connatic of Alastor Cluster, who enforces his will with the external agency of the Whelm — the Anome has no such provision to deal with threats from without. His authority rests entirely on his power to detonate the explosive torcs worn by every adult citizen of Shant; otherwise, he functions simply by enforcing cantonal law.

Although *The Anome* concludes with the solving of the mystery of the Faceless Man's identity by Etzwane and Earthman-observer Ifness and Etzwane's consequent acceptance of this ruler's duties, the novel ends with an even greater mystery left unresolved: why did the Anome not act in what is clearly a national emergency? The solution to this mystery is provided in the second Durdane novel.

In *The Brave Free Men* (1972), we see the reorganization of Shant into a political military force capable of meeting the Rogushkoi threat. After a series of intrigues and crises culminating in what nearly becomes full-scale war with Shant's neighbor, Palasedra, the remaining Rogushkoi are either exterminated or forced to flee off-planet in a saucer-shaped spacecraft. In this expulsion, both the fact of their off-world origin and the reason for the previous Anome's "artificial passivity" (XVI) is revealed: a nonhuman symbiotic race known as the Asutra has been manipulating various Shant officials, though to what end is not yet made fully clear. Etzwane, Ifness, and the Palasedran scientists who help to reveal the sinister presence of the Asutra wrongly assume that it is they who are responsible for the Rogushkoi coming to Durdane (the Asutras' presence in key human hosts being to hinder military retaliation). The novel ends with the threat to Shant ended for good and with a completely new period in Shant's history just beginning.

In the final novel, *The Asutra* (1973), the planetary focus spirals out to include first the continent Caraz, and then the world Kahei, far beyond Durdane, and finally the whole universe known to the Historical Institute. Acting on rumors that there has been Rogushkoi activity in the wilds of Caraz, Etz-wane and Ifness journey there to discover the remains of a battle between two different kinds of spaceships—bronze disks and black globes. They learn, too, that local slavers are sending humans off-planet for some unknown purpose.

In an unsuccessful attempt to secure an alien depot ship orbiting Durdane, Etzwane finds himself taken into space, to the world Kahei, where he is forced to serve a race known as the Ka in their war against the Asutra. Only when Etzwane manages to stage a "coup" and obtain passage back to Durdane for himself and his companions does he finally learn the real story. Back in Garwiy in Shant, Ifness tells him of how the Asutra, seeking to make the Ka their hosts in that form of symbiosis basic to "the Asutra dynamic" (XI), actually found the situation reversed and their kind on Kahei dominated and enslaved by the Ka and forced to perform menial tasks.

Because the Asutra were employing humans from Durdane as hosts in their efforts to liberate their captive brethren on Kahei, the Ka created the Rogushkoi and sent them to Durdane to exterminate the human communities from which the Asutra drew their hosts. With the Rogushkoi defeated, the Ka's final solution was to draw on these communities themselves to provide warriors in this conflict. Inevitably, having learned of the enslavement of humans by alien races, Earth has finally intervened, forcing both parties to return their human allies to Durdane, the Ka to surrender their Asutra, and the Asutra to abandon their attempts to take over Kahei.

Trullion: Alastor 2262

This novel (1973), the first work in a "new series," launches the "general culture" stories proper. It concerns the world of Trullion, one of three thousand inhabited planets in a volume of stars near the rim of the galaxy, nearly thirty thousand light-years across, known as Alastor Cluster.

The inhabited Alastrid worlds are controlled from the planet Numenes by a figure known as the Connatic who, as a rule, grants each planet a good deal of autonomous self-government, intervening only when the general peace stands to be threatened. In such instances, he brings in his space navy, the Whelm.

In spite of this general policy of noninterference with local customs, and despite such extreme and reclusive human societies and racial types as the Rhunes of the world Marune in a later book, we have that curious cultural paradox of "cosmopolitan provincialism" or, as we have already termed it, enlightened medievalism. Despite communication links which allow the dissemination of ideas, fashions, and tastes in that "cultural imperialism" that is "the only practicable form" (*Son of the Tree*, XII), there remains a distinct awareness of planetary isolation. A comment made by Lord Gensifer — "We are all citizens of Alastor. We are local folk, all five trillion of us" (XIV) — is valid indeed. Alastrid civilization, like that of its neighboring stellargraphical phenomenon — the Gaean Reach — is very much a "general" culture.

On the Connatic's planetary registers, Trullion is charted as planet number 2262. True to Vance's keynote of isolation, it is "the lone planet of a small white star, one spark in a spray curling out towards the cluster's edge" (I). It is a small water world, with a single narrow equatorial continent known as Merlank, a generous and fertile land hosting an easy and good-natured human population, themselves derived from a more zealous body of original settlers. (Another recurring factor in Vance's universe, seen later on a world like Maske, is the gradual softening of the tenets of a founding ideological group who sought out their new home as a place wherein to establish their own sympathetic community.) Such a bucolic existence has bred a relaxed planetary government centering on twenty prefectures and an Order of Lords. There is an aloof aristocracy at one end of the social scale, tribes of wandering nomads called Trevanyi at the other.

Only two hazards disturb the placid Trill lifestyle. The first of these are the merlings, indigenous aquatic inhabitants of Merlank's many waterways, who constantly strive to capture humans for their dinner tables. Any merlings caught on land are promptly killed; humans venturing into the water automatically qualify as merling-food. The second affliction to the idyllic Trill existence is the starmenters, notorious space pirates who take refuge among the so-called "starments" — the countless asteroids and fragments of space detritus scattered throughout the Cluster. These cold-blooded rogues have become figures of romance and legend, acquiring a certain wild glamor in spite of their depredations against the various Alastrid societies.

The story opens with Glinnes Hulden returning to his home in the Welgen Fens after ten years in the Whelm. He has resigned his commission after receiving the news of his father's death at the hands of the merlings. Upon reaching Welgen, the market town serving the Fens district, Glinnes learns that his elder brother, Shira, has been missing for two months as well, although the circumstances surrounding his disappearance are far from clear. Have the merlings gotten him, too, or has he gone off on one of the drug-crazed rambles that are a normal part of the Trill way of life?

This question becomes important for Glinnes, for on reaching his old ramshackle family home on Rabendary Island, he learns that his younger brother, Glay, and his mother, Marucha, have sold the adjacent Ambal Isle with its ancient ancestral manor house. It is a dilemma, for in the unresolved fate of Shira — the rightful master of the Hulden property — Glinnes is unable to invalidate the contract by asserting that he is the new Squire of Rabendary. Nor is he able to void the transaction by reimbursing the new owner, an austere man named Lute Casagave, who has taken for himself the name Lord Ambal, the cost of purchase, for Glay has given these funds to a certain Junius Farfan, leading figure in a new and growing ideological movement known as Fanscherade that is intent on altering forever the direction of the relaxed Trill way of life to one that is more disciplined and purposeful.

Adding insult to injury, Glinnes also learns that Glay has permitted a family of Trevanyi nomads — the Drossets, reckless itinerant folk who have little respect for a Trill's sensitivity to his cherished landscape — to camp on Rabendary Island. Glinnes evicts these unwelcome guests and is almost fed to the merlings when he runs afoul of their vengeance. It then remains for him to somehow earn sufficient money to pay off Casagave and regain Ambal Isle.

It is here that the xenographical mystery becomes a sports story, for Glinnes' only recourse is to take up hussade — the contact sport that is so popular throughout the entire "general culture" of the Alastor Cluster and the Gaean Reach. For Glinnes, this means an arduous formative period in the Gorgons, where he is subject to training under Lord Gensifer, the team's stubborn and unimaginative sponsor and leader. The few competent players, such as Glinnes, are severely handicapped by the rest. After a succession of crushing defeats, Glinnes and some key companions abandon the Gorgons to overhaul a new team, the Saurkash Tachinaros, and with this promising lineup they are able to score many rewarding victories, much to Lord Gensifer's dismay. In retaliation, the infuriated Gensifer, to teach the Tachinaros a lesson, goes so far as to substitute a visiting exhibition team for his own, but again his Gorgons are soundly trounced.

Apparently unstoppable, the Tachinaros decide to try for big money by taking on the Vertrice Karpouns at the famous Welgen Stadium, an event to which a great number of the aristocracy from the local prefectures are invited. During the game, three ships belonging to the notorious starmenter Sagmondo Bandolio drop down upon the field and take three hundred of the region's wealthiest aristocrats for ransom.

Such a daring raid could only have worked with careful inside planning through a local agent, but authorities are baffled as to who this could be. When the notification comes that the ransom monies—over thirty million ozols—are to be paid to Akadie, a local celebrity and family friend of the Huldens, suspicion naturally falls on him. Desperately anxious lest he be robbed of the amassed fortune either by the Trevanyi, the fanatical Fanschers who are in need of funds to pursue their great dream, or by the victimized nobles themselves before the starmenter's courier can come for it, Akadie initiates a set of deceptions which successfully foil the efforts of the Drossets to obtain the wealth.

But misfortune still occurs. On the very day that Akadie has turned the money over to Bandolio's messenger, news arrives that the Whelm has raided Bandolio's base, captured the pirates, and recovered the hostages. What is more, under scientific questioning, Bandolio reveals that he has not received the ransom money. Akadie is beset by demands from the various noble families that their ransom payments be returned, the general consensus being that Akadie has secreted the money for his own use. Fearing reprisals, Akadie flees to the Vale of Green Ghosts and joins the Fanscher community there, just prior to that movement's demise at the hands of enraged Trevanyi.

Two mysteries remain—the whereabouts of the thirty million ozols and the identity of the local contact who helped coordinate the starmenter raid. On his mother's behalf, Glinnes persuades Akadie to return to Welgen and there is eventually able to clear him from suspicion. The starmenter Bandolio explains that the anonymous contact who met him at night, disguised by a Gorgon hussade mask, was taller than Akadie. Pursuing his various leads, Glinnes is not only able to discover the missing money—information which he keeps to himself— but he instigates an amazing final confrontation in which Lord Gensifer is revealed to be the local agent and is taken by the merlings while trying to escape, Lute Casagave is exposed by his erstwhile colleague Bandolio as a notorious "retired" starmenter himself, and likable rogue Bandolio effects his own escape. With these revelations made, authorities are satisfied that the money is lost for good, while Glinnes has recovered Ambal Isle and a secret fortune, the morality of such an act being very much in accord with the Trill lifestyle.

The above synopsis has, of course, only made mention of the novel's main plot structure. The Glinnes–Duissane Drosset relationship and the added mystery of the itinerant journalist who turns out to be a Chief Inspector of the Whelm (and is almost certainly the Connatic himself: "I was in the neighborhood and was kept apprised of events" — XIX) add depth and color to this intricate world-picture.

As the first installment in a newly planned xenographical series, this novel is a rich offering indeed. It introduces the Alastrid cultural context itself, the sport hussade as a central cultural motif, and a host of planetary exotica unique to the Trullion setting: avness, "that melancholy dying-time of day" (IX) which makes the Welgen Fens possibly Vance's most haunting and memorable locus apart from ancient Ambroy in *Emphyrio*; the distinctive Trill customs of star-watching or taking cauch; and various concepts and institutions — whether we consider the Trevanyi idea of *Forlostwenna* or the terrible expedient of the prutanshyr as a means of punishing criminals. (The suggestion of what prutanshyr entails is given by the typical evocative implication. Vance has always been fascinated by the grimmer side of human nature and the ingenuity man has shown in fabricating instruments of torture and death. The prutanshyr and something like the Exhibitory in *The Dogtown Tourist Agency* merely serve to highlight the local equivalents of gas chambers, guillotines, and garroting posts. As such an institution, the prutanshyr is possibly rivalled as a means of execution only by the ingenious "expulsion" into Bauredel featured in *Emphyrio*.)

A less dramatically emphasized feature of the Trullion novel is the permissive nature of Trill society, sketched in by references to love-drugs like cauch, by allusions to the liberal social attitudes behind star-watching, by the jocular reference to a nine-year-old's loss of virginity, and so on. This *is* an alien world — (in spite of such haunting familiarities as mention of Welshmen, Zeus, Dido, and Gorgons (X) — and, while we can look for earthly parallels in European and Oceanic societies (just as we cannot condemn the prutanshyr without reappraising such local institutions as the guillotine and the garrote), we are to remember this essential alienness.

The Gray Prince

The Gray Prince (1974) could well be the classic xenographical novel. It has an ingenious twofold xenological mystery as its center — two planetary treks that are integral both in revealing the "local" and physical realities of Koryphon and in advancing the plot — and it blends together into a cohesive whole two human-derived alien cultures (the Uldras and the Wind-runners), two nonhuman races (the erjins and the morphotes), plus an assortment of paranormal skills and a viable "enlightened medievalism" (in all planetary societies save that of the cosmopolitan Outkers of Szintarre). The cultural "collisions" that occur are numerous indeed, and at every conceivable level of interest.

Orbiting its sun Methuen, Koryphon is a world in an entirely different section of the human-settled galaxy from the location of the previous novel — at such a remove that we hear of Alastor Cluster appearing as a "blazing miracle" (VIII) in the eastern sky. A planet of some antiquity in terms of settlement, Koryphon boasts two human-derived races — the Uldras of southern Uaia, inhabiting an area known as the Alouan, and the Wind-runners to the north, a people whose lifestyle centers on sailing their wind-wagons across a plateau known as the Palga. To the south, across the Persimmon Sea, is the equatorial continent of Szintarre, where the cosmopolitan society of Outkers (the name for tourists, emigrants, and off-worlders in general) centers on the fashionable resort city of Olanje. It is from here that a council of thirteen nobles — the Mull — rules all of Koryphon, in theory at least.

In Koryphon's recent past, a group of space pirates landed and forced some Uldra chieftains to cede certain choice areas in the Alouan, thus forming the great Domains where, two hundred years later, a new landed aristocracy still lives, using Uldra "Treaty" tribes to work the bountiful estates. These Submission Treaties and the presence of the self-appointed Alouan "land barons" cause considerable consternation among the fashionably conscientious folk of Szintarre, but the holdings have been somewhat sanctioned by tradition and so generally accepted — at least, that is, until a new local Uldra chieftain calling himself the Gray Prince begins encouraging the Redemptionists — a group committed to restoring the Treaty lands to the Uldras — into more direct action. The Gray Prince is dedicated to this same task. It is a fashionable cause, especially now that the Redemptionists have so striking a figurehead.

Two even more exotic aspects of normal Koryphon life are the erjins and morphotes — quasi-intelligent creatures apparently indigenous to Koryphon, although in the case of the erjins there is scant fossil evidence to reinforce such an assumption. The behavior and motivations of the morphotes are incomprehensible, and while some claim the erjins are fully sentient, this fact has not been satisfactorily demonstrated, and they are popularly regarded as "clever animals" (XIV).

The novel opens with Schaine Madduc, a member of the ruling family of Morningswake Domain, returning home to Koryphon after five years at school on the world Tanquil, a self-imposed exile following a disagreement with her father. She is greeted at Olanje spaceport by her brother Kelse, a partial cripple with prosthetic arm and leg replacements for the limbs lost during an attack by a wild erjin when he was younger.

They meet Gerd Jemasze, their family friend from a neighboring Domain, and over dinner Kelse reads them a letter from his father, Uther Madduc, who is at present up on the Palga Plateau among the Wind-runners investigating an old mystery—trying to discover once and for all how the normally wild erjins are trained and domesticated for sale in Olanje as servants and footmen, or for use as mounts by the Uldras. Uther writes that he has "a wonderful story to tell... a most prodigious and extraordinary joke" (I), and that he will meet them on the following day at Galigong, a seaport on the Uaian coast, and share it with them. Such good-humored ebullience is most uncharacteristic of Schaine's father, and they are all curious as to what Uther's "wonderful story" can be.

At an Olanje party that evening, a young cosmopolitan named Elvo Glissam becomes infatuated with Schaine. Elvo supports a society that opposes the use of erjins as beasts of burden. He criticizes their exploitation both by the Outkers of Szintarre and the Uldras of Uaia and condemns their domestication at the hands of the Wind-runners, who profit from such "enslavement" by exchanging "broken" erjins for accessories for their wind-wagons. Elvo is also sympathetic to the Redemptionists, who oppose the privileges of the land barons. So that he can have first-hand acquaintance with both wild erjins and the advantages enjoyed by the Treaty Uldras living on the Domain lands, Schaine invites him back to Morningswake on the following day when she goes with Kelse and Gerd to join her father.

It is at this same party at Villa Mirasol that we see a typical cross-section of the Olanje intellectual elite and learn more of their various commitments. One of the guests is the popular leader of the Retent Uldras (or Blues, as they are called), the Gray Prince, and much to Schaine's amazement he turns out to be none other than the Madducs' childhood ward, Muffin, the young Uldra who slew the erjin that maimed Kelse. Muffin has become a proud and self-possessed revolutionary figure, making the most of the current vogue enjoyed by his Pan-Uldra movement.

After various discourses highlighting the opposing viewpoints in the Domains/Pan-Uldra and erjin questions, the novel's action shifts to the following morning, with Schaine, Kelse, Gerd, and Elvo setting off for Galigong by aircar. They wait there long after Uther Madduc is due to have arrived, and then trace his scheduled flight path to where his aircar is discovered shot down and wrecked. Uther Madduc's body is found in the wreckage.

Before they can land, their own aircar is attacked by an Uldra sky-shark (as the Uldras call their armed one-man flying platforms), and they are forced down as well. Stranded, they must fight off a party of hostile Uldras mounted on erjins and then make a hundred-mile cross-country journey to Morningswake. This is the first of the novel's two planetary treks, and it is used to reveal more about the Uldras, the "wild" erjins, and the Koryphon locus in general, providing an opportunity for an analysis of fundamental concepts and differing life-views.

Safely back at Morningswake, on the morning after Uther Madduc's funeral, Schaine and Kelse receive a visit from the Gray Prince, ostensibly to pay his respects, but in reality he wishes to pursue an old passion for Schaine and use his new status to test certain conventions of Madduc hospitality — namely, the right to be admitted to the Great Hall, a privilege traditionally denied Uldras. Kelse refuses him this courtesy, explaining to an angry Schaine that the erstwhile Muffin carefully chose his moment to visit. Kelse's reasoning is that when the Gray Prince comes as an Outker, he will be accorded Outker privileges. Ordering lunch to be served on the terrace, Kelse adds insult to injury by inviting the head stockman, an Uldra mystic and old friend of Uther Madduc's named Kurgech, to join them. Muffin leaves in a fury.

Kelse, Elvo, and Gerd Jemasze are left to ponder the mystery of Uther's joke. Using the autopilot from the wrecked aircar and Uther's own notebook, they establish his route up to the Palga plateau, to where he landed at No. 2 Depot and tricked a

certain Wind-runner priest named Poliamides into showing him
the erjin training center. One entry in the notebook is most intriguing, for it says: "Of bittersweet ironies this is the prime...
and if any dare to question our right and our justice, I can and
will pin him to the wall of his own doctrinaire absurdity" (VI).
This would seem to suggest some vital connection with the circumstances of their own occupancy of the Alouan Domains,
and consequently Gerd, Elvo, and Kurgech undertake to duplicate Uther's route to learn what lies behind the mystery.
Due to Wind-runner apprehensions about Uldra raids, aircars
are banned from the skies over the Palga, and therefore, after
reaching No. 2 Depot, Gerd and his companions must continue
by surface transport.

Now begins the second planetary trek, one that reveals life
among the Wind-runners on the limitless grasslands—the
"sarai"—of the Palga. It is as intricate and exotic a human-derived culture as Vance has yet contrived.

Through a Wind-runner priest named Moffamides, they
obtain a land-yawl and protective "fiaps"—talismans—to safeguard their expedition. Then they set out upon the sarai to locate Uther's guide, Poliamides, who has gone, so Moffamides
tells them, to the forest of the Aluban. After a series of adventures involving a thief-wagon (thus revealing the uselessness of
Moffamides' talismans) and a black schooner belonging to a
party of avenging Srenki, the travellers reach the Aluban, only
to discover Poliamides' skeletal remains. This is more than just
a joke perpetrated against them by a pranksterish Wind-
runner priest, for Moffamides has meant them to die there,
obviously to prevent any investigations into the erjin trade by
Outkers, especially by one like Elvo Glissam who is sympathetic
to that formidable movement dedicated to emancipating the
creatures. "Becalmed" a short distance from the Aluban forest,
the travellers are waylaid by Moffamides, who uses Wind-runner magic against them. Kurgech retaliates with Uldra magic
of his own, and they are able to capture Moffamides and use

an Uldra "crazy-box" to interrogate him. They learn that Uther Madduc was taken to the Place of Rose-and-Gold at Al Fador, where the erjins are trained, and eventually they find and follow his track until it ends. Then Moffamides, under whatever compulsion Kurgech has placed upon him, warns them that "an erjin prince" (X) is watching them. With Moffamides acting as interpreter, they request directions to the training station. The erjin first tries to mislead the travellers and then, failing to deceive them, is destroyed by Gerd Jemasze when it suddenly turns on them.

The party then makes its own way to the Place of Rose-and-Gold, discovering it to be an elaborate, many-tiered shrine covered with ancient glyphs depicting warring erjins and morphotes using energy weapons and flying machines. Puzzled by the significance of this monument, the travellers proceed on to Al Fador itself and see the training compounds and some erjins with the men who are allegedly their trainers. The travellers are pursued and cornered by erjins, but Kurgech is able to send a "mind-message" (XI) to one of his Uldra kinsmen at Morningswake, and Kelse promptly brings an armed aircar to their aid.

Back at Morningswake, changes are occurring with startling rapidity. The Redemptionists have persuaded the Mull to issue an edict stating that all treaty lands — with the exception of the manor houses themselves and ten adjoining acres — are to be handed back to the Uldra tribes. The Uldras launch armed incursions into Domain territory to assert this point, and the land barons combine to form a protective militia in retaliation. Also, the Gray Prince pays Schaine a clandestine visit, still anxious to press his love for her and prepared to force her to comply with his wishes. He makes the claim on her of having saved Kelse from the erjin, but Gerd Jemasze has followed Muffin and heard his words. He shows himself and reveals a long-concealed truth: that Muffin actually stood by and watched the erjin mutilate Kelse, destroying the creature only when he saw Schaine approaching.

This confrontation is followed by another of a more general kind as the Mull and the land barons' newly formed "Order of Uaia" clash over the future of the Domains. The land barons demand Mull protection against further Uldra depredations; the Mull insists that its edict be honored. In return, the Mull is accused of condoning the enslavement of intelligent indigenes — the erjins. The Mull demands proof of this, maintaining that erjins are quasi-intelligent animals.

To settle the matter, Gerd and Kelse conduct the Mull representatives on a tour of the Place of Rose-and-Gold monument and the Al Fador "training" installation. It is there that they are told by an old erjin that the supposedly docile erjins throughout Szintarre and the Alouan are in fact warriors, and that they have already been given the telepathic signal to launch their campaign to regain Koryphon for their own race. The Outkers of Olanje are completely unprepared for this insurrection from within by what were formerly compliant menials, and it is only after a retaliatory expedition is mounted by the land barons that this erjin uprising is crushed.

Seeking advantage from the disrupted state of affairs, the Gray Prince sends his Uldras against the land barons. But now the Order of Uaia is a more effective force and the Uldras too are defeated. This leaves matters almost exactly as they stood before the abortive erjin coup — the Gray Prince demanding the return of the hereditary Uldra tribal lands; the Mull deliberating in their favor; the land barons determined to resist. The novel culminates in a formal session of the Mull, at which the various claimants put forward their cases.

It is now, in the face of the Gray Prince's demands, that Gerd Jemasze reveals the full substance of Uther Madduc's "wonderful joke": how the morphotes are the world's true indigenes, once masters of a sophisticated technological civilization that was conquered by invaders from space—the erjins. Across the subsequent millennia, both races degenerated, their territories being seized by the earliest human settlers on Koryphon who later adapted to become the Uldras and Wind-runners.

Thus the farce is made complete. If the land barons are to surrender their Domain lands, so then must the Outkers, Uldras, and Wind-runners relinquish their holdings as well, all the way down to the original occupants—the morphotes. The novel closes with the Mull's edict being rescinded, and the Gray Prince—always an opportunist—leaves Koryphon altogether. Quite appropriately, the closing moment of the novel presents us with a morphote, ever watching and—waiting?

The Gray Prince is a topical and provocative novel in that it takes on issues such as racialism, political and social morality, the notions of justice and freedom, etc.—relocating them in a safely removed context. It illustrates that remark made by one of Keith Laumer's characters in "Protest Note" (1966): "If two monkeys want the same banana, in the end one will have it, and the other will cry morality."[2]

We are dealing here with different cultural ethics at variance. On concluding the novel, the reader has been through most of the classic human conflicts (over love, ideologies, moralities, economic and political advantage, and so on) with the added advantage of seeing these conflicts thrown into relief by the objectification of context. Koryphon is not Earth—we are observing a complex cultural profile with "ant farm" detachment. The human condition is thus quantified as a number of constantly recurring phenomena, which we are to consider more as ethical pragmatists like the Connatic than with cynicism.

Again, Vance provides all manner of entries to be added to the xenographer's lexicon: behavioral concepts like "kill-fury," *xheng*, and *aurau*; local institutions involving star-watching, karoos, kachembas, blasphemy masks; special minorities like the wittols and the Srenki, and so on. It is a rich tapestry indeed.

Showboat World

This novel (1975) brings us back to Big Planet, "the innermost planet of the yellow star Phaedra" (*Prolog*) featured in the earlier novel of that name. A vast, metal-poor world 25,000 miles in diameter, with climate and gravity quite close to that of Earth, Big Planet has become an enormous clearinghouse for countless groups of terrestrial dissidents.

> Big Planet lies beyond the frontier of terrestrial law, and has been settled by groups impatient with restraint, or determined to live by unorthodox tenets of conduct: nonconformists, anarchists, fugitives, religious dissidents, misanthropes, deviants, freaks. The tremendous expanses of Big Planet indifferently absorb them all.
>
> In a few isolated districts something like civilization exists, though always in some more or less usual variant. Elsewhere, beyond the environs of small communities, law is only as strong as local custom, or, as often, nonexistent.... The habits of life are infinitely varied, as over the centuries the heterogeneous groups, isolated and inbred, have diversified to florid extremes. (*Prolog*)

Ever in pursuit of compatibility, we can easily see Big Planet as one of those "planets suitable for colonization by dissident groups" (*Star King*, III) sought after by the locaters from the Oikumene in the Demon Princes trilogy—settled, developed, and culturally "patchworked" until, by the time of the Gaean Reach and *Showboat World*, it is exactly the spectacular phenomenon best suited to Vance's interests, permitting endless variations for cultural taxonomy, countless opportunities for planetary treks and travelogs. The Prolog to the most recent Big Planet novel, taken from the *Handbook of the Inhabited Worlds*, has that same benign philosophical attitude so much a part of the Connatic, and of Vance himself.

> The savants of Earth have long pondered and analyzed and argued the circumstances of Big Planet. A hundred zealots have urged the imposition of terrestrial discipline, that law and order be brought to Big Planet, but those who defend the status quo have always had the final pronouncement: "Big Planet represents for us that tantalizing vision of the land beyond the frontier where bravery, resource and daring are more important than the mastery of urban abstractions. The original settlers made great sacrifices to win freedom for themselves. In the process they willy-nilly determined the destiny of their descendants, so now the new

generations share the idiosyncracies of the old, or indeed extend them to new limits. Who can deem this good or bad? Who can define justice or correctness or truth? If law is brought to Big Planet, if this glorious diversity is stifled, the dissidents are once again disenfranchised; once again they must move on, to havens even more remote. (*Prolog*)

Big Planet itself is probably showing us this world at a much earlier period. It has the usual classic ingredients of any Vance piece—the trek-and-travelog basis, the exotic adventure and central mystery (as well as those other, lesser mysteries of the route that are solved by cultural analysis—the workings of Kirstendale society, the secret of the Myrtlesea Oracle, etc.). It is an earlier work, too, in the sense that it tends to polarize good and evil into extremes, unlike the later books where relative goods and evils prevail. Charley Lysidder is a villain more of the order of a Demon Prince. In an important sense, he would see himself as doing for Big Planet what Harry Creath did on Ballenkarch in *Son of the Tree*.

In the later book, *Showboat World*, this polarization is nowhere near as rigorous. If Apollon Zamp is a hero, he is a Falstaffian one: self-serving and stubborn, an unscrupulous rogue and a pompous old fool. There is a potential for villains and evil around every river bend, wherever there exists another moral or legal code, another self-contained society. There are few blacks and whites, only telling grays.

Showboat World opens with a close focus onto the Lower Vissel of Lune XXIII South, and the strong competition that exists among a group of rival showboat captains and their troupes, working out of a very atypical "cosmopolitan" center, Coble. Flamboyant, self-opinionated men for the most part, these captains would see themselves as both artists and entrepreneurs, taking cultural enlightenment to the diverse pockets of humanity scattered along the Vissel and its tributaries.

The plot of the novel initially involves the rivalry between two such captains in particular—Apollon Zamp and Garth

Ashgale—over the privilege to voyage far north and perform at the Grand Festival at Mornune before King Waldemar of Soyvanesse. Out of a mixture of greed and personal vanity, these two men attempt all sorts of chicanery, constantly endeavoring to foil one another's best efforts at winning the right to attend the Mornune festival. Ashgale deliberately neglects to tell Zamp of the selection contest to be held at Lanteen; Zamp in return scuttles Ashgale's showboat, thus disqualifying him from the adjudication. Then, after Zamp has deviously won the selection, Ashgale arranges events so that Zamp's showboat, *The Miraldra's Enchantment*, is burned during a routine river-stop performance at Port Whant two days later.

Barely escaping with their lives, Zamp and his troupe make for Coble on Surmise Bay, but there Zamp is faced with another dilemma. He holds the silver invitation plaque to the Grand Festival but has no showboat and no troupe with which to make use of it. Out of pocket after the fateful debacle at Port Whant, Zamp is shunned by his former company, who refuse to have any further dealings with him.

A solution is provided by Dame Blanche-Aster, a personable though solemn young woman who has attached herself to Zamp's company earlier, following his success at the Lanteen contest, and who has displayed no small concern at the prospect of playing at the Mornune festival. It is by her wiles, exercised on Zamp's behalf, that she is able to persuade Throdorus Gassoon, the pedantic, over-cautious and unadventurous master of the museum-ship *Universal Pancomium* to undertake the long voyage upriver to Mornune, using his renovated vessel as the new *Miraldra's Enchantment*. Blanche-Aster has flattered Gassoon's image of himself as a scholar and disseminator of cultural enlightenment and ancient lore to less fortunate folk, inducing him to exalt King Waldemar with a performance of the ancient Earth masterpiece, *Macbeth*.

Ever the showman, Zamp immediately locks horns with

Gassoon over the nature of their production, Zamp insisting on a musical score and the inclusion of a number of more sensational and spectacular modifications, Gassoon determined to preserve the integrity of the original script. Their constant bickering conveniently conceals Blanche-Aster's own carefully hidden motives for her involvement in the affair. She presents a different face to each so as to maintain the ill-suited partnership that is making the Mornune voyage possible.

After various adventures along the route, they reach their destination, and now the novel's attention shifts to the local cultural focus of the intricate Mornune society, with its sovereignty held by the ruling member of whatever noble house receives a Tabard woven by the Magic Loom, a marvelous device constructed by the first kings of Soyvanesse. Three such Tabards have so far been produced by the Loom. The first was the legendary Green and Gold Tabard of Destiny woven for the House of Doro and finally lost during an insurrection; the second, the Blue and Gold Tabard was produced for the usurping House of Erme and also lost during a battle; the third, the Scarlet and Gold Tabard, is that currently worn by the present King Waldemar.

As it turns out, the conditions of the Grand Festival are far less appealing than might be wished. As an added inducement to the amassed showboats to give of their very best, Waldemar has decreed that a penalty will be imposed on whichever troupe provides the poorest entertainment. The six showboats strive to outdo each other, and on the final evening of the scheduled performances, Zamp and Gassoon stage their production of *Macbeth*.

It is during this performance that Blanche-Aster, playing the part of Lady Macbeth, throws off her robe to reveal that she is wearing the supposedly lost Blue and Gold Tabard. She has returned home to Soyvanesse to reclaim her throne, her Tabard automatically invalidating Waldemar's later one. But then Gassoon, playing the role of Duncan, rushes on to learn the reason for the interruption only to create an even greater disturbance. For, in an effort to lend Duncan a more regal air, Gassoon has selected from among his collection of antique garments gathered from all over Big Planet, none other than the legendary Green and Gold Tabard itself. Superseding the others, this Tabard automatically makes Gassoon king of Soyvanesse. He straightaway proclaims that *The Miraldra's Enchantment* has won the contest prize, and that Blanche-Aster is to be his bride.

Four days later, after Zamp has set off downriver back towards Coble, amply rewarded, Gassoon is seen galloping along the bank of the river. Taken on board, he tells Zamp of how the Green and Gold Tabard literally fell apart with age, and that, realizing what this would signify, he decided to rejoin his "good comrade Apollon Zamp" (XV). The two captains are left to discuss their good fortunes, their shared wealth, and their future plans.

Showboat World, in some aspects of tone and plotting, is distinctly reminiscent of Vance's earlier novel, *Space Opera*. In both works, there is an entrepreneur figure commanding a ship and troupe intent on enlightening the masses of other cultures. Dame Isabel Grayce goes forth with grand operas on a cultural-exchange program to Rlaru and the worlds along the way. Showboat captains Apollon Zamp and Throdorus Gassoon mean to win a contest at Mornune with a performance of an ancient classic. In each novel events are determined by a scheming young female — Madoc Roswyn and Dame Blanche-Aster — who "seduces" the various key members of the respective expeditions so as to pursue her own plans.

Furthermore, *Showboat World* illustrates those other basic elements of Vance's xenographical approach. The shortage of metal plus the unique circumstances of Big Planet's original settlement produces a medieval cultural profile for the various planetary societies and ensures an extreme provincialism for all the "showcased" communities. Through the river circuits played by the showboats and the voyage to Mornune, we are given the planetary trek/travelog, and with Blanche-Aster's objectives and the conventions of accession in the realm of Soyvanesse, we have the central xenological mystery to be solved.

Illustrated as well is the essential difference between a xenographer like Vance and a writer like Poul Anderson, for Anderson's novels concern mostly nonhuman alien cultures being examined from without by human visitors (e.g., *The Man Who Counts*, 1958; *World without Stars*, 1967; *Fire Time*, 1974; etc.). Even his human-derived cultures are generally approached this way. Vance, on the other hand, apart from dealing almost exclusively with human alien cultures (even the Tschai novels only partly violate this approach), has them examined from within by one of their own members, whether it is Apollon Zamp, Ghyl Tarvoke, or Jubal Droad. There are exceptions, of course (Miro Hetzel, Adam Reith, Kirth Gersen), but these are comparatively rare.

A charge related to this is that Anderson is more concerned with xenological adventure than xenological mystery. Generally speaking, he does not make as much use of his xenological puzzles and therefore his cultural analyses as Vance does (nor does he have the latter's experience as a conventional mystery writer, doling out clues while carefully withholding solutions). Anderson keeps few secrets that are essential to the plot. In *The Man Who Counts*, when we are finally told that the Drak'ho and the Lannacha belong to the same race (their different breeding cycles determined by custom rather than evolution), there is none of the pleasure of revelation that comes from, say, the denouement of *The Gray Prince*.

This does not diminish Anderson's achievement in any sense, but rather points out a difference in approach. Whereas both writers are concerned with the exotic adventure, we can split hairs and say that Anderson is more the straight adventure writer, the straight xenologist, pursuing alien encounters, first confrontations and such (e.g., *Question and Answer*, 1956), while Vance is more the compleat xenographer — detailing a particular world as thoroughly as he can without compromising the mystery element of his adventure. To compare one of Anderson's worlds, like Diomedes, with Trullion, Halma, or Koryphon in Vance's universe would be a foolish and misplaced exercise. There is little basis for comparison, each writer seeing his xenographical task differently.

Marune: Alastor 933

With the possible exception of *Maske: Thaery*, Vance's most complex "general culture" work in initial conception is *Marune: Alastor 933* (1975), largely because of the unique character of Marune itself and the "peculiar Rhune dispositions" (II) that have come to exist because of it.

Once again, we are in Alastor Cluster, under the suzerainty of the Connatic. Marune is a small, rugged world "almost at the Cold Edge, in the Fontinella Wisp" (II), orbiting one sun in "an isolated system of four dwarfs respectively orange, blue, green, and red" (IV). It is a world originally settled by a terrestrial-derived race known as the Majars, who were later supplanted as the planet's ruling inhabitants by a second derivative human race of "aloof and eccentric warrior-scholars" (II) — the Rhunes, themselves contained in turn by the cosmopolitan Alastrid culture when the Connatic was forced to bring in the Whelm to end the Rhune persecution of the Majars. Because of their hostile proclivities, the Rhunes were subsequently denied access to energy weapons and any form of modern transportation, thus adding to an already distinctly medieval cultural profile.

At the time of the novel, the Majars have become a moribund race, a community of ten thousand descendants in the low hills to the south of the world's solitary cosmopolitan outpost, Port Mar. The Rhunes, on the other hand, number well over a hundred thousand and are a vital and flourishing people occupying a series of rigidly feudalistic polities — the Rhune Realms — in the mountains to the east. Theirs is a profoundly complex society, intricately affected by Marune's shifting relationship to its four suns, completely disdainful of any customs and cultural forms not their own. All areas of conduct are regulated by the most exacting protocol. Marital relationships, for instance — a state known as *trisme* — are arranged for advantage, nothing more. Such matters as sexual activity, eating in clear view of others, etc., are considered disgusting — an indication of the contempt felt for the inhabitants of Port Mar and the other Earth-worlds. Only at the monthly occurrence "mirk," when none of the suns is in the sky, is there a relaxation of these social rigors. During "mirk," the normally circumspect Rhunes go forth masked and disguised to commit all sorts of crimes and atrocities — what are known as "mirk-deeds" — but even this peculiar phenomenon has been strictly conventionalized within the Rhune social and behavioral calendar.

The narrative opens with the local focus of Carfaunge, a spaceport on the world Bruse-Tansel, Alastor 1102. A young man with amnesia, dressed in a nondescript manner, with his hair hacked short and no identification, is brought to the notice of port officials. Lacking facilities to deal with such a predicament, they have no other recourse than to put him to work at one of the dye-camps, so that he might earn his passage to the Connatic's hospital on Numenes, and there obtain the proper treatment.

Pardero, as the young man is called, finally reaches Numenes and is there subjected to a complex series of tests aimed at establishing his "anthropometry, physiological indices, details as to . . . somatic chemistry, psychic profile" (II) and so on. After weeks of intense scrutiny, it is revealed to him that he is "a Rhune from the Rhune Realms, east of Port Mar on the North Continent of Marune, Alastor 933" (II).

Following further weeks of cultural reorientation, Pardero finally returns home to Marune, determined above all else to learn his true identity and that of the enemy who sent him so far across the Cluster, obviously meaning him never to return. From inquiries made in Port Mar, Pardero learns that he is none other than Efraim, the new "kaiark" or ruler of the Rhune Realm of Scharrode, and that he has arrived home just in time to prevent the succession of his kinsman, Destian, to this position following the death of his father in a military engagement against bandits allegedly from a neighboring Realm, Gorgetto.

It is clear at once that Efraim's untimely arrival has seriously discommoded the plans of Destian, his "mother" Singhalissa and "sister" Sthelany, as well as rendering inoperable certain key alliances with the powerful neighboring Realm of Eccord which would permit both a joint leadership with the Eccord kaiark, Rainlle, and cede to Eccord that part of Scharrode known as Whispering Ridge, where Rianlle dearly wishes to build a pavilion.

Efraim arrives at Benbuphar Strang, the fortress-capital of Scharrode, in the company of a young Port Mar cosmopolite named Matho Lorcas, the same young man who had acted as impromptu guide to New Town some six months before for a group of young Rhune nobles—Efraim, Destian, Sthelany, and Rianlle's "daughter" Maerio—during a formal visit by Scharrode and Eccord royalty to Port Mar. On learning that he was last seen alone in the company of this Lorcas on the eve of his disappearance, Efraim has sought him out, only to become convinced that this personable young Port Mar vagabond is not the enemy he seeks. Moreover, on learning of Efraim's fate following that highly improper excursion in New Town, Lorcas has introduced Efraim to one Skogel, who in turn suggests that Efraim's amnesia is due to his having been given Fwai-chi shag to eat—a drug derived from the extrusions on the skin of Marune's peaceful autochthones.

Consequently, in order to pursue a former infatuation for Sthelany and to accumulate memorable experiences, Lorcas accompanies Efraim back to Scharrode. But from the moment of their arrival, they are caught up in the intrigues of Singha-lissa, Destian, and Sthelany and embroiled in all manner of slights and social embarrassments designed to capitalize on Efraim's affliction and thus induce the council of nobles to regard him as unfit for royal duties.

In terms of the Rhune Code, it is not at all surprising that there is such indignation and active resentment. For, as Lorcas tells him, "You are a Rhune no longer" (V). During his brief exile, Efraim has necessarily undergone an enforced cosmopolitan cultural orientation, so that he can see himself as ruling "a beautiful mountain realm from a castle of archaic glamor" (VI), an observation made with more cosmopolitan detachment than any Rhune could bring to bear. Inevitably, as a result of the same new perspective, the strict conventions of Rhune society—the taboos on eating or showing affection in public, the strict injunction against sexual activities except during the monthly occurrence of "mirk"—appear as narrow-minded eccentricity.

> He speculated as to the advisability of innovation: why should the Rhunes conduct themselves with such exaggerated daintiness when trillions of other folk feasted in public, with never a concern for their alimentary processes? His own single example would only arouse revulsion and censure; he must think further on the matter. (VI)

Efraim's position becomes increasingly awkward. He must act as kaiark without an adequate knowledge of customs and protocol, discover the identities of both his enemy and his father's murderer, and withstand the very real political pressures placed on him by Rianlle of Eccord to give over Whispering Ridge as a gesture of goodwill between the two realms—a gesture Efraim is unable to make because of a prior verbal agreement between the Fwai-chi and Efraim's late father, guaranteeing them perpetual rights to the land. And all the while there are the continual schemes of Singhalissa, Destian, and Sthelany to oppose Efraim, culminating in an unspeakable act of premeditated murder disguised as a mirk-deed which Efraim only just manages to escape, although an unsuspecting Lorcas is less fortunate and is murdered in his stead.

Efraim's dilemma is still unresolved. Rianlle's requests for Whispering Ridge become more and more insistent, tinged with reminders of Eccord's superior military and strategic position, and Efraim's other problems are dwarfed into insignificance by the need for a suitable evasion. This is provided by the timely arrival of a group of Fwai-chi, who come to the gate of the castle. They wish to help prove the existence of the verbal contract and give Efraim one of their drugs, a dangerous potion they have so far withheld because of the great risks involved in its use.

The Fwai-chi drug works and Efraim's memory comes flooding back. He recalls the events of that fateful evening six months before, of how he left Lorcas and on his way back to the hotel came upon the noble Rianlle leaving a Port Mar bordello (a delightfully low touch this, reinforcing the idea of our essential humanity in yet another way). Mortified at having been recognized, Rianlle insisted on their taking refreshments, and so was able to slip Efraim the amnesia-inducing drug and send him off-planet. Efraim also recalls how, during his stupor, he overheard Rianlle and Singhalissa discussing an alliance between themselves and their respective realms, through which Rianlle would obtain Whispering Ridge — a key religious spot for the Fwai-chi — and so levy a toll upon them in precious stones and elixirs.

Rather than have his "unorthodoxy" and treachery made public, Rianlle forgoes all claims to the territory and gives Maerio in *trisme* to Efraim. It is revealed that Destian, Singhalissa, and Sthelany are guilty of the murders of Lorcas and Efraim's father, and they are summarily banished.

At the novel's close, it is clear that this is the dawn of a new age for the Rhunes, that they are in fact a divergent strand of humanity in the initial stages of readapting to the universal culture. Had their depredations against the Majars not caused the intervention of the cosmopolitan Alastrid forces and the subsequent creation of an off-world enclave — Port Mar — the Rhunes would have continued in their cycle of differentiation beyond all hope of recovery. As it is, in *Marune: Alastor 933*, we have caught the Rhunes before this permanent "alienation" has occurred. It is important to note that Efraim is not the first "tainted" Rhune (presenting quite an exception because of the exceptional circumstances contributing to his "indoctrination"), but that Rianlle himself had broken with the strictures of the Code without these external contributing factors. As he says to Efraim upon being discovered leaving the bordello:

> "Ah, well, you must not judge me too harshly. Unfortunately for myself, I am expected to represent the apotheosis of Rhune gallantry. The pressures become overwhelming. Come along; we will take a hot drink together as the folk do without shame here at Port Mar." (XIII)

Perhaps the only problem for the reader, having been primed along with Pardero on Numenes for the complex culture that is to come, is that we meet few Rhunes sufficiently untainted to convince us fully of their uniqueness as a people. There is not enough "local" Rhune "orthodoxy" to counter that cosmopolitan "orthodoxy" with which we are already familiar. To find this, we must turn instead to secondary characters like the Majar desk clerk at the Royal Rhune Hotel or Matho Lorcas for commentaries on the Rhune psyche.

The Dogtown Tourist Agency

In this novel (1975), we have an effectuator, Miro Hetzel, employed by Palladian Micronics to investigate a company known only as Istagam, which has undercut interstellar competition in the manufacture of vital electronic components. Nothing is known of Istagam other than the traffic of its products through the port city of Axistil on the planet Maz, a small ancient world swinging "round the white dwarf sun Khis, in company with a large frigid moon" (III).

Maz is unique in that it marks the border for three coterminous interstellar empires — Liss, Olefract, and Gaean — and is jointly governed by a Triarchy of all three. The nonhuman powers are decidedly xenophobic and shun all intercourse with humankind (and presumably with one another). Nevertheless, Hetzel's principals are concerned that Istagam may be the front for a Liss or Olefract operation seeking to flood Gaean markets through an outlet on Maz.

Compounding the Istagam mystery still further are the Gomaz, a race of sentient autochthones who have developed for themselves an intricate feudalistic society of rival castles and constantly warring tribes. Because of past insurrections, these "septs" are strictly disallowed the use of energy weapons of any kind.

Upon reaching Axistil, Miro Hetzel has difficulty in pursuing his investigations. The Gaean Triarch refuses even to see him privately to discuss Istagam, and Hetzel is left to make inquiries at the local tourist agency of the novel's title. There he learns that Byrrhis, a local Gaean with extensive tourist holdings — magnificent resorts in deserted Gomaz castles, conducted tour facilities, etc. — quite probably has knowledge of Istagam, but as Byrrhis is not on hand either, Hetzel can make little use of this information until several further dramatic events take place.

Determined to make contact with Sir Estevan Tristo, the Gaean Triarch, Hetzel plans to attend a scheduled Triarchic session at the Triskelion. He is delayed by unseen enemies who gas him, but he reaches the Triskelion in time to discover that the Liss and Olefract Triarchs and two visiting Gomaz chieftains of the Ubaikh sept have been assassinated by "a crazy young Gaean" (IV). As luck would have it, Hetzel later finds this person sitting disconsolately on a park bench. His name is Gidion Dirby and, if his story is to be believed, he has been the unfortunate victim of a most astonishing program of brainwashing that has left him convinced that he has been brutally victimized by a man resembling the Gaean Triarch. He tells Hetzel how, falling on hard times, he was involved in what could only be the smuggling of contraband "man-stuff" (XII) to the Gomaz, which in turn led him to be imprisoned and subjected to a particularly nasty process of aversion therapy at the hands of this man.

When his tormentors finally released him, destitute and without papers, Dirby went at once to report his experience to the authorities at the Triarchic session, just in time to be implicated in the multiple assassinations of the Liss and Olefract Triarchs and Gomaz leaders and the attempted murder of Sir Estevan Tristo. In the ensuing confusion, however, Dirby was able to escape arrest.

Hetzel is intrigued by Dirby's story, by the elaborate plot used to direct events towards the elimination of all three Triarchs, and decides to assist, aware, too, that any such assistance must, under the circumstances, invariably take him nearer the elusive subject of his industrial espionage for Palladian Micronics. Leaving Dirby in the "neutral" territory of the Beyranion Hotel, Hetzel sets out by rented aircar to the hinterland to question the remaining Gomaz chieftain who survived the Triskelion assassinations. It is a difficult conversation, but Hetzel does learn that the rival Gomaz sept of the Kzyk, enemies of the Ubaikh, have "the secrets of metal and energy" and have become "suppliants" to Gaean will (IX). The Ubaikh chieftains had gone to Axistil to protest such "favors to the Kzyk" when the murders had occurred (IX).

Following this interview, Hetzel sojourns to one of Byrrhis's castle inns with Janika, the girl from the tourist agency, and there begins to piece together a solution to the mystery surrounding Istagam and the Gomaz. It is a picture in which the Kzyk provide cheap labor in exchange for illicit Gaean technological aid supplied by Istagam.

En route back to Axistil with his conclusions, Hetzel's aircar is forced down, sabotaged, the power cells drained. Hetzel and Janika are compelled to make a cross-country trek to the airbus depot near the Kzyk castle, with an unwilling member of an Ubaikh war party as guide. At the castle, they witness a spectacular siege as the Ubaikh launch their Class III war against the Kzyk. During this superficially local affair, there appears a disguised Liss patrol boat which proceeds to strike at the Kzyk castle. When a Gaean aircar attempts to retaliate, it is destroyed, upon which the Liss craft withdraws, leaving the rival Gomaz septs to their own devices now that illegal alien interference has been eliminated.

Hetzel and Janika return to Axistil by airbus and there, using the Ubaikh chieftain to indicate from what part of the Triskelion council chamber the fatal blasts originated, Hetzel is able to identify the murderer, an agent who has acted on Byrrhis's orders to prevent the Triarchs from taking action against the Istagam operation. By shifting the blame onto Dirby, they meant to escape suspicion altogether.

The death of Byrrhis (presumably at the hands of Liss agents) resolves matters further. He has been supplying the indentured Kzyk with a synthesized virility hormone — *chir* — a chemical vital to their procreative cycle, in return for their labor, the profits from Istagam being channelled into the various resort inns across the planet.

What begins as a story of industrial espionage on an interstellar scale becomes a tale of political intrigue, interracial legalities, and cultural embargo. Once again, cultural analysis of the native Gomaz, their complex motivations and worldview, is made central to these other events. There is the usual planetary trek for "showcasing" an alien world and its people; the marked medieval cast surrounding Axistil, the resorts, and the sept castles; the air of backwater provincialism and isolation attending the whole Maz locus. There is the wry humor of the Casimir Wuldfache subplot and a surprising density of peripheral material (the Liss and Olefract cultures) in what is in so many ways a much more mature reworking of the sort of indigenous planetary culture found in that earlier Magnus Ridolph short story, "The Kokod Warriors" (1952).

Maske: Thaery

This most recent of the "general culture" novels (1976) is also a story of espionage. A young local agent attempts to expose the plans of a respected and important noble who would forever change the face of his world out of a desire for personal gain. Like *Emphyrio* and *The Dogtown Tourist Agency*, *Maske: Thaery* concerns economic matters overlaying those other related issues of political, ideological, and racial conflict, and pursues the theme of tourism developed in the previous novel.

Vance takes as his focus the land of Thaery on the world of Maske, one of two worlds in a double-planet formation swinging close together around Mora, a lonely star situated beyond the Gaean Reach in a desolate region known as the Great Hole. In spite of its typical isolation, Maske has known innumerable waves of human migration, at least one in the so distant past that it has specialized into a most unique human racial type — the Saidanese — who likewise have settled Maske's sister world, Skay.

The most recent wave is of a less divergent humanity, and it is from the people of Thaery (descended from a reactionary ideological group from Diosophede who came to Maske in fourteen ships) that Vance takes his hero, Jubal Droad, the younger son of a landed family in the recalcitrant Thariot district of Glentlin. As a Glint, Jubal is traditionally discouraged from seeking a place in the more promising vocations and so must seek his future livelihood elsewhere. His older brother, Trewe, as the Droad of Droad House, would of course give him employment on their family estate, but the prospect of life as a gamekeeper or bailiff holds little attraction for Jubal. Alternatively, he might leave Thaery and join that maritime race, the Sea-Nationals, forever sailing their ships around the world; or emigrate — an extreme alternative indeed, for an Alien Influence Act and a Mandate of Isolation prevent the return of emigrants once they have gone off-planet.

Jubal's solution to his dilemma is to go into "Yallow," that time between youth and maturity when the young Thariot becomes a wanderer and travels through the thirteen districts, maintaining roads and fences and assisting in the upkeep of the landscape. It is a time to be cherished for its memories and adventures, for when Yallow ends, youth has "officially" ended as well, and the Thariot is expected to become a responsible and orderly member of Thariot society.

During his Yallow ramblings, Jubal hears rumors from an innkeeper about spaceships landing in the hinterland, bringing Saidanese from the neighboring world, Skay, for who-knows-what evil ends? Jubal regards this information with considerable skepticism and goes out with three Djan (as those Saidanese native to Maske are called) to rebuild a retaining wall and roadway that have been destroyed in a rock slide. His efforts come to naught, for no sooner has a makeshift trail been restored than a Thariot leading a party of Djan warriors disregards Jubal's warnings and insists on using it. By doing so, they cause another rockfall in their passing, and Jubal is injured.

As we learn later, it is during his convalescence that Jubal traces the route taken by these travelers and discovers that it leads to a place that shows the imprints where spaceships have landed. Someone has gone off-planet and returned. Searching the area for clues, Jubal unearths some exotic off-world clothing in a nearby garbage pit.

Upon his complete recovery, Jubal returns to Glentlin and Droad House, determined to take out a warrant against the anonymous Thariot who behaved so recklessly. Even while making these avowals, a litigator arrives at Droad House interested in purchasing that peninsula of Droad land known as Cape Junchion on behalf of a noble but anonymous Thariot client. Trewe Droad refuses and the litigator departs, warning them that such a decision may not be to their best advantage.

Although Jubal has undertaken Yellow, his wanderlust is far from satisfied. Still restless, he visits his uncle Vaidro, who gives him a letter of introduction to a certain Nai the Hever, an important magnate in the Thariot capital, Wysrod. The town of Wysrod on Duskerl Bay, with the Marine Parade, Travan Square, and the Cham, and its eccentric hacks, becomes the "close focus" for the main action of the novel, although Jubal's later adventures take him farther afield—to Erdstone Pool in Wellas, and off-planet to Eiselbar (*Maske: Thaery* gives us not one but two planetary settings and three distinct and separate cultures). It is from Wysrod that the Parloury rules Thaery—made up of Five Servants traditionally drawn from the five most powerful Thariot "ilks" or families.

Reaching Wysrod, Jubal immediately presents himself at Nai the Hever's house up on the Cham but from the first makes a poor impression, largely because of his self-consciousness as a Glint. Nai the Hever is not available, but by insisting that his letter is both personal and urgent, Jubal is allowed to accompany his daughter, the Lady Mieltrude, to an important session of the Parloury, where as one of the Five Servants, Nai the Hever is engaged in the important matter of deciding whether or not to certify a certain popular and powerful young noble named Ramus Ymph as a suitable successor to the Ymph Servant who has recently died. Opinion is divided as to the suitability of Ramus as a candidate for this position, for while he is a dynamic and competent personality, many feel that he is too intent on changing the old ways.

As Ramus is addressing the assembly, Jubal is astonished to recognize him as none other than the Thariot who led the Djan troop and ignored his warning. When he imparts this knowledge to Nai the Hever, telling him of the subsequent discoveries of spaceship landing sites, the Servant makes the fateful decision that prevents Ramus from gaining his desired foothold in the Parloury. Afterwards, for reasons that are later made clear, Nai the Hever refuses to prosecute Ramus Ymph under the Alien Influences Act. The Ymphs are a powerful ilk and not to be intimidated lightly. Furthermore, although Nai the Hever seems to have no great love for Jubal, he does give him a position working in Department Three of the Sanitation and Hygiene Office, a section which Jubal later learns from Sune—the beguiling young woman who is Mieltrude's friend and confidante—to be "the secret intelligence bureau" (VIII).

No sooner has he commenced his duties there than he is served with a warrant from the Faithful Retribution Company (one of the more colorful Wysrod institutions—an organization existing solely to carry out revenge) on a charge of slandering Ramus Ymph: a contract that has been taken out by Nai the Hever's daughter Mieltrude. As Ramus Ymph's fiancée, she is presumably concerned with avenging herself on the one who prevented Ramus from becoming a Servant. With the aid of a Sea-National companion, Shrack, Jubal is able to turn the tables on the agents sent to carry out this retribution.

In retaliation, Jubal takes out a warrant against Mieltrude and thereby prompts Nai the Hever into using him in a more direct capacity. He informs Jubal that the parcel of clothing worn by Ramus while off-planet has been traced to a world in the Gaean Reach—Eiselbar, a planet orbiting a giant yellow star, Bhutra. Disguised as a tourist, Jubal is sent to Kyash on Eiselbar in an attempt to discover Ramus's purpose for having gone there.

It is now that we are given the second xenographical study. Eisel society is a complex affair, with its birth-debts (to be paid by offspring to their parents); its strict balance of obligations; its extreme attitudes against theft of any kind; its elaborate and constant use of music exactly appropriate to any given occasion (a complete glossary is included); its skeuomorphic architecture; and its economy based on a highly-developed tourist industry and on the export of chemicals derived from indigenous mobile slimes.

Jubal's inquiries at Kyash soon reveal that Ramus Ymph

had come to Eiselbar ostensibly as a rug dealer, selling Djan tapestries at ridiculously prohibitive prices in order to buy a space-yacht and to arrange some sort of deal through the People's Joy Tourist Agency—an organization specializing in arranging itineraries for "modules" of forty tourists at a time.

No sooner has Jubal returned to Maske with this information than Ramus shows his hand in another way. He has evidently persuaded one of Jubal's misguided blood relatives, Cadmus Off-Droad, to seize the Droad estate by force, and has assisted him with arms and Djan warriors in exchange for Cape Junchion, although there is no direct proof of this. When Cadmus' plans are thwarted, a masked figure manages to escape by sea—a figure Jubal later identifies from fingerprints to be Ramus Ymph. Still, Nai the Hever is reluctant to bring matters into the open. He tells Jubal: "I want placid relations with the Ymphs until certain patterns reveal themselves" (XIV).

Convinced that Nai the Hever's prevarications conceal a conviction that the Ymphs must soon dispose of Jubal, the young Glint takes matters into his own hands. After all, in his plans to secure Cape Junchion, Ramus Ymph has now been responsible for the destruction of Droad House and the deaths and maiming of Droad kinsmen, as well as his quite numerous crimes against the state. It would seem that there is a different kind of justice for the rich than for the poor.

Allegedly to enforce the warrant he formerly took out against her, Jubal kidnaps Mieltrude and takes her aboard Shrack's boat, the *Clanche*. When he learns that Ramus has chartered another vessel and is bound for Wellas—that truly amazing homeland of the human-derived Waels—he has the *Clanche* set off in pursuit. En route, Mieltrude reveals that her supposed friend Sune is Ramus' mistress and that it was she who forged Mieltrude's signature and took out the warrant against Jubal.

They follow Ramus to Erdstone Pool in Wellas, Jubal finally confronting him before the Sen, the council of Waels, to whom Ramus has presented a plan for using Wellas coastal lands for "depots" and "commercial enclaves" (XVII). Disguised as a Wael, Jubal questions Ramus' intentions further and finally uncovers the full extent of his schemes. Through the People's Joy Tourist Agency on Eiselbar, Ramus meant to bring modules of tourists to Maske, and, having failed to obtain Cape Junchion as a site for his resorts, he now means to locate his resort facilities on the Wellas littoral. In order to implement such a program, he is prepared to use off-world assistance to quell any opposition from the Sea-Nationals and the Thariots—in short, to effectively master the whole planet and open it up for off-world development.

For his deceptions, the Waels inflict a terrible punishment on Ramus, and the *Clanche* returns to Wysrod. There, Jubal is reconciled both with Nai the Hever and Mieltrude, and by dint of his cunning is able to arrange for the Ymphs to finance the rebuilding of Droad House.

As the culminating work in the "general culture" series to date, *Maske: Thaery* is true to the clearly defined xenographical conventions established in the preceding novels. With its two maps, its truly dense prologue, its six glossary entries and countless footnotes (explaining such terms as "strochane," "smaidair," "ankhe," "culbrass," etc.), what is, as always, essentially an exotic mystery story becomes Vance's most lush "travelog" and possibly his most formidable novel in background conception so far.

8. Jack Vance: Science Fiction Stylist*

RICHARD TIEDMAN

I

THE ANALYSIS OF STYLE is a singularly difficult objective. One is always oppressed by the tasks of tracing the subtle silent influence by which a notable writer first shapes and then develops his mode of expression until it reflects an individual and original use of language. If this evades easy definition, it is still readily identifiable when found—a kind of linear mastery of materials that attacks and compels, a unique handling and synthesis in the use of words that renders life to a printed page. These attributes are sadly lacking in most present-day writers, both of science fiction and mainstream literature. Without prior knowledge, very few are identifiable by an examination of one page from their works. So many of their books are subdued in tone and stinted in color, utilizing only the middle register of possibilities.

The exceptions stand out. For example, whatever the actual value of Ray Bradbury's work, his laconic, compressed prose can never be mistaken for anyone else's; nor, after a few pages,

*A somewhat different version of this essay was published as a monograph in Indiana by Coulson Publications. Copyright ©1965 by Richard Tiedman.

can Robert Heinlein's mastery of colloquial dialogue, in conjunction with his clear, unvarnished mode of exposition, be miscredited. Jack Vance likewise is one of a mere handful whose argument is enhanced by a personally distinguished means.

Style is a characteristic manner of expression, and it may vary enormously among different writers. Generally speaking, there are two approaches by which a writer leaves his stylistic fingerprints, and both are legitimate and desirable means to that end. The first is when the author's personality is allowed to suffuse and color the texture. Here the narrative, to an extent, assumes the viewpoint of the writer; his psychology, values, temperament, and opinions are sufficient to establish this "characteristic" tone. Robert Heinlein is probably the preeminent writer among those who display this technique. Heinlein rarely, if at all, attempts to make an effect with words outside of their purely referential associations. They serve as a means to an end. Though the craftsmanship in most of his books is exemplary, there are few striking effects of imagery or rhythm. As Sam Moskowitz has observed, Heinlein has "sacrificed the aesthetics of the individual passage to achieve the unified poetry of the whole." He may be recognized by certain mannerisms and clichés, but more especially by the unmistakable cast and tone of mind that permeate his pages.

As might be expected, a single sentence or paragraph removed from its context is usually neither remarkable nor readily identifiable. It takes a few pages before the Heinlein "touch" becomes apparent. His style, then, has little to do with the technical aspects of prose. In this respect he exerts little influence on the prose style of others as his fiction is to a large extent a reflection of his emotional composite makeup. Writers who have superficially affected his manner by an incorporation of snippets from his books have succeeded only in spotlighting their own vacuity. Moskowitz's statement that Heinlein's most important influence on science fiction has been stylistic is, therefore, difficult to approve. His deserved success is that of an original mind — imaginative innovation conveyed through unobtrusive and natural prose.

The risk inherent in a style of this kind is that the writer may allow vestiges of personality to intrude in odd places. Heinlein has usually been successful in avoiding this hazard. However, in his recent novels the diminution of plot interest, feebleness of characters, and deterioration of prose have been made doubly apparent by an irritating ubiquitousness of authorial presence. Obviously, care must be exercised in the creation of a style of this manner.

Jack Vance typifies a radically different approach to the problem of personal style. As in the case of Heinlein, anyone who has read one or two books by Vance would have no difficulty in assigning selected passages to their correct author, with the distinction that while Heinlein requires a few pages to be read, with Vance it is possible to guess his authorship from a few sentences. His stories are attended by a very personal and unmistakable method of sentence construction, rhythmic variety, and extravagant imagery — all controlled with great technical dexterity. In opposition to Heinlein, Vance's personality is in evidence not through choice of content but in manner of expression. This is as subjective an approach to writing as it is an objective and impersonal approach to fiction.

Vance apparently wants everything — plot, social structures, characterization — to spring into form with its own interior life, thus retaining individual autonomy. The reader will witness a complete absence of any personal animus or overt deduction. In Vance, the reader sees, senses, and is shown, rather than being told. Thus he is drawn into an unconscious and immediate participation in events. The tiresome and garrulous polemics of Heinlein's later books find no parallel in Vance's works. Vance prefers that stylistic identity rest at a distance from authorial identity.

The dangers inherent in this approach are quite different from those of Heinlein's. In attempting a more individual style, the most circumspect care is necessary lest this degenerate into self-parody. With a writer like Ray Bradbury, who affects a very idiosyncratic style, this is an ever-present threat. The mark of Vance's achievement is that although his style is the result of conscious effort, it reads as naturally and as plausibly as Heinlein at his best. This is a result of a careful and precise use of personal mannerisms. (Of course, these two approaches are not mutually exclusive, and a writer like Bradbury may utilize both methods.)

How does Vance's style differ from that of others? First, in his use of uncommon words; the stories are bedecked with rare words, exotic idiom, and rich texture. The unusual word (unusual to spoken conversation) is used to produce the utmost variety of color and effect. The language is consistently rich yet such exotic words do not seem to intrude even though in a more haphazard context they would tend to obfuscate the flow of narration. Given the breadth and spaciousness of Vance's settings, the choice of a more circumspect "language" would hardly do justice to the products of his imagination. Besides, how much more elegant to be "subaqueated" rather than drowned (*The Languages of Pao*).

However, in his use of dialogue Vance often prefers more common words, those of sensation and action. His dialogues, with their swift-paced use of ellipses and often humorous bent, form a necessary contrast to the broad descriptive passages of his mature novels.

Much of Vance's readability stems from the rhythmic variety of his sentences. In scenes of flux or turmoil the syntax becomes crisp, lapidary — yet completely arhythmic. This is not necessarily remarkable, of course, but Vance usually manages a cadence unmistakably his own. He is fond of using verbs and adjectives in unadorned consecutive sequences. This sentence is a typical, if somewhat extreme, example in a purely descriptive vein:

The clouds of the early approaching evening storm gathered, rose, fell,

> shifted, swirled; glowing and changing in every tone of gold, orange-brown, gold-brown and dusty violet. (*The Dragon Masters*, III)

Similarly, many sentences are made up of a succession of short clauses, with the connectives eliminated to gain force. Here a paragraph ends abruptly — pungent, concise, with a Vancian twist:

> Vision retreated; hearing hummed, flagged, departed; time swam, spun... (*New Bodies for Old*, III)

He knows the value of a sudden change in vocabulary and rhythm, as the good writer is master of both the ample and the brief modes of expression. Vance's more recondite wording and languorous rhythms are reserved for descriptive scenes.

With deceptive ease he alternates scenic effects, narration, and dialogue in a smoothly welded panorama, infusing the whole with an actualizing impulse. As Vance wants to make every moment adventive and imperative, he rarely lapses into reveries of mere word painting; indeed, not a passage can be accused of the excessive flatulence of D. H. Lawrence rhapsodizing over a field of flowers. Purely descriptive passages are relatively short, sketched in with strong colors and scattered through the narrative texture in such a way that the story is never impeded. The reader always has a sense of continuous narrative superimposed over the depth of background. Here is an excellent example of Vance's ability to invest a passage with vividness:

> The cottage, the forest, the village were situated halfway up the face of a slope, vast beyond Earthly conception. Above, Glystra could see no sharp termination or ridge; the land melted into the pale blue distance. Below was a vista so grand and airy that after the first few miles the eye could sense only the spread of territory, meadows and forest becoming a green, blue, beige blur. (*Big Planet*, III)

His individuality is intrinsic to almost every line; the opening of "The Kokod Warriors," with its unusual construction and picturesque simile, is unmistakably Vancian:

Magnus Ridolph sat on the glass jetty at Providencia, fingering a quarti-quartino of Blue Ruin. At his back rose Grantee Head; before him spread Mille Lles Ocean and the myriad little islands, each with its trees and neo-classic villa. A magnificent blue sky extended overhead; and at his feet, under the glass floor of the jetty, lay Coral Canyon, with schools of sea-moths flashing and flickering like metal snowflakes.

Unlike certain writers with pronounced stylistic traits, such as Bradbury, it cannot be said that Vance's style is limited by a lack of internal contrast. The reader who is not partial to Bradbury is apt to weary of the continuous repetition of technical mannerisms. Vance avoids this pitfall by a judicious pacing of both syntax and event, at the same time maintaining a variegated congruity of mood.

Yet it is a dangerous style to imitate. It verges on that borderline where virtues may defect — the colorful become garish, the verdant become lush, the opulent become grandiose, the elegant become mannered. The utmost discipline is needed to keep its appointed course. That Vance is able to tread this "razor's edge" with hardly a slip points up an interesting anomaly in his makeup. We may quote Arthur Jean Cox's interesting article, "The Anatomy of Science Fiction" (*Inside*, June 1963): "What should be noted is that his intellect is abstract and formal; it would be bleak, except that he correctively emphasizes what is sensuous." And: "He sees history as a pattern, society as modes and styles of conduct, persons as social types." Cox apprehends the apparent contradiction in Vance's writing, but possibly errs in stating that his "intellect is abstract and formal." It is true that his plots reflect at times a rigorous formalization; this, however, is merely framework, and not indicative of temper. Vance does show a disinterested and analytically inclined literary bent, but this is a result of objectivity and his desire to let the story speak for itself, without commentary. What is sensuous, is so in the context of appealing to or being perceived by the senses, rather than in the connotation of being voluptuous or licentious. This combination of the "abstract" and "formal" with the "sensuous" serves to act as a check and balance, and the chasm of uncontrolled expression is thereby avoided.

Style is the image of character, and Cox would probably agree that humor, gaiety, and lightness of touch that interpenetrate even Vance's more somber novels (e.g., *To Live Forever*) could, no matter how regimented the structure, never be called bleak. The style is a result of a conscious and deliberate awareness which disguises the workings of the author's artistic objectivity even as it accomplishes his purpose of transforming the printed page into sentient experience.

In contrasting Vance's plots with his manner of presentation on a comparative basis, most readers would agree he is more successful in his handling of the latter. Here he shows a higher degree of consistency and judgment. Sometimes, as in "Parapsyche," he displays a less than firm articulation of theme, and at any rate it is unusual when theme is in advance of style (*The Languages of Pao* is an obvious exception). The reader may feel at times that the whole does not equal the sum of the parts, that the entire gamut of possibility has not been completely consummated, and that the sweep and swiftness of the style have deflected his awareness of the fact. Probably Vance's greatest weakness lies in the area of plot improbabilities or, more specifically, improbable events. Sometimes the threads of design are pulled into a pattern by incidents of a too-happy fortuitousness: the vitamin episode in *Big Planet* fails to convince, while the contrived close of "The King of Thieves" falls flat. Another occasional fault is the failure to unify all the thematic threads of a story: the abbreviated ending to "I-C-A-BEM" is unsatisfactory; the accumulated plot threads are left dangling in limbo as the story slams to its unexpected close. Perhaps in this novelette Vance's story-telling prowess is his own undoing. "I-C-A-BEM" is a semi-satire on the machinations of undercover government agents. At the end Vance proceeds to make a satiric point; the reader who has been intrigued would prefer the sacrifice of the point in order to continue the story — an instructive error in the dangers of worth. When, however, theme, structure, and delivery are in equal harmony, as in *To Live Forever* or "The Miracle Workers," the resultant product need defer to no one.

The plots of Vance's earlier novels tended to be mosaic in structure — that is, accretive rather than projective. They moved forward by the accumulation of incidents in sectional episodes, tied together by transitional interludes to form a unified whole. *Big Planet* and *The Dying Earth* are the best examples of this technique. There is a distinction between the episodic and the merely fragmentary; in these novels, as in Heinlein's excellent *Citizen of the Galaxy*, the episodic structure gives the sequences the compacted unity of a short story within the context of the larger design.

The profuse texture of Vance's novels is due to the accretion of material rather than any complexity in narration. Vance prefers, unlike van Vogt, straightforward development rather than multiple strands of action. He does not care to implement and heighten tension, as van Vogt does, in the third person. Van Vogt uses what may be called an antinarrative technique all his own, which operates by the resolution or partial resolution of eight hundred- to thousand-word sequences. The result gives the impression of breakneck speed and a sense of continuous anticipation — if the author's ingenuity is equal to the task of getting out of the cul-de-sac such an approach is likely to engender. (If not, calamitous anticlimax is the result). Using this technique, van Vogt has been noticeably successful — despite the fact that his characters often seem to be puppets on strings, set to quiver by the author's hand.

Vance prefers to work below the reader's conscious attention: sequences are resolved at least seemingly by the natural exigencies of the situation and by characters whose acts and viewpoints are reflected by their temperaments. This is not to say one method is superior to the other, merely that the views are distinctly opposed. Vance's qualities unfold to better advantage in a more naturalistic and leisurely exposition.

Unlike van Vogt's labyrinthine structures, Vance's plots are relatively simple, however much encrusted with subsidiary material incidental to the story line. Cox in his 1963 essay is very perceptive on this point: "He [Vance] keenly responds to the specifics of social form, the 'patterns of culture' as expressed in conduct, manners, styles of dress, housing, crafts, artifacts, etc. — of which he has sent up a pyrotechnic display over the past twenty years." It is this baroque verve and effusion in the conjuring of imaginative detail work that give the novels their interior resonance and continuity of impression. In *The Dying Earth*, *Big Planet*, and *To Live Forever*, Vance is brilliantly resourceful in evoking his fictional backgrounds, the imposed interplay of scene taking on a concrete reality of its own. In this quality he is supreme; "eclipse is first, and the rest nowhere." It is this quality that lends much of his fiction its evocative verisimilitude. Thomas Mann remarked, "Style is the accommodation to the subject." Vance, we feel, often reverses the process. The emancipation of detail work from the relative unimportance of background elaboration is a hallmark of Vance's style; no other writer in the field forges his settings so profusely and so carefully, and with such consistency of nomenclature. Poul Anderson states in a short sketch: "Here [*The Dying Earth*], as often elsewhere, Vance employs sheer word magic, haunting and absolutely right names, Ascolais, The Melantine Gulf, Kaiin, The Ide of Kauchique, the Land of the Falling Wall, Liane the Wayfarer, Turzan of Miir, the Spell of the Slow Hour...." The list could be multiplied endlessly. In this boundless inventiveness in the coining of proper names, Vance has succeeded in giving an emotional value and substance to his geography.

Imagination requires knowledge to control and order its outpouring into significant and meaningful forms. According to Anderson, Vance is a voracious reader, possesses a technical education, and has traveled extensively. This varied background manifests itself in a scattering of miscellaneous learning on a wide number of subjects. This knowledge, however, is in-

tegrated and subordinate, free from pedantic overtones; it or-
naments but does not obscure the structure.

It is difficult to assess influences on Vance's style. The individuality of the writing was apparent from the beginning, albeit
in somewhat crude form. Perhaps faint parallels can be drawn
to E. R. Eddison and Abraham Merritt. While Vance's prose
is, at times, nearly as euphonious as Eddison's, it is never as
ponderous and opaque. He is far more ingenious in varying the
mood and pace than Eddison, who tended to preserve a fixed
point of view in narration. A distinction may be made in that
Eddison's ornateness springs from the prose being superimposed
on the subject matter; with Vance the reverse is true. Eddison's
grandiose style would suffer unduly if anything trivial occurred
during the course of one of his novels. For Eddison's prose to
describe triviality would be like trying to pick up needles with a
bulldozer. Fortunately, nothing happens which drops below
the level of the colossal; in time, Eddison's prose suffers from
"the fatal lullaby of a majestic style."

With Merritt, there are again similarities, and again they
are more apparent than real. Vance lacks, except in isolated
instances, the grotesque elements that are the hallmark of
Merritt's novels. Merritt had great difficulty sustaining a narrative in conjunction with the uncanny atmosphere of his stories; often the exigencies of the narrative would intrude on the
prevailing mood. Vance is often more successful; in his best
work there is a balancing of qualities, one being a function of
the other. Aside from a mutual fondness for passages describing exotic shades of color and use of recondite wording, it is
less easy to relate Vance to Merritt than Eddison.

Those in the field who had a more definite impact on his
writing were, according to Vance himself, Olaf Stapledon,
Edgar Rice Burroughs, Robert W. Chambers, and, to a lesser
extent, James Branch Cabell and Robert E. Howard. Outside
the milieu, Robert Louis Stevenson, Percival Wren, Saki, P.
G. Wodehouse, and the picaresque romances of Jeffrey Farnol

were influential. Sometimes they acted as a springboard of ideas, Stapledon especially being a vast repository of notions. Occasionally plot germs were presented: *Big Planet* was suggested by one of Wren's short stories, in which deserters from the Foreign Legion, fleeing across the desert, die one by one.

In examining these influences I found very little that strikes a Vancian chord. However, Vance states that he also admires John Ruskin, "though this is hardly fiction." In Ruskin's *Modern Painters*, Volume II, we find the following paragraph describing a painting of Angelico:

> With what comparison shall we compare... the angel choirs of Angelico with the flames on their white foreheads waving brighter as they move, and the sparkles streaming from their purple wings like the glitter of many suns upon a sounding sea, listening in the pauses of alternate song, for the prolonging of the trumpet blast, and the answering of psaltery and cymbal, throughout the endless deep, and from all the star shores of heaven.

Needless to say, there is nothing resembling this passage in Vance's work; and yet we may sense in this fantastic embroidery the faintest echo of its imagery resonating into Vance's prose, chastened into plausibility. This is a passage written in the deepest purple of a synthetic dye, and as outdated in viewpoint as in style. (But what a potent brew it is!) It takes a combination of genius and mental imbalance to write this way consistently, and Ruskin was thus doubly equipped. At any rate, Vance may have found a diluted version of this heady mixture irresistible.

Vance's development was rapid: only seven years elapsed between the relative crudeness of his first professional appearance to the considerable achievement of *Big Planet*. There was no lengthy period of painful experimentation, as in the case of Bradbury. Vance found his tack almost immediately and after some initial hesitation developed it quickly to the limit of its possibilities.

Among mainstream writers, the prose of Lawrence Durrell (for whose *Alexandria Quartet* Vance professes admiration) presents points of contact. In fact, Henry Miller's description of Durrell's work is equally applicable to Vance when he speaks of "the big passages, the panoramic frescoes—his wonderful descriptive purple passages, majestically done, marvellously elaborate and intricate, which exist in and of themselves." Both are ornate, and both find a source of vitality in their own excesses.

II

It would be preferable, perhaps, to discuss a few of Vance's early novels in great detail; in sacrificing depth for range, comments are necessarily overgeneralized. The following works are chosen to provide a representative selection of the whole.

Vance's first published story, "The World-Thinker," appeared in the Summer 1945 issue of *Thrilling Wonder Stories*. Although comparatively crude by today's standards, it contains many of the elements that were to distinguish his later style. It was written while Vance was serving in the Merchant Marines during the closing phases of the war, after he had led a checkered life in the Pacific for some years. The plot is stock enough: the stealing of a dangerous invention and consequent pursuit. The chase ends on the planet of Laoome, the World-Thinker—an incredibly ancient being who has been exiled from his home planet, Narfilhet. Laoome possesses the power to create whole worlds, complete in every detail, in a different space-time continuum. A subsequent novel, *The Dying Earth*, is presaged in a scene where Laoome loses control over his creations. Millions of gelatinous red animals fall from the sky while black pylons rise thousands of feet into the air. To complete this fantastic phantasmagoria, the sun turns into a gigantic slug which crawls down from the sky to impale itself on the pylons.

Though much inferior to his later works, "The World-Thinker" is a much better story than other dolorous efforts published during this fallow period of the mid-1940s. One is inclined to classify it as fantasy rather than science fiction—a distinction sometimes difficult to make in Vance's work. Certainly it lacks finish and discipline but not, however, imagination; the faults were soon to be overcome.

For the next five years Vance's writings appeared with a fair degree of regularity. He established a following with his Magnus Ridolph series about an elderly detective who exploits the exploiters on an intergalactic scale. Ridolph, an engaging rogue, after a series of misadventures usually turns the tables on his foes—to his profit and the reader's amusement. The most overtly amusing of the series is "The Spa of the Stars," while "The Kokod Warriors" is perhaps the best by way of its fascinating delineation of Kokod's warrior race, as well as its fine descriptive passages:

> Below passed a wonderfully various landscape: lakes and parks, meadows, cliffs, crags, sweeping hillside slopes, river valleys. Here and there Ridolph sensed shapes in the fading light—the hivelike tumbles. As the evening deepened into dove-colored night, the tumbles flickered with dancing orange sparks of illumination.

During these years Vance's technique had expanded greatly. However, until 1949 he had not essayed anything longer than novelettes. In 1950 he threw off the garments of apprenticeship.

The history of *The Dying Earth* is curious. Appearing in 1950 in a paperback edition, it made little initial impression, probably due to the limited number of copies available, and dropped into obscurity. Discriminating readers of the first edition began to proclaim its quality; by 1956 it had become an eagerly sought-after collector's item, almost impossible to come by. Fortunately, in 1962 Lancer Books reprinted it as part of their "Limited Edition" series. It has since been reissued in paperback and hardcover.

Vance's efflorescence, latent in the short stories, finds its full achievement here. His work until *The Dying Earth* had been promising but somewhat dilatory; now, after five years of experience, he moved out onto a larger canvas with assurance. The novel is divided into six sections of approximately equal length. All take place in the same setting: the Earth of the fabulously distant future. The sun has become merely a glowing ember, and through the dim day and darker night strange creatures wander. Each section is complete in itself, although characters sometimes overlap without damage to sense.

This time there is, apparently, no doubt as to classification, as wizards and magic exist in abundance. This is a fantasy Farnsworth Wright would have delighted in during *Weird Tales'* balmy days. If there is a genesis to be traced, it is perhaps to Clark Ashton Smith's "Zothique" stories of the 1930s. The latter's prose, however, makes a direct impact upon his readers; Vance is less overt: there is a dreamlike quality about *The Dying Earth* that is not so much felt as sensed. Indeed, it is the most impressionistic of all his novels, and closer to Lord Dunsany than Smith in this respect. William Hope Hodgson's *The Night Land* perhaps provided impetus for *The Dying Earth*, at least as far as the initial setting. But any other resemblance ends there; Hodgson, who possessed an extraordinary imagination, chose to write in a style so eccentric and archaically affected that only the omnivorous and forbearing reader will see *The Night Land* through its considerable length.

In *The Dying Earth* we see for the first time on a large scale what is to become a Vancian characteristic: the incorporation of extraordinary amounts of small detail woven into a rich and translucently colorful fabric, conveying this remote vision with an implicit and enveloping ambience. We see that

> [t]he Derna is a swifter, thinner river than the Scaum, its bosomy sister to the south. And where the Scaum wallows through a broad dale, purple with horse-blossom, pocked white and grey with crumbling castles, the Derna has sheered a steep canyon, overhung by forested bluffs.

And we follow its course until

> [t]he Derna, no longer a flow of clear water, pours through a network of dark canals and subterranean tubes, and finally seeps past rotting wharves into the Bay of Sanreale. ("Liane the Wayfarer")

Or the view from above the marketplace of white-walled Kaiin, where rise

> a bank of ruined columns, like broken teeth — legs to the arena built two hundred feet above the ground by Mad King Shin; beyond, in a grove of trees, the glassy dome of the palace was visible where Kandive the Golden ruled Kaiin and as much of Ascolais as one could see from a vantage on Porphiron Scar. ("Liane the Wayfarer")

The prose of *The Dying Earth* is subtly formalized, faintly archaic, perfectly forged and designed to convey emotion rather than reality. In this paragraph describing the ancient Museum of Man, we see Vance's skill in investing a scene with an ordered complexity (showing, incidentally, his indebtedness to Ruskin in his description of St. Mark's).

> The light came from an unknown source, from the air itself, as if leaking from the discrete atoms; every breath was luminous, the room floated full of invigorating glow. A great rug pelted the floor, a monster tabard woven of gold, brown, bronze, two tones of green, fuscous red and smalt blue. Beautiful works of human fashioning ranked the walls. In glorious array hung panels of rich woods, carved, chased, enamelled; scenes of olden times painted on woven fiber; formulas of color, designed to convey emotion rather than reality. To one side hung plats of wood laid on with slabs of soapstone, malachite and jade in rectangular patterns, richly varied and subtle, with miniature flecks of cinnabar, rhodochrosite and coral for warmth. Beside was a section given to disks of luminous green, flickering and fluorescent with varying blue films and moving dots of scarlet and black. Here were representations of three hundred marvelous flowers, blooms of a forgotten age, no longer extant on waning Earth; there were as many star-burst patterns, rigidly conventionalized in form, but each of subtle distinction. All these and a multitude of other creations, selected from the best human fervor. ("Guyal of Sfere")

The Ruskin "influence" has since (perhaps regrettably) diminished considerably.

During 1950, with "The Five Gold Bands" and "New Bodies for Old," Vance asserted his new-found mastery, albeit on a lesser level and scale. The first of these is an interstellar adventure novel. Sam Langtry, discoverer of space drive, has nepotically left the secret of it to his five sons. Each of the sons has cultivated a planet of his own, and succeeding Langtrys have mutated to accommodate the conditions of their particular environment. After thirty-four generations, the mutated stock of the original Langtry's sons bear only superficial resemblance to an Earthman; moreover, they still possess control of the space drive from which Earth has been excluded. The plot revolves around the attempts of Paddy Blackthorn and Fay Bursill to wrest the secret away from the monopolistic controls of the Langtry worlds. Paddy and Fay are not the cardboard stereotypes so endemic to early science fiction; they come to life for the reader and enliven the story by the strength of their personalities. This is a novel of the type *Startling* specialized in — particularly in its comic overtones, only done with even more élan and verve than others could muster (exempt Fredric Brown's classic *What Mad Universe* from this judgment). With its swift pace, humorous embellishments, and emphasis on an adventure idiom, "The Five Gold Bands" is the forerunner of the direction Vance was to take for the next four years.

"New Bodies for Old" is perhaps a more original conception. An organization has perfected a method of transferring memory from one brain to another; an old man may become young simply by having his memory transferred to another body. Unfortunately, the young victim is then trapped in the body of its former tenant. Roland Mario is thus ensnared and the plot turns on his struggle to regain his body. Vance, as usual, manages a fascinating bit of detail work with the Empyrean Tower, a gigantic pylon three miles high, built for the jaded amusement of one who has lived through fourteen different bodies. The novelette ends, as does the later *Big Planet*, on a sardonically ironic note.

"Son of the Tree" is a prelude to that vaster conception, *Big Planet*. Here is the ancient Druid religion of tree-worship transferred to a remote region of the galaxy. Kyril, planet of the Druids, is engaged in a power struggle with its traditional rivals, the Mangs. Both wish an alliance with Ballenkarch, which would tip the balance of power in their favor. The Druids attempt to transfer their religious sentiments by planting the only living shoot from Kyril's tree, a colossal growth miles high, whereby two million Druids enslave a laity of five billion peasants with a promise of arboreal immortality, on Ballenkarch. The protagonist, Joe Smith, is drawn against his will into the whirl of political machinations, treading a dangerous course between opposing factions. This novel possesses some of Vance's most memorable characters: the Druid priestess Elfane, stubborn, willful, haughty, intent on propagating her religion—in other words, a delightful vixen; Manaolo, Elfane's indefatigable suitor, with his upsurging egotism; an old woman with a great jewel on each finger, who lives on human blood; the yellow-skinned, orange-tongued Mangs; the mothlike Cils; the Belands, who wear a coat of paint for clothes; and, above all, the Bluewater Hableyat, a venerable Machiavelli arcanely plotting his objectives behind the scenes.

The next pair of stories, "Abercrombie Station" and "Cholwell's Chickens," is notable for the engaging predator of a heroine, Jean Parlier. Jean, who could give Ralph Waldo Emerson lessons in self-reliance, is one of Vance's most vivid personalities. Equally intriguing is Vance's idea of an earth satellite for fat men—free from the pull of gravity. The inhabitants of the station have developed to a state of grossness impossible on Earth: at the station what should be a mass of sagging tissue expands into a globular pink ball of flesh. Naturally, the inhabitants of the station are reluctant to leave their comfortable surroundings, with the result that, after a generation, exaggerated corpulence is the prevailing order of fashion. Poor Earl Abercrombie, the eighteen-year-old heir to the station, is something of an anachronism, being merely stout of build. Since he is something of a freak, Earl has developed some shuddersome inclinations to compensate his frustrations. He is a student of teratology and cavorts with freaks he keeps in a state of suspended animation. The chilling mercenary Jean is hired to marry Earl; the expected difficulties ensue and the story ends on a notably gruesome note, for Vance, as the freaks escape to wreak havoc on the station. Fortunately, Jean escapes destruction and returns in a sequel, "Cholwell's Chickens." This story of eight Jean Parliers is as wild as its predecessor, no small accomplishment.

Vance's reputation had been growing steadily, but no major work of his appeared in *Astounding* (later *Analog*) until 1952. This was *Telek*, which concerns itself with the effect on the mass population of a small minority group possessing the power of telekinesis. Such a theme seems tailor-made for *Astounding*; yet editor John W. Campbell had some doubts whether the story was science fiction or fantasy. Despite his trepidation, the reader poll picked *Telek* overwhelmingly as the best story in the issue.

With *Big Planet* (1952), we come to Vance's favorite kind of story. *Big Planet*, with its vast landscapes, teeming oceans, sky-piercing mountains, variety of customs and admixture of seemingly irreconcilable contradictions, seems to excite in Vance's mind the most intense empathy. In general, writers gravitate to the kind of thing they do best. *Big Planet* is the natural culmination of his creative efforts to that date. The stories written afterward, heralded by *Telek*, begin a new period.

Big Planet is a huge low-gravity world that functions as a refuge for various persecuted groups from Earth. Settling on Big Planet, where there is endless room for expansion, they have evolved into heterogeneous groups that have developed in wildly improbable ways. But now a leader has arisen, the Bajarnum of Beaujolais, who is attempting to unify these unallied throngs. Claude Glystra and a group of experts are sent from Earth to investigate these proceedings. The ship is sabotaged and crashes on Big Planet. Glystra and his fellows begin the forty-thousand-mile hike to Earth Enclave on foot. The reader is presented with a vivid succession of scenes as they wend their way through

Tsalambar Woods, Nomadland, past Edelweiss, the river Oust, Swamp Island, down the monoline through the Hiberian March, Kirstendale, along Lake Pellitante, across the desert toward Myrtilesee Fountain. (XIX)

The vast panorama of the Big Planet landscape spreads out before the reader in a vivid succession of images. Here Vance succeeds in creating an impression of reality in depth: that beyond the characters and vistas observed directly, the reader's awareness spans beyond the horizons of recorded fact to the creation and actualizing of further possibilities. We feel the pulse and ferment of Big Planet life portrayed in prose whose amplitude and richness are so congenial to its display. The animation of the imagination renders the reader's engagement complete. In these aspects Vance recalls Robert E. Howard's Hyborean Age and Eddison's colossal literary tapestries.

One is rarely overtly aware of the skill with which Vance keeps his scenes and characters progressing, so freshly is the narrative implemented and endowed with a fluid and continuous flow. And who but Vance would think of the incredible (but workable) economic and social structure of Kirstendale, or this sort of incidental touch:

> During the afternoon Sir Walden took them to what he called a "pressing." It proved to be a ceremonial squeezing of essence from a vat of flower petals.... The children bore tiny cups through the crowd, each containing a few drops of essence. Sir Walden said, "Bring your tongue almost to the liquid, but do not quite taste it."
>
> Glystra bent his head, followed the instructions. A wave of pungent fragrance swept through his throat, his nose, his entire head. His eyes swam, his head reeled, momentarily dizzy in a kind of floral ecstasy.
>
> "Exquisite," he gasped when he was able to speak.
>
> Sir Walden nodded. "That was the Baie-Jolie press. Next will be a heavy Purple Woodmint, then a Marine Garden, then a Rose Thyme, and last my favorite, the fascinating Meadow Harvest Sachet." (XII)

Big Planet may lack the substrata of underlying cogency and intellectual control which distinguish *To Live Forever* or "The Miracle Workers," but taken on its own terms — and a good novel needs no other — it sets the highest standard in a purely entertainment vein.

It is the nadir of Vance's misfortunes that one of his best works should have been published in the issue of *Startling Stories* following Philip José Farmer's "The Lovers." That story was a tremendous tour de force and stirred reader controversy that continued unabated for a year. Reaction to *Big Planet* was blunted (need I say unjustly) in the hubbub; but after this unfortunate beginning, *Big Planet* is now recognized as a classic in the field.

Strangely, it is immediately after the publication of *Big Planet* that we come to Vance's potboiler. *Vandals of the Void* was written as part of Winston's Juvenile series. The opening paragraph is Vancian in tone, but he is scarcely recognizable elsewhere. One receives the impression that the novel is scaled down for younger readers. It is nowhere even remotely approachable to the least of Robert A. Heinlein's superb series for Scribner's.

"Brain of the Galaxy," from the same period, is a better example of Vance's skill in the shorter lengths. There have been numerous science fiction stories with fish hooks embedded in the opening (Henry Kuttner's "The Fairy Chessmen" is a notable example), but Vance is not satisfied with just one. The story opens with five episodes, utterly unconnected with one another. Arthur Caversham of 22nd-century Boston finds himself without clothes at a coming-out party; Bearwald the Halforn fights the unhuman Brands from Mount Medallion; Ceistan searches the dead city of Therlatch for the lost crown and Shield Parchment and is tempted by a maiden; Dobnor Daksat competes with the master dream-makers at the imagicon; Ergan the trader undergoes the treatment of the Rac Torturers.

At this juncture the reader is as intrigued as he is mystified. Vance provides a perfectly logical answer to unify these episodes. The sequences are hypnotic dreams experienced by candidates for the post of Galactic Prime. Since in the dreams only basic attitudes manifest themselves, each episode provides an accurate qualitative test of the individual's ability to react to situations contrived to test varying aspects of character and ability. The five separate parts of the opening detail the reactions of the present Galactic Prime, who is competing against candidates from the entire galaxy. The Prime's score is the highest registered, yet renewal of his position is denied him by a typically Vancian twist of irony.

This excellent story contains one of Vance's happiest inspirations in the fourth of the opening sequences. The imagicon is a huge amphitheater, within which are six forty-foot screens. By a device, the competitors are able to project their mental visualizations onto the screens. Dobnor Daksat competes with the master dream-makers of the galaxy; each player in turn conjures up an image which he can alter at will. Pulakt Havjorska begins with a green jewel dripping a rain of blue and silver drops which strike a black ground and disappear in little orange explosions. Ghisel Ghang imagines a complex kaleidoscopic pattern which vanishes and reappears in a complete new suit of colors. As the composition goes on, the visualizations become longer and more complex until the master dreams are reached: the growth and decay of a beautiful city; the creation of a multiple series of fire bursts; the reactions of a marble statue brought to life. The imagicon is such an original conception that one wishes Vance would incorporate it in another story.

"Dodkin's Job" and "Ullward's Retreat" are short stories of a different bent. The first is an ebullient satire on the ultra-organized society. Luke Grogatch, formerly of high station, has descended to the ignominious position of Flunky/Class D/Unskilled. From his present job as nightshift swamper at the Sewer Maintenance Department, he gloomily contemplates the last two rungs his descent may bring him — confess nonconformity and be shuffled off to the Disorganized House, or become a Junior Executive. Shudderingly rejecting these dolorous alternatives, Luke daydreams of a more sumptuous life: "AAA nutrition, a suite of rooms for his exclusive use, Special Coupons by the bale," and, best of all, "Class 7 Erotic Processing, or even Class 6, or 5." But Luke's captious, sarcastic and out-spoken temper bar admittance to such grandeurs—unques-tioning obedience is the order of the day. An order to the effect that he must check his shovel at the Sewer Maintenance Ware-house, perhaps taking precious hours away from his Class 12 Erotic Processing, bursts the bonds of Luke's not-too-firmly wrought patience. Tenaciously he ascends from echelon to higher echelon, from sinecure to sinecure, in hopes of reversing such inconveniences to Luke Grogatch. (Luke thinks of himself in the third person as a way of objectifying his misfortunes.) When Luke finally reaches the topmost peak of the monster organization, a devastating surprise awaits him and the reader. Vance's satire in this story is much nearer the surface than in *I-C-A-BEM*, providing a much closer coincidence between aims and effect. Here his tongue-in-cheek laughter can be heard throughout.

"Ullward's Retreat" is a variation on the theme provided by "Dodkin's Job," with the difference that society's woes are here intrinsic rather than imposed. Here, however, the play of Vancian irony is lighter. The population of Earth has increased stupendously; mere space in which to exist has become a mass sought-after fetish. Bruham Ullward, who prior to acquiring his wealth through digestive pastilles lived out of a locker, takes great pleasure in showing his friend his elegant and, above all, spacious apartment. This is equipped with expensive sets of vi-sion panels which provide the illusion of miles of space in a small area, a necessary adjunct to measure status and ease the claustrophobia-minded. Ullward's whole existence centers around his retreat, a sort of definition of ego by possession. Ullward, in J. M. Keyne's words, "is rooted in nothing; he is void and without content; he lives and feeds on his immediate surroundings; he is an instrument and a player at the same time which plays on the company and is played on by them too." To increase the admiration of his guests, Ullward decides to de-plete one-half of his fortune by purchasing the partial rights to a planet. Here, in unlimited space, he makes hectic plans for his first brace of guests. These, however, find conditions not so salubrious or so naturalistic as that provided by the vision panels, and scuttle back to Earth at the first opportunity. Ullward, discontented with solitary approbation, follows and the story ends, predictably, as Ullward welcomes friends to his elegant apartment.

With the demise of *Startling Stories* and its companions in 1955, Vance found his main market of publication ended. Editor Samuel Mines and his predecessor Sam Merwin had been among the last standard-bearers of the "story-for-its-own-sake" school, in contrast to the sometime involute cerebration advocated by John W. Campbell and *Astounding/Analog*. Vance had been one of the leading writers for Mines, but, sensing the trend, he had since incorporated elements of social and scientific extrapolation into his work.

"Gift of Gab" poses an interesting problem: how to communicate with an alien race that has never developed a language. The Dekabrachs are an intelligent race of sea-creatures whose mass empathy has obviated the need for direct communication. The plot hinges on the Earthman's need to make contact with a captured Dekabrach. Vance solves the problem with consummate ingenuity.

With *To Live Forever* (1956), we come to the most brilliant and important of Vance's early works. In ingenuity of plot and mastery of prose, it is probably the quintessential assertion of sheer individuality among his novels of this period. Unlike some of his lesser works—"Parapsyche," for instance—here his technique keeps pace with his imagination, producing a novel that both grips the emotions and fascinates the intellect.

The scene is set on the Earth of the distant future, which has been riven by the Malthusian Chaos. The remnants of humanity live in Clarges, "the last metropolis of the world." Beyond Clarges, Kypre, Sous-Ventre, the Gondwanese Empire, Singhalien, Nova Roma, retain a semblance of civilized if barbaric order within their boundaries. Clarges, though, has not only regained the lost knowledge of the past but progressed far beyond it. A system of achieving immortality has been developed, and, because population must be limited to available space, only those who earn it through achievement can obtain the prize. A giant brain called the Acturian records and judges the achievements of the individual. The population is divided into five groups, called phyle: Brood, whose lifespan is calibrated at eighty-two years; Wedge, which adds ten more; Arrant, or Third, gives another sixteen; and Verge, which adds twenty years. Finally, the ultimate reward: Amaranth—immortality. The rate of progress through phyle is called slope. Those winning through to Amaranth cannot even be killed through accidental physical injury; each has a set of duplicate surrogates, each one empathized to the individual Amaranth. If he is killed, one of the surrogates takes his place, equipped with an identical body and identical memories. Then there are the Glarks, who take no part in the competition.

Grayven Warlock, once of the Amaranth Society, has been convicted of murder—the supreme crime in Clarges' social order. He escapes but is assumed dead. Warlock develops a scheme to reappear as one of his own surrogates, but seven years must pass before he can be classed as legally dead. In the interim he works at Carnevale, a safety valve for those who seek relief from the race for slope. Before the allotted time passes, his deception is discovered by the Jacynth Martin, an Amaranth. Warlock kills her, but when the surrogate is activated it vows vengeance on Warlock. Warlock's struggle to gain his lost position and his conflict with the Jacynth form the surface basis of the plot.

This novel is, even for Vance, extremely elaborate and embroidered; hardly any detail is touched on without an embellishmental flourish. Here the full Vancian orchestra is displayed in a way that exhibits his baroque tendencies at their apogee. The society of Clarges is dealt with in all its complex manifestations, including such typical Vancian touches as the Aquefacts of Reinhold Biebursson, and the pantomimes of The Anastasia de Fancourt. The life of Clarges is continually reflected in chains of relationship; Carnevale and the palliatories are the polar end products of the "pull of opposing emotions." In these incidental touches as well as in his copious and never-failing felicity of descriptive phrases, Vance lights the interior life of Clarges to a degree that, by comparison, the backgrounds of many other writers present only the merest adumbration.

In Vance's novels of pure entertainment the interest lies in the surface of the narrative; *To Live Forever* has a subsidiary focus of interest which, instead of being dispersed two-dimensionally, is locked and concentrated into an essential unity by adding a third dimension through a symbolic presentation. Warlock is the sublimation of discontent, the product of the synthetic social system, both pinnacle and end. From Amaranth he is thrust into the social malaise and dilemma of the lower phyle with all their unendurable tensions and strains. He must rise again; the system is never questioned. Vance gives us a hint in the naming of his lead character: first "Warlock" (a traitor to his order; a deceiver; a monster), then "Waylock," which delineates his situation to a nicety. Warlock's problem is ineluctable; his symbolic dilemma is that of all Clarges. He is held up as a traitor and monster by others, when he is really the refined essence of themselves. At the end, Warlock breaks the power of the Acturian; the population, robbed of life, rushes forward to kill the traitor; Basil Thinkoup, purveyor of sane morality, calling out for order and calm, is crushed.

Perhaps this ending needs to be more fully explicated; the closing pages in particular are, in P. Schuyler Miller's view, "controversial." Yet this is quite in keeping with Vance's tendency not to come around full circle, but to leave something unsaid on the verge of accomplishment. We see the same distaste for ending on the tonic, so to speak, in *Telek* and "Gift of Gab." What undermines these pages slightly is that Waylock's dilemma is enlarged to encompass all of Clarges. Warlock's drive, energy, and personality have colored and given thrust and momentum to the essential theme; to have it removed at the very climax for the impersonal face of the mob lessens the total effect. As so often happens, an enlargement of perspective entails a scene viewed at a great distance. Yet it is hard to see how the difficulty was to be avoided, and certainly it does not retroactively affect the novel as a whole.

In form, texture, and manner, *To Live Forever* is far removed from *Big Planet*; it is remarkable that Vance can vary his style so markedly and still retain for the reader a sense of unmistakable identity. This applies in manifest ways. The emotional and atmospheric coloring of *To Live Forever* is painted with a palette of more somber and subdued hues, but more subtly shaded and richly various in its finely judged gradations of nuance; the prose is closer textured and of greater weight and density than that which so successfully illuminates the sunlit vistas of *Big Planet*. This perhaps is not due so much to deliberate technical manipulations as the good writer's intuitive adaptation to the requirements of his creation. The special quality and atmosphere of Clarges, and indeed the whole novel, is caught wonderfully in the opening paragraphs:

> Clarges, the last metropolis of the world, stretched thirty miles along the north shore of the Chant River, not far above the broadening of the Chant into its estuary.
>
> Clarges was an ancient city; structures, monuments, manors, old taverns, docks and warehouses two or even three thousand years old were common. The citizens of the Reach cherished these links with the past, drawing from them an unconscious comfort, a mystical sense of identification with the continuity of the city. The unique variation of the free-enterprise system by which they lived, however, urged them to innovation; as a result Clarges was a curious medley of the hoary and the novel, and the citizens — in this as in other ways — suffered the pull of opposing emotions.
>
> There never had been such a city as Clarges for grandeur and somber beauty. From the Mercery rose towers like tourmaline crystals, tall enough to intercept passing clouds; surrounding were great shops, theaters and apartment blocks; then came the suburbs, the industrial purlieus, the nondescript backlands extending out past the range of vision. The best

residential areas — Balliasse, Eardiston, Vandoon, Temple Cloud — occupied hillsides north and south overlooking the river. Everywhere was motion, the quiver of vitality, the sense of human effort. A million windows flickered in the sunlight, vehicles darkened the boulevards, shoals of aircraft meshed along the avenues of the air. Men and women walked briskly along the streets to their destinations, wasting no time.

Structurally it is undoubtedly the more difficult work because of the necessity of rendering the complex interrelated texture of Clarges as opposed to the rhapsodic movement needed to convey the mélange of Big Planet. Yet the framework on which the web of ideas is erected is firm and convincing; content and style fuse to present this tenebrous vision before the reader. It maintains a midcourse between the naturalism of *Big Planet* and the deliberate artificiality of *The Dying Earth*. In the stories written since, Vance has ranged on both sides, harking back to *The Dying Earth* in *The Dragon Masters* and the idiom, with variations, of his adventure stories of the early fifties in *Star King*.

Semantics, philology, and their effect on basic psychological attitudes are the conceptual core for Vance's next novel, *The Languages of Pao* (1957). Unlike A. E. van Vogt's *The World of Null-A*, its introduction into plot is functional rather than decorative. The idea that the structure of a language is the determining factor in individual and collective motivation is quite an original basis for a science fiction story. "The Paonese sentence did not so much describe an act as it presented a picture of a situation.... There were no verbs, no adjectives; no formal word comparison such as *good, better, best*." As a result of the peculiarities of their language, the Paonese are an extremely homogeneous population; every person thinks, acts, and talks very much like every other. When a new language is introduced, the Paonese reverse their previous attitudes and become a vigorous, progressive race. The original Pao is the antithesis of Big Planet; and therein lies part of its weakness. The Paonese by their very nature are incurably dull; their conversation helps to enliven proceedings a bit.

Vance's prose, usually so facile, is strangely ineffective here, its normally bright colors diluted into gray halftones. Moreover, the originality of the plot is not consummated by inner detail work; thus, Pao never achieves the vibrancy of Clarges or Big Planet; his powers of invention are operating on a considerably lesser level. Despite the depressed level of description, much of the dialogue is delightful, with its multiple connotations and formalized complexity. Perhaps a surfeit of third-person writing accounts for the lack of immediacy and intensity here; as a result, the story suffers from static periods. S. E. Cotts calls the book "disappointing in view of the excellence of some of the underlying ideas"; P. Schuyler Miller takes a more enthusiastic view. While there can be no doubt that this is second-order Vance, the novel will retain reader interest for the originality of its conceptions.

"Parapsyche" (1958) is the novel furthest removed from the main sequence of Vance's development. It shows that, with him, content and style are not inseparably fused, for his usual identifying touches are almost completely absent. The novel could have been written by nearly any competent writer of that period. How strange to censure a Vance story for lack of style! Perhaps a more conventional mode was chosen because of the contemporary Earthbound setting.

If the style is conventional, the thematic material is the reverse. It expounds a theory that parapsychological phenomena are manifestations of the collective unconscious and that there are nonmetaphysical reasons for such happenings. There are all sorts of objections that could be made to these ideas; Vance, however, makes clear that he advances them in a purely speculative manner. In a preface to the novel he notes, "Captious readers may raise their eyebrows at the last few pages. Even the author's credulity is strained." If the author is not entirely convinced, the reader is hardly likely to be more sympathetic. In fact, the controversial nature of the plot is not helped by thin characterization, sometimes vapid dialogue, and tenuous binding up of plot threads—which tend to fray out distressingly.

As a final blow to reader credulity, the main character is resurrected, after being assumed dead, with no explanation at all — this in the best Hollywood tradition of the happy ending. As another indication of Vance's seeming lack of interest, the last sentence echoes the final one of *To Live Forever* with amazing fidelity.

The novel borders very close to fantasy in its freewheeling conjecture. Yet while not exhibiting the characteristic Vancian touches, it retains, at least, the clarity of his better works. And this is perhaps the reason why Vance's style is not suited, despite his success in *The Dying Earth*, to fantasy; a more ambiguous, less clearly defined prose than his would make a better impression in "Parapsyche." There is nothing in Vance's output to compare with the opening pages of Fritz Leiber's *Destiny Times Three*, to choose an example whose atmospheric tenor would have better suited "Parapsyche," where unseen forces are impalpably felt lurking on the consciousness, caught in flashes of light and sensed in darkness; nothing comparable to the peculiarly distorted and feverish air of shadowy twilight through which Leiber's characters move, like those in a dream, their thoughts strangely gaped and distorted. The opening of *Destiny Times Three* ("in ghastly, shivering streamers of green and blue, like northern lights, the closing hues of the fourth Hoderson symchromy called 'the Yggdrasil,' shuddered down toward visual silence") is very Vancian in idea and superficial manner, yet so very different in tone and effect, as if to indicate the variousness of language. Leiber makes these effects by a sort of tonal uncertainty, producing tensions extremely delicate and provocative, providing a sort of sensory framework which sustains and heightens the mystery of the opening. Vance does not display at any time an inclination for these types of effects. The novels seldom make use of impressionistic modes — no imperceptible mergings. Instead, practically all atmospheric effects, like all coloristic, are thrown into high relief by the diffusion of light and shade in sharply differentiated chiaroscuro. "Parapsyche" perhaps calls for the Leiber approach. It must be admitted that, in comparison to *Destiny Times Three*, "Parapsyche" seems somewhat pedestrian. It is apt to provoke strongly ambivalent views among readers; yet in assessing its value in comparison to other of Vance's novels, it must be reckoned near the bottom.

With "The Miracle Workers" (1958), Vance made his last appearance to date in *Astounding/Analog*. To read this short novel after "Parapsyche" is to graduate to an altogether higher level of achievement, for if maintaining and reflecting theme and narrative in sustained unanimity, and combining interesting characterization with ingenuity of plot are essential, this may be reckoned his best effort. It may not reach the heights of *To Live Forever* in profusion of detail or richness of language, but in unity and sureness of procedure it is superior. Vance's novels tend to vary in worth considerably, not only comparatively, but internally within themselves. In "The Miracle Workers" he opens confidently and maintains a high level of quality throughout.

Like the later *The Dragon Masters*, the story deals with the evolution of Earthmen stranded in a remote region of the galaxy (and it is no reflection on that Hugo award-winning story to state that "The Miracle Workers" is the better of the two). The Earthmen inhabitants of Pangborn through the generations have lost all technical knowledge of their precursors; much equipment from past ages is operative, but the knowledge of repair and upkeep has been lost in the mists of time. Instead of a society based on empirical scientific procedures, the Earthmen have degenerated into small warring city-states aided by jinxmen, cabalmen, and spellbinders. As the story opens, Lord Faide, master of Faide Keep, is carrying out his imperialistic designs against the rival Keep of Lord Ballant. Instead of sieges and catapults, the invasion is made by Faide's head jinxman, Hein Huss, aided by apprentices who telepathically enter the minds of the enemy warriors, inducing various unpleasant physical sensations. Once contact has been established, the men of

Ballant Keep, made susceptible by generations of fear and conviction, are at the mercy of Hein Huss, unless their own jinxman
is capable of countering the "hoodoo." This, Anderson Grimes,
the Ballant jinxman, fails to do. Returning from his successful
conquest, Lord Faide is attacked by the original inhabitants of
Pangborn, the First Folk. Ignominiously defeated, he returns
to Faide Keep to nourish revengeful plots. Since the First Folk
know nothing of jinxmanship, which is actually self-induced,
they cannot be hoodooed. How the supposedly bumbling Sam
Salazar defeats the attack of the First Folk by a return to the
"mystical" methods of the ancients is the axis of the story.

"The Miracle Workers" is a study of, as is *Telek*, the completely divergent paths which an isolated society may take if a
small group is invested with extraordinary powers. In both
cases, society readjusts and centers itself around the empow-
ered few. In both instances, the majority retrogresses as competition is superfluous in light of the unattainable. In *Telek*, the
obvious solution is attained; either all Teleks must be eliminated, or all must become Teleks. But in "The Miracle Workers"
the jinxmen are adjuncts to the Keep masters; however, the entire social system is based on their powers, without which it
would collapse. Why the jinxmen have not caballed against
their masters, setting up a dictatorial system of their own as
the Teleks did, is obvious, since successful jinxmanship is a
form of self-hypnosis which requires a constantly replenished
environment as a basis for its operation. Without the jinxmen,
the society as a matter of course would return to empirical procedures. One only has to turn to ancient (and not too ancient)
India and China to see how, once accustomed and ordained
thinking becomes thoroughly entrenched, it acts as a self-
inhibiting factor. "The Miracle Workers" demonstrates how
purely imaginary chains can be used to bind a susceptible pop-
ulace. Each of the great jinxmen has possession of a demon,
not in actuality, but in accepted belief — and what is not disputed soon becomes fact. The jinxmen can mesmerize men in-

to seeing the image of a demon to breed fear and terror or they can induce into the warriors the characteristics of differing demons. Thus Anderson Grimes' Everid is "a force absolutely brutal and blunt, terrifying in its indomitable vigor"; Isak Comandore's Keyrill is instinct with crafty malice; the Dant of Hein Huss is swift and agile — all, though, are singularly horrible in their physical manifestations. When warriors are "demon possessed," they take on the attributes of the demon in question.

One aspect in which this story is superior to *The Dragon Masters* is in its more interesting characterization: the dyspeptic Lord Faide, his dreams of conquest dissolved by their very success; the phlegmatic Hein Huss, who finds the summit of achievement a similar cul-de-sac, and who acts as a foil to the waspish Isak Comandore, nourishing his ambitions in what he cannot see is a crumbling order of existence, completely self-deceiving in the acceptance of his own illusion; and supposedly bumbling, inept Sam Salazar, endowed with pawky humor and intransigent perseverance, undermining the whole structure of belief. These characters are sharply sketched and monolithic in their outlook and simplicity. The story still takes precedence — hence a perspective somewhat withdrawn as compared to the work of the early fifties where the reader tended to become immersed in a character's point of view. Here Vance has made an obvious effort to simplify and chasten his style. The ostensible profusion and decoration of *To Live Forever* are almost completely eschewed. This normalization of method is made, perhaps, because of a wish for the plot line to stand out in clear lineaments, and not to be impeded or obfuscated by his penchant for arabesque-like digressions. Still, unlike "Parapsyche," Vance is recognizable in every paragraph. Here one feels he wrote, more than any other of his stories, in a way that completely satisfied him. "The Miracle Workers" retains the typical Vancian rhythms without the personal rhetoric. One's preference must probably be made on the basis of the individual equation. The point is dwelt on because the stories written since reflect a similarity of method which may be indicative of an equilibrium in the quest for mode which would balance and reconcile the best of his various styles without mannerism or repetition. One misses the glowing texture of *To Live Forever* and yet finds no source of disaffection or want in "The Miracle Workers." It is not in the least a transitional work, but a consummated achievement, and the average reader is apt to judge its personal eclecticism more satisfying.

That this is true is reflected by the readers' poll for that issue of *Astounding/Analog*, which easily put "The Miracle Workers" in first place. Since *Telek* also had garnered the palm, and "Gift of Gab" rated second behind Eric Frank Russell's excellent "Call Him Dead," it is difficult to understand why editor Campbell had not seen fit to publish more of Vance's work. It must be remembered, however, that in the past Campbell had always been more interested in pleasing himself than the reader (certainly an editor's prerogative, and in this case a fortunate one for science fiction, as it raised standards in the genre and adjusted readers' tastes to encompass a more serious view than before). The difficulty crops up over stories that were submitted which avoided the Campbellian restrictions of what constituted an *Astounding/Analog* story. A case in point is that virtually all of Ray Bradbury's stories of the period 1945-1950 were initially submitted to Campbell — and rejected. The wonder is not that they were turned down, but that Bradbury could suspect that Campbell would publish any of these stories, for one would have to look far before finding two people in the same endeavor with less in common than Ray Bradbury and John W. Campbell. But when Vance adjusted himself to accommodate Campbell's predilections, he wrote three excellent novelettes — so perhaps there is something to be said for writing an "*Astounding/Analog*" story.

It was in *Galaxy* in 1962 that *The Dragon Masters* appeared, which later won a Hugo award for Vance at the 1963 World

Convention—recognition long overdue. Like "The Miracle Workers," it deals with an isolated world, cut off from Earth in the outward expansion. Here, too, the remnants have banded together in small warring city-states.

Joaz Banbeck leads a progressive and scientifically regimented state at Banbeck Vale, while the "jocose and wrathful" Ervis Carcolo foments his imperialistic design from the euphemistically named Happy Valley. Before the coming of the Basics, unhuman aliens from space who periodically raid the vales for captives, the Carcolos had enjoyed a dominance over their neighbors. Their reign of power now interrupted, Carcolo plots to regain the former ascendancy of Happy Valley. Both sides are now aided by dragons—Juggers, Fiends, Blue Horrors, Long Horned Murderers, each bred from Basic captives into specialized species. A third factor is the native Sacerdotes, whose pacific creed forbids action even against the Basics, but who have designs of their own. "Beyond caution or dismay," Carcolo sends his men and dragons against Banbeck Vale in ventures foredoomed by his obstinacy and lack of foresight. Indeed, the character of Carcolo could easily be read as a satire on dictators. During his misadventures the Basics return, throwing the critical situation into chaos which resolves in Joaz Banbeck's favor.

P. Schuyler Miller called *The Dragon Masters* a grand, spellbinding job of imagination-stretching rather like *The Dying Earth* in tone. Despite many felicities it is not quite the equal of that story or its more obvious counterpart, "The Miracle Workers," which possesses more genuine Vancian élan as well as a plot which serves to unify the component elements into a more compact and related narrative. Nevertheless, the Hugo award was thoroughly justified.

Vance's first novel of the Demon Princes series, *Star King* (1963), is like a mature comment on his adventure stories of the early fifties. It is a pure entertainment, neither grinding axes nor propagating personal designs.

Kirth Gersen's family, excepting his grandfather, has been killed in a raid by Malagate the Woe, a Star King: a being approximately human physically but with a completely alien stock of motivations. Gersen has been trained by his grandfather in every form of physical and mental combat; living an ascetic life, his immediate purpose is the destruction of Malagate. Gersen obtains from Lugo Teehalt a filament detailing the location of a paradise-like planet. Gersen traces the filament to three administrators of Sea Province University, one of whom, under the circumstances, must be Malagate. But which of the three? With them Gersen embarks on a trip to the discovered planet, with the razor-edge problem of trapping Malagate into exposing himself.

This is an adventure novel with carryovers from Vance's detective writing. (The admixture proves as effective as in Asimov's *The Caves of Steel*.) What is interesting is the contrapuntal development of the narrative in conjunction with prefaces to the chapters. A. E. van Vogt in his Null-A novels headed the chapters with quotes from A. H. S. Korzybski's *Science and Sanity*, designed to give a tincture of scientific verisimilitude. These, however, were quite short. Vance went considerably farther in quoting at length from fictitious sources and, occasionally, extant ones like Spengler's *The Decline of the West*. Thus we have extensive quotes from such pseudo-bibliography as *Men of the Oikumen* by Jan Holberk Vaenz; *The Demon Princes* by Caril Corphen; some delightful hocus-pocus from *The Avatar's Apprentice* (in scroll from the Ninth Dimension); excerpts from popular magazines such as *Cosmopolia*; segments of speeches; some pithy aphorisms; and, finally, an amusing history on naming the planets of the Rigel Concourse.

The pros and cons of this interlinear commentary can be disputed. On the one hand, it provides a spotlight for throwing, from various angles, light on the multiple aspects of the society under study. Some of the prefaces are mere embellishment, without relation to the narrative proper; others are essential to a proper understanding of the plot. Some may feel that these interpolations serve to heighten tension by breaking up and delaying the flow, begetting a continual sense of expectancy; others may feel irritation. In *Star King* the practice is completely successful, not because of the method itself, but because of the intrinsic interest of the segments.

Vance supplies the readers with his usual panoply of bright characterizations: Hildemar Dasce, a Vancian villain *in excelsis*; Detteras, whose initial dialogue with Gersen is one of the high spots of the novel; and, above all, Pallis Atwrode. Vance has a particularly happy knack for drawing these distaff portraits. Pallis Atwrode is the last in a long line of engrossing women extending from Fay Bursill of "The Five Gold Bands" through Elfane, Nancy-Thilssa, the Jacynth Martin, and, if one is in a particularly robust mood, Jean Parlier. Perhaps it was ill-judged to group the novel's best scenes immediately adjacent; Pallis Atwrode's and Detteras' dialogues with Gersen, coming as they do in the middle, give the novel the impression of slumping to either side of these sequences. This, however, is more perspective than actuality. Vance shows a rather cavalier attitude toward Pallis, as he did toward Bishop and Pianza in *Big Planet*; she is permitted one extended scene and is then relegated to passivity—a regrettable circumstance. The novel, while on the whole not quite first-order Vance, certainly ranks high in the second rank. It shows a tendency toward the incorporation of the pure entertainment story with the "concernful" quality of the *Astounding/Analog* short novels, and which may very well mirror Vance's future direction.

III

Vance's preoccupation with stylistic procedures, exploration of subsidiary details as an integral theme, and dualism of effect between stories of pure entertainment and speculative analysis have not received the mention they deserve. Indeed, the 1963

Hugo award for *The Dragon Masters* was the first widespread measure of critical approbation expressed, although he had been producing work of similar quality for at least twelve years. To explain the reputation of other writers, whose nugatory nonsense has resulted in a gaseous overinflation of their worth, is inexplicably difficult. None of these miasmic wonders has, however, risen to a Hugo award — yet. There are a number of reasons for Vance's particularly unrecognized status. First, he has devoted his time between several types of fiction other than the speculative. This cuts down on the number of stories produced; compared with such copious writers as Edmund Hamilton, the late Henry Kuttner, or Andre Norton, his output is comparatively small. Second, he has a somewhat reticent attitude toward science fiction as an organized movement. Writers like Isaac Asimov, L. Sprague de Camp and Robert Bloch have immeasurably increased their reputations by a continuous presence at various conventions. Vance is, apparently, not a coterie man.

Perhaps the primary reason, however, is that at least half of his output has been devoted to "entertainments." Arthur Jean Cox remarked in 1963 that "his stories do not involve fully enough what is uniquely science fictional. A single example may do: *Big Planet* is a memorable story, but the charm we find in it is not such as can be found only in science fiction. Vance's talent does not spontaneously express itself in that science fiction written by the more famous names. (There are two or three powerful exceptions: *Telek, To Live Forever* and, lately, *The Dragon Masters*.) However, he does have interests which can express themselves better in science fiction than elsewhere, which is why he is attracted to it; but they are not at dead center."

It is true Vance does not write "rock-bottom" science fiction, and I doubt that those who do care to have attention called to it. At any rate, the critics of the mainstream seem to be more indulgent. The arrows of pretense do not seem to have been directed at Graham Greene, whose works show a similar dualism between entertainments and his more serious political and social tracts; and even the latter are often written in the idiom of the adventure story. The preoccupation with "concernfulness" has been carried to extremes, perhaps because of a growing recognition on the part of mainstream oracles to what Cox calls a "sub-literary genus," and a consequent overzealousness on the part of adherents to conform to what they may consider "meaningful." Certainly it is true that *Big Planet* does not involve any intellectual or psychological concerns, but surely a novel of such high entertainment value should not be subjected to such ambiguous and arbitrary valuation. It, like every good novel, determines its own justification—and needs no other. Yet it cannot be denied that *To Live Forever* and "The Miracle Workers," with all their beautifully realized integrations of ideas and balance between entertainment and dexterity of intellect, satisfy more nearly those elements who would escalate science fiction in general esteem. Still, I think the story of "entertainment" is more than a mere anodyne; and it seems that Thomas Mann, whose *The Magic Mountain* is perhaps the supreme example of the pedagogical novel, agrees: he writes in an afterword to the American edition of the book: "A work of art must not be a task or an effort; it must not be undertaken against one's will. It is meant to give pleasure, to entertain and enliven. If it does not have this effect on a reader, he must put it down and turn to something else." I hope this will ease the consciences of all those who may feel they are not suffering enough in their reading. It may be pointed out that two brilliantly successful novels such as Asimov's *The Caves of Steel* and Vance's *To Live Forever* only faintly engage any extant social situation. Yet the pedants will always boost them in preference to the same authors' entertainments because of the amount of speculative analysis which acts as a web to sustain the narrative. Among the saddest developments in science fiction are the recent novels of Robert A. Heinlein, who seems to have succumbed to a surfeit of laudatory reviews and has, in consequence, tried his hand at a sort of literary hybrid—the science-fiction–mainstream novel. In attempting a continuous parallelism between the two, Heinlein fails to combine the virtues of either and dilutes the possibilities of both in a middle course that finds all that is worst in each. We may hope for his return to what is "uniquely science fiction."

Vance is not likely to be at the mercy of these swings in taste. With him, form approximates ideas: that is, each story operates on the basis (to the degree it can) of an organic development of ideas, rather than (as in Heinlein's latest works) an external straitjacketing of ideas to preordained ends. This does not mean that writers should follow Vance's example, or, indeed, anyone's; it is by an accountable individualism rather than a timorous collectivism that the cause of science fiction will be enhanced. Excellence will accommodate many paths. But as a general principle, the initial ideas should act as a trellis to the unfolding narrative. Only in this way will ends and motivation coincide. Thus, reasoning will (if cause and effect are fairly rooted interiorly and do not look beyond the life portrayed) be subject to an easily discoverable causality. When a writer disregards this rule, for any of various reasons, he is liable to find himself in the position of A. E. van Vogt after Damon Knight's summary demolition of *The World of Null-A* in his book *In Search of Wonder*. The author's views ran rampant. Vance's fiction, despite the inimitable style, is essentially impersonal and fails to spotlight any personal idiosyncracies. Unencumbered by exterior motives, Vance is content to let his ideas obtain their own development and independent conclusions. Heinlein, on the other hand, has reached his conclusions prior to the beginning, and sets out to muster as much collaborative and supporting evidence as possible before the reader.

Because of the lack of intellectual substrata in his "entertainments," Vance occasionally has been accused of being overly light, but lightness is the quality opposed to clutter, circuitousness, and redundancy. There is an erroneous opinion that only the ponderous tracts of the mighty can have more than an ephemeral existence, or meaning. Yet the depth of a book is not determined solely by the ideas used as a point of departure, but depends largely upon the degree of perception and intensity with which characters, mood, and setting are rendered. So many of Aldous Huxley's highly sophisticated and intellectually discursive novels seem to lose their grip on the reader on being finished; one recalls being highly stimulated, but is somewhat at a loss to say exactly why. There is no slowly fading afterglow of remembered mood as this passage of *Big Planet* evokes:

> Glystra walked down to the shore, to watch evening settle over the lake. Immense quiet enveloped the world, and the faint sounds from the camp only pointed up the stillness. The west was orange, green and grey; the east was washed in tenderest mauve. The wind had died completely. The lake lay flat, with a surface rich as milk.
>
> Glystra picked up a pebble, turned it over in his fingers. "Round pebble, quartz—piece of Big Planet, washed by Big Planet water, the water of Lake Pellitante, polished by the sands of the Big Planet shore...." He weighed it in his palm, half-minded to preserve it. All his life it would have the power to recreate for him this particular moment, when peace and solitude and strangeness surrounded him, with Big Planet night about to fall. (XIV)

Somehow, though, the "synthetic novel of ideas" manages to sustain a reputation longer than a thought.

When Vance or Hal Clement or Robert Heinlein at his best chooses to incorporate exterior schemes, it is done with complete fluidity, ideas and narrative intermingled in a balanced and continuous counterpoint. Only occasionally does Vance lapse, the last pages of *To Live Forever* being an instance where a theme is stated rather than implicit. But always he retains a detachment that allows an undistorted perspective.

To quote Poul Anderson: "In a period when so much science fiction is weary, flat, stale and unprofitable, the field needs his touch—needs color, imagination, originality, excitement and unobtrusively careful craftsmanship." Unfortunately, Vance's habit of dividing his time between various genres has diminished considerably what should have been exclusively science fiction's gain. Currently his energies are directed to the mystery field, in which he has had notable success; his novel, *The Man in the Cage* (1960), won the coveted Edgar Award of the Mystery Writers of America and was subsequently adapted for an hour-long television show. These mystery writing proclivities, though undoubtedly lucrative, are an obvious misalliance. His preeminent qualities seem to be almost tailor-made for science fiction and suffer in transposition to other media.

Vance's position in science fiction and fantasy remains secure because he will represent a rallying point when the days of cerebrality have worn themselves to a shadow. As there has been a swing away from the romanticism of Merwin and Mines to the sometimes austere intellectualism of Campbell, so in turn will the pendulum swing back again. This future romanticism will, however, be very different from that of the past and may well prove to be a happy combination of those opposed schools. Indeed, it may be already here. Vance in *To Live Forever* and "The Miracle Workers" provides an example of what may be done by treading a middle course. He remains, perhaps, the strongest advocate of the "story-for-its-own-sake" school, and yet, without undermining their structural balance, he has succeeded in incorporating serious themes in his work. If the trend is toward a healthy eclecticism, his influence is certain to act as a prescient force in the future of speculative fiction.

IV

The three sections above were written in 1964. Although perhaps somewhat elaborate and tendentious in argument, they do develop points which I feel are still worth making today. The space devoted to stylistic influences, however, could be considered overly assiduous. In an interview between Vance and

Peter Close (*Science Fiction Review*, November 1977), the following dialogue occurs:

> CLOSE: I think your style, themes, and plotting weren't greatly influenced by other writers.
> VANCE: This is essentially correct.

This is a conclusion I've come to agree with. Vance's connection with other writers is, at best, only apparent and superficial; he is, in fact, individual. The one possible exception to this might be *Space Opera*, apparently a futuristic parody of a Wodehouse novel, and a very amusing one.

There are, too, some serious misjudgments of certain stories. I was not fully aware in 1964 of the tendency toward what Peter Close calls the sociological and anthropological elements in Vance's fiction. I completely underestimated *The Languages of Pao*, and "The Dragon Masters" now seems to me one of Vance's most magnificently crafted stories.

In 1964, not having read any of Vance's mysteries, I was dubious about his venturing into this field. These doubts have been completely dispelled by *The Man in the Cage*, *The Deadly Isles*, and the two California novels, *The Fox Valley Murders* and *The Pleasant Grove Murders*. These last two, especially, are delightful excursions in the genre and feature in Sheriff Joe Bain one of Vance's most sympathetic heroes. And as a tour-de-force in legerdemain, Vance begins the books with the most colorful character—Sheriff Ernest (Cooch) Cucchinello—already dead and buried, yet his presence is vividly felt throughout both novels. (To see how this is accomplished, read the books!)

Also, since 1964 Vance has written prolifically, and some of these later novels are among his very best. There are the two superb sequels to *Star King* in *The Killing Machine* and *The Palace of Love*—my own favorites among his series—and the latest wonderful news is that Vance is now completing the last two novels in the sequence. Perhaps even more celebrated has been the sequel to *The Dying Earth* stories, featuring Cugel the Clever. *The Eyes of the Overworld*, though it adopts the same setting of the earlier book, is very different in tone. Cugel is a rogue and a scoundrel of infinite resource. In a world rife with virtuosic mendacity, rampant skulduggery, and treacherous double-dealing, Cugel surmounts every trial. As he justly observes, he is not called Cugel the Clever for nothing. Vance has not been given his due as a humorist; indeed, he seems to me one of the funniest writers alive, in or out of the genre, and *The Eyes of the Overworld* is his comic novel par excellence.

Emphyrio, highly praised by Joanna Russ, is undoubtedly one of the important later novels. There is, however, an underlying melancholy and sadness about the book — at least for me — that even the triumphant ending does not dispel. Both emotionally and in its setting, *Emphyrio* is something of a brown study, and I prefer Vance working with the brighter primary colors.

While "Parapsyche" was not, in my opinion, one of Vance's more successful efforts, *The Brains of Earth* is a fascinating study on some of the same themes of parapsychological phenomena and is an underrated work. "The Last Castle" is of course one of Vance's most highly praised stories and a Hugo winner for 1966. It shares a complex of themes with "The Miracle Workers" and "The Dragon Masters," and it would be good to see them published together as representative of Vance's finest work.

For sheer enjoyability, the first Alastor book, *Trullion: Alastor 2262*, is Vance at the top of his form. The invention of *hussade* and the pulse-pounding description of the games are splendidly vivid. The Vance hero is here sundered between two brothers — the extroverted Glinnes and the moody, darkly exalted Glay. Glinnes is overtly the more favored character, but I suspect Vance's sympathy is equally divided. After the rapid pace, excitement, and multihued waterscapes of this novel, its immediate successor, *The Gray Prince*, is a curiously elusive book. Arthur Jean Cox maintains that this is one of Vance's two polemical stories (the other being "Assault on a City"). This is possible although no writer in the field is less given to didactic moralizing.

One of my favorite later books is *The Blue World*. First written as a novella for *Fantastic* and later expanded with great effect to a full-length novel, it is a tale of initiation, ordeal, and change, with a magical, fairy-tale atmosphere — altogether one of Vance's most beautiful books.

Vance is, above all, a marvelous teller of tales. There is a great deal that sympathetic criticism may elicit from his works, but the task is rendered peculiarly difficult (and captivating) because, perhaps more than any other major writer in the field, his work is replete with contrary tendencies and qualifications. This leads to a perennially interesting question: What does Vance really think? In the Demon Princes series, for instance, what is his attitude toward the concept of The Institution? I would say, somewhat guardedly, that he approves, but the other side of the question is given considerable play in the novels. Vance likes to enter imaginatively into all sides of a concept; the result, often, is a kind of multifaceted ambiguity which defies easy categorization.

Isaiah Berlin, in a famous essay, divided writers and thinkers into two groups — the hedgehogs (men of one encompassing central vision) and the foxes, who, as one writer put it, "are pluralists pursuing many unrelated, even contradictory ends, moving simultaneously on many different levels." It is safe to say that Vance is, and will remain, among the foxes. If this renders critical elucidation fascinatingly difficult, those who take up the task will find in Vance's novels and stories scope for abounding riches.

Concerning Jack Vance
An Afterword by POUL ANDERSON

IT IS NOT BECAUSE he has been a good friend of mine for many years that I feel that Jack Vance is one of the finest writers that the science fiction field has ever known. There are several people dear to me personally whose stories leave me cold. But a Vance work is always a treat to read, and often much more than that.

In no particular order, his special virtues seem to me to be these: His backgrounds, including the gorgeous names he bestows, are vivid, as evocative of romance and wonder as the South Seas or Samarkand, and at the same time thoroughly believable; unlike the imaginary worlds and societies of too many writers, Vance's make basic good sense — they work. The same is true of his characters, who beneath all the glamour of alienness are real people. He always tells a story, unfashionable though the art of narration has become in some circles, and it is always a rattling good story, full of happenings. His style, his way with words, is sheerly wonderful, both crisp and poetic, often charged with subtle wit. Underlying all these qualities is a philosophy, which together with his insight into life gives his tales considerable depth.

Not so incidentally, he has also written mystery and crime fiction (semi-pseudonymously as John Holbrook Vance). Here his essential realism and his knowledge of human beings stand forth plain to see, and thus illuminate the same elements in his science fiction. I would particularly recommend *Bad Ronald* as a terrifying study of a psychopath and *The Fox Valley Murders* as a delightful piece of Californiana, a regional novel of the very best kind.

Although he has always been popular with readers, he has in a sense been incredibly neglected, at least by most critics — one good reason for my low opinion of most critics. It is pleasant to see that he now appears to be finally getting "discovered."

In person he's friendly and unpretentious, so much so that it can take new acquaintances a while to realize how much he knows and understands and thinks about. He has done a lot of different things and seen a lot of the world, and this shows in his writing. Long may Jack Vance go on.

Jack Vance: A Biographical Note

JACK VANCE has become one of the most widely read and well-respected authors of our time. He has written more than forty novels and seventy-five shorter works in the fields of fantasy, mystery, suspense, and science fiction. His first story, "The World-Thinker," appeared in *Thrilling Wonder Stories* in 1945, but it was the publication of *The Dying Earth* (1950), a picturesque novel of the twenty-millionth century, which first established Vance's reputation as a master of fantasy literature. Concurrent with his early literary career was that of screenwriter: throughout the early 1950s he was a script writer for the *Captain Video* television program. His critically acclaimed series of Demon Princes novels, begun in 1963, is science fiction of the highest caliber, elaborately styled yet fast-paced and exciting. In 1964 *The Dragon Masters* won the Hugo Award for short fiction. In 1966 *The Last Castle* won the Nebula Award for Best Novella; in 1967 it won the Hugo Award for Best Novelette.

Though better known for his fantasy and science fiction, he has also authored a number of mystery and suspense novels under his full name, John Holbrook Vance. In 1960 *The Man in the Cage*, a novel set in northern Africa, was awarded an Edgar by the Mystery Writers of America and later adapted for television. Along with other of his mysteries, it has been widely translated and published abroad. *Bad Ronald*, a suspense thriller published in 1973, has also appeared on television.

Jack Vance is especially renowned for his narrative wit, his brilliant use of color, his exotic alien scenery, and his ability to depict fully realized alien races and cultures. His hobbies include blue-water sailing and the four-string banjo. He lives in the hills above Oakland, California, with his wife Norma and son John.

Jack Vance: A Bibliography
Compiled by MARSHALL B. TYMN

ALTHOUGH not intended to be definitive, this bibliography is comprehensive in its scope and is representative of Jack Vance's total output. All items are listed in alphabetical order. The last section gives a list of important critical articles about his work. I am indebted to Kurt Cockrum and Daniel J. H. Levack, who furnished materials on Vance not readily available to me.

Books and Pamphlets

The Anome [novel]. New York: Dell, 1973 pb; Ace, 1978 pb as *The Faceless Man*.

The Asutra [novel]. New York: Dell, 1974 pb.

Bad Ronald [novel, as John Holbrook Vance]. New York: Ballantine, 1973 pb.

The Best of Jack Vance [story collection]. New York: Pocket Books, 1976 pb; Taplinger, 1978.

Big Planet [novel]. New York: Avalon, 1957; Ace, 1958 pb (bound with *Slaves of the Klau*); San Francisco: Underwood-Miller, 1978.

The Blue World [novel]. New York: Ballantine, 1966 pb; San Francisco: Underwood-Miller, 1979.

The Brains of Earth [novel]. New York: Ace, 1966 pb (bound with *The Many Worlds of Magnus Ridolph*); London: Dobson, 1975.

The Brave Free Men [novel]. New York: Dell, 1973 pb.

City of the Chasch [novel: Tschai series #1]. New York: Ace, 1968 pb; London: Dobson, 1975; [special edition, San Francisco: Underwood-Miller, 1979].

The Deadly Isles [novel, as John Holbrook Vance]. Indianapolis: Bobbs-Merrill, 1969; New York: Ace, 1971 pb.

The Dirdir [novel: Tschai series #2]. New York: Ace, 1969 pb; London: Dobson, 1975; [special edition, San Francisco: Underwood-Miller, 1980].

The Dragon Masters [novel]. New York: Ace, 1963 pb (bound with *The Five Gold Bands*); London: Dobson, 1965; rpt. Boston: Gregg Press, 1976.

The Dying Earth [unified story collection]. New York: Hillman, 1950 pb; San Francisco: Underwood-Miller, 1976.

Eight Fantasms and Magics [story collection]. New York: Macmillan, 1969; Collier, 1970 pb.

Emphyrio [novel]. Garden City, NY: Doubleday, 1969; New York: Dell, 1970 pb.

The Eyes of the Overworld [unified story collection]. New York: Ace, 1966 pb; Boston: Gregg Press, 1977; [special edition, San Francisco: Underwood-Miller, 1978].

The Face [novel: Demon Princes series #4]. New York: DAW, 1979 pb; San Francisco: Underwood-Miller, 1980.

The Faceless Man (see *The Anome*).

The Five Gold Bands [novel]. New York: Toby Press, 1953 pb (as *The Space Pirate*); Ace, 1962 pb [shorter version, bound with *The Dragon Masters*].

The Four Johns [novel, as Ellery Queen]. New York: Pocket Books, 1964; London: Gollancz, 1976 (as *Four Men Called John*).

Four Men Called John (see *The Four Johns*).

The Fox Valley Murders [novel, as John Holbrook Vance]. Indianapolis: Bobbs-Merrill, 1966; New York: Ace, 1967 pb.

Future Tense [story collection]. New York: Ballantine, 1964 pb.

Galactic Effectuator [unified story collection]. San Francisco: Underwood-Miller, 1980.

The Gray Prince [novel]. Indianapolis: Bobbs-Merrill, 1974; New York: Avon, 1975 pb.

Green Magic [story collection]. San Francisco: Underwood-Miller, 1979.

The House on Lily Street [novel]. San Francisco: Underwood-Miller, 1979.

The Houses of Iszm [novel]. New York: Ace, 1964 pb (bound with *Son of the Tree*).

Isle of Peril [novel, as Alan Wade]. New York: Mystery House, 1957.

The Killing Machine [novel; Demon Princes series #2]. New York: Berkley, 1964 pb; London: Dobson, 1967.

The Languages of Pao [novel]. New York: Avalon, 1958; Ace, 1966 pb; [special edition, San Francisco: Underwood-Miller, 1979].

The Last Castle [novel]. New York: Ace, 1967 pb (bound with *World of the Sleepers* by Tony Wayman).

The Madman Theory [novel, as Ellery Queen]. New York: Pocket Books, 1966 pb.

The Man in the Cage [novel, as John Holbrook Vance]. New York: Random House, 1960; London: Mayflower, 1961 pb.

The Many Worlds of Magnus Ridolph [story collection]. New York: Ace, 1966 pb (bound with *The Brains of Earth*); London: Dobson, 1977.

Marune: Alastor 933 [novel]. New York: Ballantine, 1975 pb.

Maske: Thaery [novel]. New York: Berkley-Putnam, 1976; Garden City, NY: Science Fiction Book Club, 1977; New York: Berkley, 1977 pb.

Monsters in Orbit [novel]. New York: Ace, 1965 pb (bound with *The World Between*); London: Dobson, 1977.

The Moon Moth and Other Stories (see *The World Between and Other Stories*).

Morreion [story]. San Francisco: Underwood-Miller, 1979.

The Palace of Love [novel: Demon Princes series #3]. New York: Berkley, 1967; London: Dobson, 1968.

The Pleasant Grove Murders [novel, as John Holbrook Vance]. Indianapolis: Bobbs-Merrill, 1967; New York: Ace, 1969 pb.

The Pnume [novel: Tschai series #4]. New York: Ace, 1970 pb; London: Dobson, 1975 [special edition, San Francisco: Underwood-Miller, 1980].

A Room to Die In [novel, as Ellery Queen]. New York: Pocket Books, 1965 pb.

Servants of the Wankh [novel: Tschai series #2]. New York: Ace, 1969 pb; London: Dobson, 1975; [special edition, San Francisco: Underwood-Miller, 1980.]

Showboat World [novel]. New York: Pyramid, 1975 pb.

Slaves of the Klau [novel]. New York: Ace, 1958 pb (bound with *Big Planet*).

Son of the Tree [novel]. New York: Ace, 1964 pb (bound with *The Houses of Iszm*).

Space Opera [novel]. New York: Pyramid, 1965 pb.

The Space Pirate (see *The Five Gold Bands*).

Star King [novel: Demon Princes series #1]. New York: Berkley, 1964 pb; London: Dobson, 1966.

Take My Face [novel, as Peter Held]. New York: Mystery House, 1957; Pyramid, 1958 pb.

To Live Forever [novel]. New York: Ballantine, 1956; Ballantine, 1956 pb.

Trullion: Alastor 2262 [novel]. New York: Ballantine, 1973 pb.

Vandals of the Void [novel]. Philadelphia: Winston, 1953; rpt. Boston: Gregg Press, 1979.

The View from Chickweed's Window [novel]. San Francisco: Underwood-Miller, 1979.

The World Between and Other Stories [story collection]. New York: Ace, 1965 pb (bound with *Monsters in Orbit*); London: Dobson, 1975 (as *The Moon Moth and Other Stories*).

The Worlds of Jack Vance [story collection]. New York: Ace, 1973 pb.

Wyst: Alastor 1716 [novel]. New York: DAW, 1978 pb.

Short Fiction

"Abercrombie Station." *Thrilling Wonder Stories* (February 1952). Collected in *The Best of Jack Vance.*

"Alfred's Ark." *New Worlds* (May 1965).

"Assault on a City." In *Universe 4*, ed., Terry Carr. New York: Random House, 1974.

"The Asutra." *Magazine of Fantasy and Science Fiction* (May 1973).

"The Bagful of Dreams." In *Flashing Swords! #4*, ed., Lin Carter. Garden City, NY: Science Fiction Book Club, 1977.

"Big Planet." *Startling Stories* (September 1952).

"Brain of the Galaxy." *Worlds Beyond* (February 1951). Collected in *The Worlds of Jack Vance* and *Eight Fantasms and Magics* as "The New Prime."

"The Brains of Earth." In *The Worlds of Jack Vance*. New York: Ace, 1973.

"The Brave Free Men." *Magazine of Fantasy and Science Fiction* (July-August 1972).

"Cholwell's Chickens." *Thrilling Wonder Stories* (August 1952).

"Cil." In *Eight Fantasms and Magics*." New York: Macmillan, 1969.

"Cosmic Hotfoot." *Startling Stories* (September 1950).

"DP!" *Avon Science Fiction & Fantasy Reader* (April 1953).

"The Devil on Salvation Bluff." In *Star Science Fiction Stories #3*, ed. Frederik Pohl. New York: Ballantine, 1955. Collected in *The Worlds of Jack Vance.*

"Dodkin's Job." *Astounding Science Fiction* (October 1959).

"The Dogtown Tourist Agency." In *Epoch*, ed., Roger Elwood and Robert Silverberg. New York: Berkley-Putnam, 1975.

"Domains of Koryphon." *Amazing* (August 1974).

"Dover Spargill's Ghastly Floater." *Marvel Science Fiction* (November 1951).

"The Dragon Masters." *Galaxy* (August 1962).

"Ecological Onslaught." *Future* (May 1953). Collected in *The Worlds of Jack Vance* as "The World Between."

"Emphyrio." *Fantastic* (June, August 1969).

"The Enchanted Princess." *Orbit Science Fiction* (November 1954).

"The Faceless Man." *Magazine of Fantasy and Science Fiction,* (February-March 1971).

"First Star I See Tonight" (as John Van See). *Malcolm's Mystery Magazine* (March 1954).

"The Five Gold Bands." *Startling Stories* (November 1950).

"Four Hundred Blackbirds." *Future* (July 1953).

"Freitzke's Turn." In *Triax*, ed., Robert Silverberg. New York: Pinnacle, 1977.

"Gateway to Strangeness." *Amazing* (August 1962). Collected in *The Best of Jack Vance* as "Sail 25."

"Gift of Gab." *Astounding Science Fiction* (September 1955).

"Golden Girl." *Marvel Science Stories* (May 1951).

"Green Magic." *Magazine of Fantasy and Science Fiction* (June 1963).

"Guyal of Sfere." In *Eight Fantasms and Magics*. New York: Macmillan, 1969.

"Hard-Luck Diggings." *Startling Stories* (July 1948).

"House Lords." *Saturn* (October 1957).

"The Houses of Iszm." *Startling Stories* (Spring 1954).

"The Howling Bounders." *Startling Stories* (March 1949).

"I-C-A-BEM." *Amazing* (October 1961).

"I'll Build Your Dream Castle." *Astounding Science Fiction* (September 1947).

"The King of Thieves." *Startling Stories* (November 1949). Collected in *The Worlds of Jack Vance*.

"The Kokod Warriors." *Thrilling Wonder Stories* (October 1952). Collected in *The Worlds of Jack Vance*.

"The Kragen." *Fantastic* (July 1964).

"The Languages of Pao." *Satellite Science Fiction* (December 1957).

"The Last Castle." *Galaxy* (April 1966). Collected in *The Best of Jack Vance*.

"Liane the Wayfarer." *Worlds Beyond* (December 1950) as "The Loom of Darkness."

"The Loom of Darkness" (see "Liane the Wayfarer").

"The Man from Zodiac." *Amazing* (August 1967).

"The Manse of Iucounu." *Magazine of Fantasy and Science Fiction*, (July 1966).

"Marune: Alastor 933." *Amazing* (July, September 1975).

"Masquerade on Dicantropus." *Startling Stories* (September 1951).

"Mazirian the Magician." In *The Spells of Seven*, ed., L. Sprague de Camp. New York: Pyramid, 1965.

"Meet Miss Universe." *Fantastic Universe* (March 1955).

"Men of the Ten Books." *Startling Stories* (March 1951).

"The Men Return." *Infinity* (July 1957). Collected in *Eight Fantasms and Magics* and *The Worlds of Jack Vance*.

"The Miracle Workers." *Astounding Science Fiction* (July 1958). Collected in *Eight Fantasms and Magics*.

"The Mitr." *Vortex*, No. 1 (1953).

"The Moon Moth." *Galaxy* (August 1961). Collected in *The Best of Jack Vance* and *The Worlds of Jack Vance*.

"Morreion." In *Flashing Swords! #1*, ed., Lin Carter. New York: Dell; Garden City, NY: Science Fiction Book Club, 1973.

"The Mountains of Magnatz." *Magazine of Fantasy and Science Fiction* (February 1966).

"The Narrow Land." *Fantastic* (July 1967).

"New Bodies for Old." *Thrilling Wonder Stories* (August 1950).

"The New Prime" (see "Brain of the Galaxy").

"Noise." *Startling Stories* (August 1952).

"Overlords of Maxus." *Thrilling Wonder Stories* (February 1951).

"The Overworld." *Magazine of Fantasy and Science Fiction* (December 1965).

"The Palace of Love." *Galaxy* (October, December 1966, February 1967).

"Parapsyche." *Amazing* (August 1958).

"Phalid's Fate." *Thrilling Wonder Stories* (December 1946).

"Phantom Milkman." *Other Worlds* (February 1956).

"The Pilgrims." *Magazine of Fantasy and Science Fiction* (June 1966).

"The Plagian Siphon." *Thrilling Wonder Stories* (October 1951).

"Planet of the Black Dust." *Startling Stories* (Summer 1946).

"Planet of the Damned." *Space Stories* (December 1952).

"The Potters of Firsk." *Astounding Science Fiction* (May 1950).

"A Practical Man's Guide." *Space Science Fiction* (August 1957).

"Rumfuddle." In *Three Trips in Time and Space*, ed., Robert Silverberg. New York: Hawthorn, 1973. Collected in *The Best of Jack Vance*.

"Sabotage on the Sulphur Planet." *Startling Stories* (June 1952).

"Sail 25" (see "Gateway to Strangeness").

"Sanatoris Short-Cut." *Startling Stories* (September 1948).

"The Secret." *Impulse* (March 1966).

"Seven Exits from Bocz." *The Rhodomagnetic Digest*, No. 2 (1952).

"The Seventeen Virgins." *Magazine of Fantasy and Science Fiction* (October 1974).

"Shape-Up." *Cosmos* (November 1953).

"Sjambak." *Worlds of If* (July 1953).

"Son of the Tree." *Thrilling Wonder Stories* (June 1951).

"The Sorcerer Pharesm." *Magazine of Fantasy and Science Fiction* (April 1966).

"The Spa of the Stars." *Startling Stories* (July 1950).

"The Star King." *Galaxy* (December 1963, February 1964).

"The Sub-Standard Sardines." *Startling Stories* (January 1949).

"Sulwen's Planet." In *The Farthest Reaches*, ed., Joseph Elder. New York: Trident, 1968.

"Telek." *Astounding Science Fiction* (January 1952). Collected in *Eight Fantasms and Magics*.

"Temple of Han." *Planet Stories* (July 1951).

"Three-Legged Joe." *Startling Stories* (January 1953).

"Trullion: Alastor 2262." *Amazing* (March, June 1973).

"Turjan of Miir." In *The Young Magicians*, ed., Lin Carter. New York: Ballantine, 1969.

"Ullward's Retreat." *Galaxy* (December 1958). Collected in *The Best of Jack Vance*.

"Ultimate Quest" (as John Holbrook). *Super Science Stories* (September 1950).

"The Unspeakable McInch." *Startling Stories* (November 1948).
"When the Five Moons Rise." *Cosmos* (March 1954). Collected in *Eight Fantasms and Magics.*
"Where Hesperus Falls." *Fantastic Universe* (October 1956).
"Winner Lose All." *Galaxy* (December 1951).
"The World Between" (see "Ecological Onslaught").
"The World-Thinker." *Thrilling Wonder Stories* (Summer 1945).
"Worlds of Origin." *Super Science Fiction* (February 1958).

General

"Adventure on Phobos" [teleplay]. *Captain Video*, 1953.
"Black Planet Academy" [teleplay]. *Captain Video*, 1953.
"A Bottle from Space" [teleplay]. *Captain Video*, 1953.
"Dark Empire" [teleplay]. *Captain Video*, 1952.
"End of Nowhere" [teleplay]. *Captain Video*, 1953.
"An Interview with Jack Vance" [by Peter Close]. *Science Fiction Review* (November 1977).
"Mercury Observatory" [teleplay, with Robert Richardson]. *Captain Video*, 1952.
"A Talk with Jack Vance" [interview by Tim Underwood]. *The Many Worlds of Jack Vance*, No. 1 (Spring 1977).

Criticism and Reference

Allen, Paul C. "Of Swords and Sorcery." *Fantasy Crossroads* (August 1976).
Ash, Brian. "Jack Vance." In *Who's Who in Science Fiction*. New York: Taplinger, 1976.
Boardman, John. "Durdane: Or Is It America." *Amra*, No. 61 (1974).
Cox, Arthur Jean. "The Boredom of Fantasy." *Riverside Quarterly*, No. 1 (1964).
Dickinson, Mike. "Romance & Hardening Arteries: A Reappraisal of the SF of Jack Vance." *Vector*, No. 95 (1979).
Dowling, Terry. "The Art of Xenography: Jack Vance's 'General Culture' Novels." *Science Fiction* (December 1978).
"The Dragon Masters." In *Survey of Science Fiction Literature*, ed., Frank N. Magill. Englewood Cliffs, NJ: Salem Press, 1979.
"The Dying Earth." In *Fantasy Literature: A Core Collection and Reference Guide*, ed., Marshall B. Tymn, et al. New York: R. R. Bowker, 1979.
"The Dying Earth." In *Survey of Science Fiction Literature*, ed., Frank N. Magill. Englewood Cliffs, NJ: Salem Press, 1979.
Edwards, Malcolm. "A Study in Anomie." *The Many Worlds of Jack Vance /Horns of Elfland*, No. 2 (1978).
"The Eyes of the Overworld." In *Fantasy Literature: A Core Collection and Reference Guide*, ed., Marshall B. Tymn, et al. New York: R. R. Bowker, 1979.

Honor to Finuka (Vance fanzine, 1979). Kurt Cockrum and Martha K. Koester. 309 Allston #16, Boston, MA 02146.

"Jack Vance." In *The Encyclopedia of Science Fiction*, ed., Peter Nicholls. Garden City, NY: Doubleday, 1979.

"The Languages of Pao." In *Survey of Science Fiction Literature*, ed., Frank N. Magill. Englewood Cliffs, NJ: Salem Press, 1979.

"The Last Castle." In *Survey of Science Fiction Literature*, ed., Frank N. Magill. Englewood Cliffs, NJ: Salem Press, 1979.

Levak, Daniel J. H., and Tim Underwood. *Fantasms: A Bibliography of the Literature of Jack Vance*. San Francisco: Underwood-Miller, 1978.

McFerran, Dave. "The Magic of the Dying Earth." *Anduril*, 6 (1976).

Robson, Alan. "Jack Vance—The Magic and the Mystery." *Science Fiction Forum* (Winter 1977).

Searles, Baird, et al. "Jack Vance." In *A Reader's Guide to Science Fiction*. New York: Avon Books, 1979.

Notes*

CHAPTER 3: ARTHUR JEAN COX

1. I did not know then that Vance had written this book, at least in part, in Positano, Italy, the setting of his unpublished suspense novel, *Strange People, Queer Notions*, in which his dissatisfaction with Europe is most undisguisedly expressed..
2. It is only in *The Gray Prince* (1974; otherwise, "Domains of Koryphon") that the self-confidence seems to falter. Indeed, the author seems somehow troubled. Elvo Glissam, whom many would take to be the hero, suffers a curious fate—he is never the same after he is killed. Speaking in a marvelling voice, he fades out of the last pages, and one actually has the baffled impression that the author has forgotten him. This unsatisfactory elimination of a major element (Glissam) suggests that something has interfered with the proper working out of the story.
3. In a catalog (No. 12) published in 1977 by Roy A. Squires, Glendale, California, offering for sale some Vance manuscripts.
4. My notion of catatonia is derived from several sources, but primarily from *Introduction to the Theory and Practice of the Szondi Test* by Susan K. Deri (1949).
5. I do not invoke Rousseau to inflate my subject; the connection is pertinent. Rousseau's concern in the *First Discourse* (1750) is with "the ever more powerful existence of the *public*, that human entity which is defined by its urban habitat, its multitudinousness, and its ready accessibility to opinion." Here I am following the summary given by Lionel Trilling: "The individual who lives in this new circumstance is subject to the constant influence, the literal *in-flowing* of the mental processes of others,

---

*NOTE: There are no notes for Chapters 1, 2, 5, 6, and 8.

which, in the degree that they stimulate or enlarge his consciousness, make it less his own. He finds it ever more difficult to know what his own self is and what being true to it consists in. It is with the psychological and moral consequences of the modern public dispensation in mind that Rousseau invents his famous savage, one of whose defining traits is the perfect autonomy of his consciousness" (*Sincerity and Authenticity: Six Lectures*, Charles Eliot Norton Lectures for 1969-1970, Cambridge, Mass.: Harvard University Press, 1972, pp. 61-62).

No one who has read "Assault on a City" can fail to see how aptly descriptive this is of its thematic thrust. (For Rousseau's "savage" substitute "The Insufferable Red-Headed Daughter of Commander Tynott, O.T.E.") I have no idea whether or not Vance has read Rousseau — or Trilling, who devoted so much of his later life to an impassioned, shrewd, and subtle questioning of what Vance the science-fiction writer terms "urbanity" — but it hardly seems to matter. Vance is surely capable of developing a parallel line of thought.

6. There is even, though perhaps not surprisingly, a "cult" book with the title *The Exploration of Inner Space.*

CHAPTER 4: DON HERRON

1. Quoted in an interview by Peter Close, *The Many Worlds of Jack Vance*, Vol. 1, No. 1 (Spring 1977), privately published by Robert Offutt, Jr.
2. Ibid.
3. Clark Ashton Smith, "The Dark Eidolon," *Out of Space and Time*, Sauk City, Wis.: Arkham House, 1942. This story first appeared in *Weird Tales* (January 1935).
4. Robert Briney, writing in *Destiny*, a fan magazine, Nos. 4-5 (Summer-Fall 1951).
5. Ibid. Briney noted at the time that Vance and Smith "have the same producing phrase."
6. Smith, "The Testament of Athammaus," *Out of Space and Time*. This story originally appeared in *Weird Tales* (October 1932).
7. Smith, "The Coming of the White Worm," *Lost Worlds*, Sauk City, Wis.: Arkham House, 1944. This story originally appeared in *Stirring Science Stories* (April 1941).
8. Smith's good friend George F. Haas once pointed out to me that Smith had the *blossoms* of his menacing plants devouring the men. Strictly speaking, this usage is incorrect, since carnivorous plants such as the Venus's flytrap eat with their leaves. The blossoms are the sexual parts of the plant — a fact perhaps not lost on Smith.
9. Smith, "The Seed from the Sepulcher," *Tales of Science and Sorcery*, Sauk City, Wis.: Arkham House, 1964. This story originally appeared in *Weird Tales* (October 1933).
10. Smith, "The Door to Saturn," *Lost Worlds*. This story originally appeared in *Strange Tales* (January 1932).

11. Ibid.
12. Smith, "The Dweller in the Gulf," *The Abominations of Yondo*, Sauk City, Wis.: Arkham House, 1960. L. Sprague de Camp, writing in the fanzine *Amra*, Vol. 2, No. 13 (1960), called this story "probably the most gruesome science-fiction story ever written."
13. Smith, "The Seven Geases," *Lost Worlds*. This story originally appeared in *Weird Tales* (October 1934).
14. Ibid.
15. Ibid.
16. Lin Carter, in *Amra*, Vol. 2, No. 48 (August 1968).
17. Carter has written a few so-called "posthumous collaborations" using a combined Clark Ashton Smith–Lin Carter by-line. Of course Smith had nothing to do with the writing of these stories. Yet Carter has made a strong effort to bring off Smith's style in hopes of adding some credence to the use of Smith's name. His efforts in this respect have failed because of a too slavish attempt to copy; Carter's "The Utmost Abomination" – an apt title – is merely a rewriting of Smith's "The Double Shadow."
18. Smith, "The Door to Saturn," *Lost Worlds*.
19. Smith, "The Coming of the White Worm," *Lost Worlds*.
20. Briney, *Destiny*.
21. Arthur F. Hillman, in *Fantasy Review*, Vol. III, No. 13 (February-March 1949), Walter Gillings, publisher. It is interesting to note that this review finds Smith's brand of SF "better" than the humanistic kind, and that it is nearly contemporary with Briney's review which reverses the opinion. Also, Vance's initial sales came in the middle and late 1940s, when the humanistic trend was gaining dominance in the field. Perhaps Vance's inherent interest in humanistic themes was reinforced by their acceptance and saleability in the available markets.
22. H. P. Lovecraft, in a letter to Smith postmarked October 17, 1930. In this same context Lovecraft remarked that Smith had a sense of the cosmic "to a supreme degree."
23. Harry Morris, editor/publisher, "Clark Ashton Smith," in the fanzine *Nyctalops*, No. 7 (August 1972), p. 19.

CHAPTER 7: TERRY DOWLING

1. Joanna Russ, "Books," *The Magazine of Fantasy and Science Fiction* (January 1970).
2. Keith Laumer, "Protest Note," *Galactic Diplomat*, New York: Berkley Medallion, 1966.

Contributors

PETER CLOSE is a British sociologist living in London. He is a contributor to *Science Fiction Review* and is currently working on a full-length book dealing with the literature of Jack Vance.

ARTHUR JEAN COX is a science fiction writer residing in Los Angeles, California. His fiction and criticism have regularly appeared in the United States and Europe over the past two decades, most recently in *Isaac Asimov's Science Fiction Magazine*.

TERRY DOWLING is an English Master at the Business College of Sydney, Australia. He is the creator of a science fiction musical, *Amberjack*, and his essays on such contemporary authors as J. G. Ballard and Jack Vance have appeared in Australia as well as the United States.

DON HERRON is a specialist in contemporary fantasy, horror, and detective fiction. He is a past editor and contributor to *The Romanticist* and *Nyctalops*, and his critical writing has appeared in *Fate* and *The Armchair Detective*. A resident of Northern California, Mr. Herron is the author of *A Dashiell Hammett Tour-*

book and the originator and current administrator of "Literary Walks of San Francisco."

ROBERT SILVERBERG is a Hugo and Nebula Award-winning science fiction writer and is one of the field's premier editors and commentators. His current fantasy novel, *Lord Valentine's Castle*, has received wide critical acclaim and was described by *People Magazine* as "the dream of a genius." He lives in Oakland, California.

NORMAN SPINRAD is a columnist, editor, critic, screenwriter, and author of contemporary and speculative fiction. *Bug Jack Barron*, perhaps his best-known work of science fiction, was awarded the Hugo in 1969. He currently divides his time between residences in Los Angeles and New York City.

RICHARD TIEDMAN is a professional writer specializing in all aspects of music in the Western world. His was one of the earliest critical voices to be heard from outside the science fiction field. His essay, "Jack Vance: Science Fiction Stylist," foreshadowed much of the single-author focus in current science fiction criticism. He lives in Cleveland, Ohio.

MARSHALL B. TYMN, associate professor of English at Eastern Michigan University, has taught science fiction there since 1974, and is director of the Annual Conference on Teaching Science Fiction, a national workshop. Dr. Tymn is an active researcher in the science fiction field, and has edited several reference works. His publications include *A Research Guide to Science Fiction Studies*; *Index to Stories in Thematic Anthologies of Science Fiction, American Fantasy and Science Fiction*; *The Year's Scholarship in Science Fiction and Fantasy: 1972-1975*; and *Fantasy Literature: A Core Collection and Reference Guide*, as well as numerous articles and monographs. Dr. Tymn is editor of three critical and reference series: *The Annotated Guide to the*

Fantastic Magazines (Starmont House), *Masters of Science Fiction and Fantasy* (G. K. Hall), and *Contributions to the Study of Science Fiction and Fantasy* (Greenwood Press). He also serves as series bibliographer for *Writers of the 21st Century* (Taplinger) and is an advisor to *Twentieth-Century Science Fiction Writers* (St. James Press, London). Dr. Tymn is vice-president of the Science Fiction Research Association and former president of Instructors of Science Fiction in Higher Education. He is currently at work on several projects, including *The Science Fiction Reference Guide*; *Science Fiction and Fantasy Magazines*; *Science Fiction: A Reference Guide*; *A Teacher's Guide to Science Fiction and Fantasy*; *A Guide to the Literature of Horror and the Supernatural*; and *A Science Fiction Motif Index*. Dr. Tymn holds a Ph.D. in American Studies from the University of Michigan, and has published two books on the American landscape painter, Thomas Cole.

MARK WILLARD is a science fiction critic and essayist whose work has appeared in the United States and Canada. A resident of McCall, Idaho, Mr. Willard is presently at work on a concordance covering the entire body of Jack Vance's speculative literature.

Index

About the Editors

Tim Underwood and Chuck Miller are publishers specializing in hardcover fantasy and science fiction. Their illustrated collector's editions (many of which have been books by Jack Vance) hark back to the days of Howard Pyle. Under their UNDERWOOD/MILLER imprint they have recently begun a series of annotated pictorial bibliographies, dealing with the works of major authors in the science fiction genre.

About the General Editors

Martin Harry Greenberg and Joseph D. Olander are the co-editors of a number of science fiction and mystery anthologies. Dr. Greenberg is Associate Professor of Political Science at the University of Wisconsin, Green Bay. Dr. Olander is Vice President for Academic Affairs at the University of Texas, El Paso. They are currently working with Isaac Asimov on two anthologies—*Microcosmic Tales: 100 Wondrous Science Fiction Short-Short Stories* and *Miniature Mysteries: 100 Malicious Little Mystery Stories* (both Taplinger, 1980).